# MUD SOLDIERS

## Life Inside
## the New American Army

## George C. Wilson

COLLIER BOOKS

MACMILLAN PUBLISHING COMPANY

New York

COLLIER MACMILLAN CANADA
Toronto

MAXWELL MACMILLAN INTERNATIONAL
New York   Oxford   Singapore   Sydney

Collier Books                                    Collier Macmillan Canada, Inc.
Macmillan Publishing Company      1200 Eglinton Avenue East
866 Third Avenue                              Suite 200
New York, NY 10022                         Don Mills, Ontario M3C 3N1

Library of Congress Cataloging-in-Publication Data
Wilson, George C., date.
   Mud soldiers: life inside the new American Army / George C.
Wilson.—1st Collier Books ed.
     p.  cm.
   Includes index.
   ISBN 0-02-071051-8
   1. United States. Army—Military life.  2. United States. Army.
Infantry Regiment, 16th. Battalion, 2nd. Charlie Company—History.
3. Vietnamese Conflict, 1961–1975—Regimental histories—United
States.  I. Title.
[U766.W475     1991]        90-26532      CIP
355.1'0973—dc20

All photographs not otherwise credited are by the author.

Macmillan books are available at special discounts for bulk purchases for sales promotions, premiums, fund-raising, or educational use. For details, contact:

Special Sales Director
Macmillan Publishing Company
866 Third Avenue
New York, NY 10022

First Collier Books Edition 1991

10   9   8   7   6   5   4   3   2   1

Printed in the United States of America

*To American Mud Soldiers everywhere
who give so much and ask so little*

# Contents

# MUD SOLDIERS

# Introduction
# The Way We Were — and Are

The world changed for the United States and its Army in 1966.

The can-do nation, the one that had never lost a war, found itself bogged down in a seemingly unwinnable war in South Vietnam.

Until 1966, President Lyndon B. Johnson and Defense Secretary Robert S. McNamara had assured the American people that Vietnam was just a "conflict" that the United States could win with its left hand.

Reserve units need not be mobilized, they said. Industry need not be put on a war footing. Rationing was not necessary. Americans could have both guns and butter. No sweat. The general populace would not be inconvenienced by this little war 10,000 miles away.

But by 1966 President Johnson and Secretary McNamara realized they had underestimated the determination of the Vietcong and North Vietnamese to win the civil war and what it would take to vanquish them.

Johnson and McNamara, also in 1966, felt the waves of public protest by adults and young people alike. The American press, particularly television, helped build up these waves by beaming the horrors of war from the battlefield to the American living room. This was a first.

Johnson, McNamara, Secretary of State Dean Rusk and other

1

American leaders found that they could not explain to the nation's satisfaction why this supposedly little war somewhere in Southeast Asia was killing almost 100 American soldiers every week and wounding another 600.

President Johnson in his State of the Union Address of January 12, 1966, could not summon up a rallying cry, like World War II's "Berlin by Christmas." All he could do was plead for steadfastness and promise to try to negotiate a way out of the war.

Less than a month later, on February 4, 1966, a troubled Senate Foreign Relations Committee began questioning the justification for the Vietnam War in nationally televised hearings. Another first for the polarizing United States of 1966.

The poles of the national debate over Vietnam became: "get all the way in; get all the way out." President Johnson did neither. In 1966 he ordered twice as many troops to Vietnam—389,000 compared to 181,392 in 1965. Too few soldiers to win the war; too many to lose it. "We are using that force and only that force that is necessary to stop this aggression," Johnson said on February 23, 1966. The "eyedropper" strategy.

But by doubling the number of American troops on the ground in 1966, Johnson did enable his Vietnam field commanders to send out their own combat units to take over the South Vietnamese Army's supposed job of searching out and killing the Vietcong and North Vietnamese main force battalions.

One such field commander was Major General William E. DePuy, the short, feisty, do-or-die commander of the First Infantry Division, known as The Big Red One. One of his rifle companies within The Big Red One was Charlie Company of the Second Battalion of the Sixteenth Infantry Regiment. And one of the Vietcong main force battalions DePuy was trying to find and destroy was D-800.

DePuy's idea was to send small units into the jungle to find a Vietcong force like D-800 and then pounce on it with overwhelming troops and firepower. He reasoned that—thanks to troop-carrying helicopters and tracked vehicles, artillery, gunships, and bombers—American commanders could reinforce their units faster than the enemy could reinforce his.

Charlie Company found D-800 on April 11, 1966. This time the crack Vietcong battalion chose to stand and fight the Americans rather than melt into the jungle. The Vietcong surrounded the American rifle company. It had to fight for its life.

2

Charlie Company's bloody stand turned out to be a microcosm of the cruel dilemma that closed in on American forces in Vietnam. If they fought hard and died in great numbers, as Charlie Company did, their losses fueled the protest movement back home against the war and the draft. If the American forces did not fight hard and kill the enemy, they could neither win the war nor impel the enemy to negotiate an end to it. DePuy and fellow commanders were expected somehow to win battles in Vietnam without losing too many men doing it. After Charlie Company's costly battle, General Harold K. Johnson, Army Chief of Staff, flew to Vietnam and told DePuy face to face that the American people would stop supporting the war if such high casualties continued.

High casualties did continue. Thousands of young men fled to Canada or took other steps to dodge the draft rather than fill the holes in Charlie Company and other combat units in Vietnam. These draft dodgers and protesters "deserve our sympathy and respect," said Chairman J. W. Fulbright (D-Ark.) of the Senate Foreign Relations Committee on April 21, 1966, ten days after Charlie Company was almost annihilated in its unheralded stand in the jungle.

Other soldiers kept dying.

By 1968, President Johnson realized that he, too, had become a casualty of the Vietnam War. He announced he would not run for re-election. His successor, President Richard M. Nixon, promised to end both the war and the draft. Nixon named a commission in 1969 to find a way to man the American armed forces entirely with volunteers. American troops, mostly draftees, left Vietnam in 1973 without winning the war despite their heroic efforts. Draft calls ended that same year. The great national experiment called the All Volunteer Force, or AVF, began. Could the United States recruit and field a quality military by relying entirely on volunteers?

For the AVF to be successful, the Presidential panel warned, military leaders would have to accept a new reality. They would have to compete in the marketplace with private industry for quality young men and women. Congress would help by raising the starting pay of these new soldiers. But America's post-Vietnam military could no longer count on the federal government to draft men to fill billets. The Army, Navy, Air Force, and Marine Corps would have to sell themselves to American teenagers or go short.

The Charlie Company that fought for its life in Vietnam in 1966 typified the spearpoint of the old Army relying heavily on draftees. The very same Charlie Company waiting for the call to battle in 1989 typifies the spearpoint of the new Army composed entirely of volunteers.

Army infantry battalions and companies are like civilian high schools in that their headquarters, usually brick buildings, stand generation after generation and house the teachers who train successive generations of students. An infantry battalion is roughly the size of a high school with 800 teachers and students. The teachers in the Army's case are officers and sergeants while the students are the soldiers. An infantry company within a battalion is like one of the four classes of about 200 students within a high school.

Battalions and companies, again like high schools and their classes, establish traditions that carry over from one generation of soldiers to the next. The headquarters of the Second Battalion of the Sixteenth Infantry Division is a brick building on Custer Hill at Fort Riley, Kansas. The headquarters of its Charlie Company is within another brick building nearby. The battalion was constituted on May 3, 1861. It fought in the Civil War and every other U.S. war except Korea since then, winning Presidential Unit Citations, streamers and medals for its valor. These trophies are displayed at the Fort Riley headquarters. Charlie Company members past and present not only take pride in the accomplishments of their parent Sixteenth Infantry Regiment and Second Battalion, along with the First Infantry Division to which those outfits were assigned in 1917 for World War I, but in what the company did all by itself. Charlie Company's performance in Vietnam is a celebrated case in point.

Charlie Company fought so valiantly on April 11 and 12, 1966, that it won the Valorous Unit Award. The streamer hailing the company's performance in that battle is embroidered COURTENAY PLANTATION and is displayed at Fort Riley. A picture of Sergeant James W. Robinson Jr., a hero of that battle who won the Medal of Honor, hangs in both the battalion and company headquarters at Riley. The new generation of soldiers who fill the billets in the same Charlie Company, few of whom were born when Robinson died hurling grenades at the .50-caliber machine gun that was chewing up his company, look at the streamer and Robinson's picture and take inspiration from them.

4

*Mud Soldiers* focuses on that same Charlie Company to give a then-and-now portrait of a typical combat unit that would be among the first to go to war. If the Charlie companies within the fighting part of the American Army have the willingness, skill, and leadership to hold in any next war, the nation can feel comforted. If they do not have these qualities, the nation must worry and do something to correct the shortcomings. Infantrymen within rifle companies must fight the enemy up close, sometimes hand to hand. They must put up with all kinds of miserable conditions, including living in the mud. The term "Mud Soldiers" is one of affectionate respect for the combat infantrymen who have it hardest and die soonest in most of our wars. General John W. Vessey Jr., chairman of the Joint Chiefs of Staff under President Reagan, took pride in calling himself a Mud Soldier, for example.

I start off the book with Charlie Company's horrific 1966 battle to portray what we ask our Mud Soldiers to do and what they must be able to do as long as the United States faces the risk of having to fight wars on land. To reconstruct Charlie Company's 1966 battle, I tracked down survivors and interviewed them extensively. Some broke into tears in reliving the trauma of that day and night. I sent the survivors draft after draft of my reconstruction of the battle until they agreed that the account which opens the book is as accurate as their memories and available documents can make it.

It struck me as one of history's ironies that the 1966 Charlie Company draftees, by sacrificing themselves so heroically and in such great numbers, helped end the draft that yanked them into the Vietnam jungle. Their losses played a direct role in clearing the way for today's attempt to build an Army entirely of volunteers. *Mud Soldiers* takes the reader across the generational bridge from the U.S. Army of Vietnam to the U.S. Army of today by putting him inside this Charlie Company. To do this, I lived with the post-Vietnam Charlie Company, sometimes in the mud, off and on for more than a year. I not only chronicled the volunteers' development as soldiers who will take the point for the nation in any next war, but came to know them as second sons. I also watched how they were led in two weeks of day and night battles against mock Soviet forces where everything was like actual combat except the bullets, which were simulated by laser beams. I saw worrisome cracks in our first line of defense.

The Mud Soldiers I came to know so well got off the bus at Fort

Benning, Georgia, in July 1987, with long hair, gold chains and dreams of what they were going to be like after negotiating the difficult passages from civilian to soldier, from boy to man. More than 200 of these raw recruits, mostly teenagers, trained as Delta Company at Benning. Half of them were then sent to Fort Riley in October 1987, as infantry graduates ready to constitute the new Charlie Company of Vietnam fame. I followed the graduates from Benning to Riley and chronicled their first year of ups and downs as professional soldiers.

I concluded that these Mud Soldiers are today's invisible patriots who will not fail us in war but whom we are failing in peace by not recognizing and fulfilling their expectations. Recruiting high-quality volunteers for such combat units as Charlie Company is becoming more difficult as this book goes to press, serving notice of trouble ahead. Congressional leaders are pushing to broaden the All Volunteer Force experiment by requiring young men and women who want to get federal loans or grants for education to serve either in the combat branches of the military or in some other public service capacity. *Mud Soldiers* is an account from the inside of where the fighting part of the American Army stands today and what must happen tomorrow for it to be all it can be at the time the nation is re-addressing the question of who should bear the burden of defending the country.

—GCW
January 1989

# 1. Legacy

The farthest thing from Johnny Libs's mind as he sat on the edge of the jungle clearing in Vietnam on the sunny Easter afternoon of April 10, 1966, was that he would have to shoot someone dead in thirty seconds. His thoughts had instead been pushed away from the Vietnam War and toward home by the chaplain standing before Charlie Company preaching the Easter sermon. The Protestant chaplain had been vaulted by helicopter from the safe world of the rear to the murderous one of the jungle 40 miles east of Saigon near the village of Xa Cam My. His crisp clothes and full face bespoke the fenced safety and hot-meal comfort of one of those fortresses the Americans were building around Saigon. The man of God was preaching to young men who had been transformed by the war from what-the-hell teenagers to stealthy soldiers living by the jungle commandment: Kill or be killed.

"Think of your loved ones back home," the preacher told the ragged soldiers sitting under the trees in front of him. "They will be going to church on Easter and praying for you."

"I don't think that's going to do us much good this time," Libs told himself. "Not where they're sending us tomorrow."

First Lieutenant John Wells Libs, 23, was leader of 2d Platoon, Charlie Company, Second Battalion, Sixteenth Infantry Regiment within the First Infantry Division, known as The Big Red One. He knew as he sat in the sun vainly trying to keep his mind on the chaplain's words that if the Vietcong struck in force tomorrow, as

7

his commanders predicted, he would not only have to run his own platoon of thirty-five men, but the whole damn Charlie Company. The company going to the field would number 134 men. The rest of Charlie Company's 157 were in the rear or out of action because of injuries, leaves or other reasons that always reduce the number of trigger-pullers available for a fight. He knew the odds were against him surviving Division's new strategy of dangling a small American force in front of a big Vietcong one to entice them to stand and fight. So Johnny Libs this sunny Easter afternoon tried to soak up the warmth and transport himself back to his hometown, Evansville, Indiana.

He had been warmed in Evansville by a thick blanket of security and happiness: house, family, money, car, friends, prestige. Johnny Libs had been athletic, bright and popular in high school. Even though he was only 5 feet 9 and 160 pounds, he was fast and agile. He captained the Memorial High School football team; ran the 100- and 220-yard dashes on the track team; was vice president of the class; earned high grades; dated lots of pretty girls. He graduated in 1960, went to St. Louis University and then transferred to Loyola University in New Orleans where the males had to join the Army ROTC whether they liked it or not. He was definitely an or-not until he went through infantry training at Fort Sill, Oklahoma, in the summer before his senior year at Loyola.

At Sill he discovered a way to live his boyhood dreams of playing John Wayne in the jungle without looking juvenile. He would join the infantry and lead a platoon in battle. Advancing through the woods to knock out an enemy machine gun without getting gunned down took skill and daring. And it was fun! Energizing. Enlivening. Flirting with death made him feel more alive than ever before. Damn! There is something to this Army after all, he concluded.

Libs vowed to become a blue-corded infantryman, a soldier who often had to go into the mud but got the dirty jobs done whether anybody outside the special fraternity realized it or not. The motto of the infantry platoon leader, "Follow me!" suited Johnny Libs just fine. He related to the mud soldier's bastardization of the 23rd Psalm: "Yea, though I walk through the valley of the shadow of death, I will fear no evil: for I am the meanest son of a bitch in the valley."

But the United States Army had other ideas for Libs, J. W.,

serial number 054 167 25, when it commissioned him a second lieutenant upon his graduation from Loyola in 1964. Vietnam was just a little skirmish way out there somewhere. President Lyndon B. Johnson had not yet gotten Congress to sign that blank check called the Gulf of Tonkin Resolution. Libs had studied business and finance in college, largely at Army expense, so the Army decided: We need this guy to be a finance officer more than a trigger-puller in a jungle nobody cares about.

"Fuck this," Libs said to himself after a few months of listening to boring lectures at the Army finance school at Fort Benjamin Harrison in Indianapolis, "I'm going infantry." He pulled every string he could reach, including those his family, who owned a big candy business in Evansville, had tied to Senator Vance Hartke of Indiana. "You've got it all wrong, Lieutenant," his superiors at Benjamin Harrison kept telling him. "You go from the infantry to here, not from here to the infantry. You're not going anyplace."

But Libs outmaneuvered them, got transferred to the infantry and took the basic course for junior officers at Fort Benning in Columbus, Georgia, "Home of the Infantry." He went on to earn his Ranger tab. He liked the roughest parts of Ranger training the best. He kept volunteering for Vietnam until the First Division at Fort Riley, Kansas, sent him there in June 1965.

The preacher's Easter sermon about Christ's Resurrection struck Libs as just the opposite of what he had been experiencing in Vietnam for the last ten months. He had been exposed to Death, not Resurrection. Overexposed. He would never get used to holding a dying soldier in his arms, assuring him, "You'll be all right," and then watching him turn gray, white—then die.

"Hey, Chaplain!" Libs asked the crisp man of the cloth in silent questions jumping up in his mind, "do you have any idea how tough it is to live in Vietnam after the kids you've loved and led die? Do you have any idea how hard it is to wash their blood out of your brain?"

Every time the high command flew his 2d Platoon out of the jungle and back to base camp for three days' rest before sending it out for another thirty days of killing and being killed chasing Vietcong, Libs tried to wash the blood out with Budweiser. No amount of beer did it. Nor did trying to bury himself body and soul in a woman he hardly knew. He had tried that on an R & R—rest and recreation—leave in Tokyo. He thought it was working and overstayed his leave by two weeks, asking himself: "So what are they going to do to me for going AWOL—send me to Vietnam?"

The stolen days of leave failed to wash away either the blood or the war. He returned to his platoon. It was the only place where people understood his disease of hollowness, fear, anger and guilt. His AWOL caused a brief flap at headquarters, but nothing major. It was never put on paper. His superiors needed Libs too much in the jungle to take the time to court-martial him. Johnny Libs had gotten real good at finding and killing VC.

The chaplain finished his Easter sermon at 4:45 P.M., gave the benediction to the weary Army company seated in front of him, looked over their bowed heads and saw a sight so startling that he called out, "What's that?"

Libs snapped his head around. Three Vietcong in black pajamas and web belts were walking across the far end of the clearing about 400 yards away. They appeared to be scouts.

"Come on, you sons of bitches," Libs shouted to his platoon. "Let's get 'em!"

He and the soldiers nearest him jumped up, slammed on their helmets and ran in spread formation toward the Vietcong. Private First Class Phillip J. Hall was lugging an M-60 machine gun. Sergeant Lawson H. "Ernst" Passmore and Corporal Otis Lee Flake, Libs's radioman, had M-16s. Another trooper tried to rig up his M-79 grenade launcher as he ran. They unloosed this arsenal while sprinting through the knee-high grass outside the Courtenay rubber plantation. Other platoons were firing at the same time. It sounded like the Mad Minute fire demonstration at Benning. One Vietcong went down. A second turned back to grab the downed man's rifle and got hit himself. He fell. The third kept running across the clearing, made it to the woods and disappeared.

"We got two of the bastards!" somebody shouted.

Libs, who had run a ten-flat 100-yard dash in high school back in Evansville another life ago, arrived on the scene first. He saw that one scout was already dead and the other one horribly wounded but conscious. A main artery near the groin of the wounded VC was gushing blood.

"Where's D-800?" Libs demanded.

The dying Vietcong spit on Libs. Libs grabbed the bleeding

man's balls and squeezed hard. The Vietcong screamed out a stream of Vietnamese words.

"What's he saying?" Libs asked of the Vietnamese interpreter who, carrying an M-1 carbine, had just reached the scene. He was standing on Libs's left, studying the dying Vietcong.

"He's from an independent unit and was out on patrol," the interpreter said.

Radioman Flake, standing on Libs's right, knew the scout had said more than that. Flake had spent enough time with the Vietnamese tea girls in the Melody Bar and other joints along Saigon's Tu Do Street to understand a fair amount of Vietnamese. Flake had definitely heard the dying scout mention D-800.

"Sir!" Flake said to Libs after the wounded Vietcong had died and the officer and his radioman were walking back toward Charlie Company's encampment, "That interpreter didn't tell you what the guy said."

"Come on now, Flake. This is important."

"I know for sure, sir, that he said he was from D-800 and was sent out to find us."

Division intelligence had expressed suspicions about Charlie Company's Vietnamese interpreter but had no hard proof. Libs resolved to watch him closely from now on, but he had bigger worries at the moment. A bigger Vietcong unit might be snaking through the woods right now to catch the Americans by surprise this Easter afternoon.

"Hall!" Libs shouted to machine-gunner Hall. "Get your ass back in position and set up the 60. Everybody else, back on the perimeter! The bad guys are here."

An officer and sergeant from another platoon ran up to view the bodies of the Vietcong scouts. The sergeant had always talked tough, but also fought tough. He had this weird habit, though, of overdoing it by cutting ears off dead Vietcong. He did his thing to the two dead scouts, to the disgust of other troopers looking on silently.

Libs rushed up to Captain William R. Nolen, commander of Charlie Company, who was back in the woods at the edge of the clearing where the service had just been conducted. The sandy-haired, religious, unassuming Nolen was brand new in Vietnam. He had never been in a big firefight. Lieutenant Colonel William S. Hathaway, battalion commander, had told Nolen to listen to what Libs had to say, to realize that this gung-ho first lieutenant had been in country long enough to know how to kill rather than be killed.

"Sir, we've got to get out of this position," Libs told Nolen. "Flake tells me these guys are attached to D-800. We've got to move over there," Libs said, pointing to the northwest corner of the clearing. "And let's ambush the bodies."

Lieutenant Kenneth M. Alderson, executive officer of Charlie Company, worried about what the Vietcong scout who had escaped into the woods would tell his commanders. The scout obviously had been able to judge the position, size and probably intent of the American rifle company seemingly far from other elements of the First Division.

The company pulled itself together. A few hours later it moved as quietly as it could—which was not very quiet—into the woods at the other end of the clearing. One small ambush team was sent out to a concealed position in killing range of the bodies in case Vietcong came to retrieve them. Another ambush squad lay along the trail the scouts had been following when they were shot.

Just before dusk, the *thwacka-thwacka* of a Huey helicopter announced the arrival of Major General William E. DePuy, the new, aggressive commander of the First Infantry Division. The helicopter had the white horns of a steer painted on its side to symbolize the helicopter company's nickname, the Long Horns. DePuy's two stars were painted on the helicopter's nose.

"Here comes that old son of a bitch Willy DePuy who loves to fight," Libs said admiringly as the general's chopper settled onto the clearing. He remembered with a smile how, right after taking command of the Big Red One, DePuy had gathered all the First Division officers together and decreed: "I will never, ever hear again over the radio, 'I'm pinned down. I'm breaking contact.' I hear it, that officer is relieved immediately. You're never pinned down. Period." DePuy told them that if they needed it, artillery could be fired extremely close to their perimeter.

DePuy wanted his officers to charge, to break out of any encirclement, to kill even if it meant being killed. He wanted to win this war in a hurry. Period. Libs said "right on" to himself at the time. He cheered the aggressiveness DePuy had triggered since taking over from the cautious Major General Jonathan O. Seaman in February 1966. Libs, like DePuy, believed in the war and wanted to win it or die trying. He was eager to hear what Old

12

Willy had to say about Charlie Company's part tomorrow in the big push called Operation Abilene.

The plan was for the Second and Third brigades of the First Infantry Division to send small units through Phuoc Tuy and Long Khanh provinces to search out and destroy Vietcong. So far, Abilene had turned out to be mostly search, not much destroy. DePuy hoped Charlie Company would find the big prize, the Vietcong's D-800 Battalion.

"You guys are out here alone," DePuy told the officers of Charlie Company. "By all intelligence, D-800 is nearby. Your chances of getting hit tonight are very good. Our artillery has got you bracketed in."

No win-one-for-the-Gipper talk. Just some cold truth spoken quietly by a general who obviously knew something big was going to happen. Then the big man flew away, leaving Libs to worry as Easter darkened into the ever-dangerous night of Vietnam.

As Libs saw it, DePuy was sending Charlie Company out as bait in hopes of catching the elusive, first-line Vietcong battalion of 400 troops and a backup force of women and children. Simple but perhaps fatal. Charlie Company would be kept far enough away from other companies in the battalion to persuade D-800 commanders they had caught an isolated American unit. The jungle was too thick to reinforce the company by helicopter. DePuy would deny after the battle that he had sent out Charlie Company as bait. He assumed Charlie Company, like every outfit he sent out into the bush, could be reinforced if it suddenly ran into heavy trouble. Another company was supposed to be close enough to come to Charlie's rescue.

What if D-800 struck Charlie Company tonight? Libs fretted. DePuy's helicopter arrival and departure probably had enabled D-800 to know Charlie Company's general location, even though it had moved a short distance since his departure. Were the Vietcong commanders deploying their mortars right now? Would their infantry hit between now and dawn? Libs was nervous, edgy, scared. He dared not lie down, far less sleep. He walked around his platoon hour after hour, checking with his men and staring out into the black clearing, looking for movement. His men had not dug foxholes to sleep in or fire from. Those not on guard were taking mud soldier catnaps on the ground.

"How ya doing?" Libs asked his men at every stop on his ceaseless rounds.

13

"Hear anything? See anything?"

"Anything going on out there with the bodies? Hear any talk at all? Smell anything?"

"Sir, it's quiet as hell out here," was the universal response from the men lying at the edge of the jungle.

"Get as many Z's as you can. This is going to be a long night; an even longer tomorrow."

In his rounds, Libs ran into Lieutenant Martin L. Kroah Jr., 30, 3d Platoon's leader, doing the same thing. Libs and Kroah had foxhole adoration for each other, an emotion that no one who has not felt it could understand. They had watched each other under the pressure of battle. Libs saw in Kroah a wild-assed former sergeant who knew how to fight and win. Kroah saw in Libs "a cocky little bastard" who was all soldier in the field and all hell-raiser like himself in the rear.

Kroah's life before joining the Army had been as hard as Libs's had been easy. His parents were divorced. His mother worked as a waitress. Marty bagged groceries for thirty-five cents an hour at Montressor's Market in his home town of Brockway, Pennsylvania. A tall, stringy kid standing 6 feet and weighing 137 pounds, Marty had a job that left no time for after-school sports. He did play the trumpet in the marching band. Montressor's would let him leave the market thirty minutes before the half of football games so he could go home, put on his band uniform and march up and down the field with his trumpet. He could not stay to watch the second half of the game; he had to be back at the market. That was just the way life was in Brockway for Marty Kroah.

After graduating from high school in 1953, Marty saw his options as working at Montressor's or the local glass factory. The Army looked like a way out of Brockway and up in life. He joined; became a paratrooper to get the extra $50 a month jump pay, sending it home to his mother; rose quickly to staff sergeant, was selected for the Non-Commissioned Officer's Academy, the Army's little West Point; and was commissioned a second lieutenant at Fort Benning's Officer Candidate School in 1962 after nine years of enlisted service. Kroah joined Charlie Company as 3d Platoon leader in October 1965.

Libs and Kroah realized this Easter night that they had allowed themselves to grow too close to each other. The loss of one would devastate the other. Marty must have sensed one of them would die in the battle with D-800. He discarded his tough demeanor long enough to put his right arm around Johnny Libs's shoulders and speak about dying in the code of mud soldiers: "Well, we're going to get the shit kicked out of us tomorrow."

"Yeah," Libs replied. "But we found D-800. We're going to kick ass, Marty."

"Yeah. I know you got Nolen's ear. Watch him."

"Marty, he'll be OK," Libs said of the green company commander. He said Nolen had told him earlier in that evening, "I'll be calling on you for a lot of help." Libs said he had replied: "I'll sure be there, Captain, no problem."

Libs liked Nolen's quiet manner. Bluster often covered weakness and incompetence in combat; quietness usually meant strength. An education at West Point or any other military college did not count for much in a firefight. Libs had learned during his ten months in Vietnam that character, guts, coolness and competence were what counted. But Nolen was so damn green. This Citadel graduate, this cherry—is he going to do something that will get us all killed? Executive Officer Alderson, who would accompany the unit into the field, was less worried about Nolen. He considered his religious commanding officer intelligent and open to advice from more experienced subordinates.

Libs also fretted about how Lieutenant George C. Steinberg, 4th Platoon commander, an intellectual but not a jungle fighter, and Second Lieutenant Smith A. Devoe, 1st Platoon leader, newly arrived in the country, would stand up against the 3-to-1 odds Charlie Company would confront if D-800 struck. "Oh well," Libs consoled himself, "I'll have Marty."

Dawn of April 11, 1966, neared without the Vietcong hitting Charlie Company. The men roused themselves for stand-to at 5:30 A.M. The soldiers took fighting positions during stand-to in case the enemy launched a pre-dawn attack. Nothing happened.

The troops opened C-ration cans of peaches and fruit cake for breakfast, or whatever else they were not sick of eating. They filled canteens, loaded up with ammunition, massaged sore feet, mounted up for another hot walk 10,000 miles from where they wanted to be. One sergeant, in what fellow troopers regarded as another one of his faked injuries, said he had sprained his ankle and could not go out on the mission. He was flown out of the clearing along with the bodies of the two dead Vietcong that intelligence officers in the rear wanted to examine.

15

"Marty," Nolen said, "I want you to be point."

Kroah thought this was unfair. His 3d Platoon seemed to have done more than its share of spearheading the company into one dangerous patch of jungle after another. Kroah did not protest. He figured Nolen wanted one experienced platoon leader out front and the other one, Libs, bringing up the rear. Nolen himself would stay in the middle of the formation. Steinberg's 4th Platoon would follow Kroah's 3d; Devoe's 1st Platoon would be third in the weaving line of four platoons constituting Charlie Company.

"Today is not just another walk in the woods," Kroah told himself as his platoon pushed off due north at 7:30 A.M. on April 11, 1966. He felt fearful and relieved at the same time. He could not explain the currents and crosscurrents coursing through him. Something was different. He knew it.

An American rifle company pushing through thick jungle is like four tiny, independent armies connected to each other only by radio. Vietnam's triple-canopy jungle, plus tree trunks, vines, brush, all conspired to block vision not only between the four platoons but between the men in one platoon. A trooper pushing through dense undergrowth and thick trees often lost sight of the man nearest him, making his advance toward hidden enemy troops all the more unnerving. Two hours into the march the soldiers discovered ominous trenches, 300 yards long and 4 feet deep. The Vietcong obviously had prepared to defend this patch of jungle.

At 11 A.M., Kroah's platoon swung west. Eleven minutes later it discovered a well-used trail running east to west. Nolen ordered patrols sent out in all four directions of the trail to probe for Vietcong and their encampments. The troopers stayed off the trail itself to avoid ambushes and booby traps. The troopers not out on patrol grabbed more C-rations for lunch, sipped from canteens.

*Snap! Snap!*

Marty heard one of his troopers he could not see firing off two rounds from his M-16. He rushed to the man, learned he had seen two Vietcong but missed them. It was 12:15 P.M. "Be more alert!," Kroah ordered. "If you see another one, let me know."

No sooner had Kroah turned away from the private than he heard him shout, "Hey! We just saw another one!"

There were no more sightings for a while. Kroah's 3d Platoon stopped for lunch. They kept their eyes on the trail where the first three Vietcong had been sighted. They finished their C-ration lunch and began moving again. A shot rang out; one of Kroah's soldiers fell. Kroah's radioman, Jasper Carpenter, fired off his M-16.

"What are you shooting at?" Kroah asked Carpenter.

"I saw three VC going into the ground!"

Kroah figured the Vietcong had slipped into a bunker on the jungle floor. He grabbed the telephone-shaped hand set off the PRC 25 radio carried by Private First Class Carpenter, a married man with children who talked and looked like the red-necked Alabaman he was. Captain Nolen's radio call sign was Charlie Six and Kroah's November Six.

"Charlie Six. This is November Six. We had sighting of three VC."

"November Six. This is Charlie Six. Kill your three Charlies?"

"Charlie Six. This is November Six. No, but they saw us."

"November Six. Charlie Six. What do you think we should do?"

"Charlie Six. November Six. Find out where they're going."

"November Six. Charlie Six. That's affirm."

Had the Vietcong sent out a few elusive snipers to draw Charlie Company deeper into the jungle and closer to the base camp of D-800? Should Charlie Company stop right there and call for reinforcements this early afternoon? Or should it try to locate the enemy so it would know what was out there in the jungle? An infantry commander in combat is damned if he is not aggressive enough and damned if he is too aggressive. DePuy had left no doubt he wanted to find and smash D-800. Nolen decided to probe deeper.

Libs, bringing up the rear of Charlie Company, was probing, too. Private First Class Phil Hall was out on the left flank of 2d Platoon feeling very vulnerable. The 21-year-old Hall, of Eagle, Wisconsin, wondered if he had gotten himself into more adventure than he bargained for when he chucked the job of bagging fertilizer in Whitewater, Wisconsin, for this job of infantryman. The husky six-footer was carrying a pump-action 12-gauge shotgun, which the Army used early in the war, and the ammunition for the M-60 machine gun. His buddy, Specialist Four John Noyce, had the 60 itself. Other buddies like John Fulford, Jackie Lancaster, Gil DeLao and Ernst Passmore were out here someplace in the dense growth. Their black humor and support was was what made life in the field bearable, sometimes even enjoyable.

*Pop! Pop! Pop! Pop! Pop!*

Somebody was shooting at Hall. He could not see him. Hall sat down on the jungle floor, shotgun across his knees, and strained to see who was out there in the trees and thick underbrush.

Libs heard the shots in his own area. Kroah had radioed earlier that he was taking sporadic fire from hit-and-run snipers. Libs knew now that the Vietcong had riflemen deployed at the front and rear of the company. The Vietcong could be trying to surround the company or draw it into a prepared killing zone.

Nolen ordered Steinberg's 4th Platoon to move forward to reinforce the left flank of Kroah's 3d Platoon. The Vietcong opened up on 4th Platoon as it moved up at 12:50 P.M., killing one soldier and wounding a second. This meant the company would have to set up a defensive perimeter around the killed and wounded if and when the medivac helicopters arrived to hoist them out of the jungle, if that was even possible through the triple canopy of treetops. First Platoon radioed that it was receiving fire. Then the firing stopped.

Libs feared the Vietcong were using the time to surround the scattered elements of Charlie Company. This would make it easy for them to annihilate each small group. To save itself from piecemeal destruction, the company would have to form a circle and cover the area outside it with interlocking fire.

"Charlie Six," Libs radioed to Nolen. "This is Mike Six. Roll up the wagons now!"

The long, twisting snake that is an American rifle company searching for an enemy cannot coil up quickly. Libs ran from man to man, pushing each one into his firing position on the slowly forming circle.

"Now don't fucking move," Libs ordered. "Shoot anything that moves, but watch your ammunition."

The 2d Platoon circled away from Hall, leaving him farther out on the flank. He was still sitting with the shotgun on his knees, scanning the thick weave of jungle. He spotted twelve Vietcong apparently going to their part of the noose forming around Charlie Company. Some wore black pajamas, others khaki uniforms. The khaki was ominous. It indicated first-line officers were directing the farmer-soldiers in black pajamas.

"Lieutenant!" Hall shouted to Libs. "I got people out here with khaki uniforms on!"

The Vietcong blasted at the patch of jungle where the voice had come from. Hall saw bullets hitting the ground all around him. None hit him. He could not see the enemy unless he raised his head above the bushes hiding him. Every time he did that, more fire came at him.

"Withdraw!" Libs yelled to Hall. "Withdraw! Get back here inside the perimeter!"

Hall began to stand up. He saw a Vietcong in black pajamas and a floppy hat walking toward him. He raised the shotgun, pulled the trigger and pumped again and again until the man in front of him fell. Hall sprinted toward the platoon's perimeter. He spotted an ant berm and dove behind it. A small soldier named Owens was already hiding there.

"Are you hit?" Owens asked.

"Fuck no," Hall responded. He tucked up his body, rolled toward the perimeter for several yards, then jumped up to sprint the last 20 yards. The Vietcong fired at him during his dash. Notoriously poor marksmen, they missed. Owens, a green trooper, stayed hidden behind the anthill.

"Hey, now I'm pinned down out here!" Noyce yelled from his hiding place outside the perimeter. He had the M-60 machine gun.

"Come on, Noyce," Hall shouted back. "I made it out of there. You can make it in."

"Get your ass in here, Noyce!" Libs commanded. "We need the 60."

Noyce sprinted for the perimeter and made it in despite the spray of bullets shot at him. Noyce and Hall set up the machine gun on the perimeter and waited for the Vietcong attack.

At the front of the column, Kroah and his 3d Platoon kept getting fire as the battle slowly developed. Kroah and Sergeant Rolf Schoolman moved ahead of their men to determine where most of the firing was coming from. Kroah thought he had located the hot spot and called in ranging rounds.

"Fox Six," Kroah radioed to First Lieutenant Francis Fox, the artillery forward observer traveling with the company, after the ranging rounds hit the right patch of jungle. "This is November Six. That's good enough. Fire for effect." Ten rounds, two from each of the five 105mm artillery pieces in the rear, came whooshing in. Kroah heard screams from his own men behind

19

him. Libs at the same time saw men being cut down in his area in the rear of the company. Nobody would ever know for sure who killed the soldiers with this friendly fire. One report estimated five troopers were killed and another dozen wounded by the errant artillery fire. It was confusing who was killing whom because of the combination of sniper and artillery fire that created sudden chaos around 2 P.M. Kroah blamed himself because he had called in degrees (360 in a circle) instead of mils (6,400 in a circle) in adjusting the incoming artillery rounds. Libs blamed Major M, an artillery officer in the rear. The Army calls such death by friendly fire fratricide. It happens in the close quarters of jungle fighting.

Vietcong snipers opened on Kroah's platoon after the artillery had stopped. Several of his men got wounded. He answered a nervous call from Nolen on the radio.

"November Six, Charlie Six," Nolen began. "We're going to pull back."

"Charlie Six. November Six. I can't do that. I've got more wounded than effectives."

"November Six. Charlie Six. Better figure something out. We're pulling out."

Nolen ordered his platoons to pull back from the most intense fire, which seemed to be directed at the front of the company formation. He hoped to avoid encirclement of the whole company, even if he had to lose the point platoon commanded by Kroah that was now in danger of being overrun. It was too late. The company had put itself too far into the closing noose. The other platoons found they could not move, either, without drawing heavy fire. Every time a soldier tried to go into a low crawl, snipers in the trees would spot the movement and shoot at him.

"November Six. Charlie Six. Looks like they've got us encircled. We're not going anyplace."

Two Air Force Huskie helicopters arrived at 3 P.M. to evacuate the men who had been killed or wounded from sniper fire and the misdirected rounds of artillery. Troopers cut a hole in the treetops so the choppers could lower a bullet-shaped jungle penetrator down to the jungle floor. Air Force Captain Harold D. Salem maneuvered his helicopter over the hole in the trees and hovered. Airman First Class William H. Pitsenbarger, 21, of Piqua, Ohio, pulled down one of the jungle penetrator's spring-loaded seats, straddled it and signaled Sergeant Gerald Hammond to release the steel cable that would lower him down to the smoking battleground 200 feet below.

Executive Officer Alderson, radio in hand to coordinate the evacuation, was astonished by the sight of an airman dressed in freshly pressed fatigues and a flak jacket and carrying two .38-caliber pistols on his body voluntarily lowering himself into the mud soldiers' smoking hell. "This Saigon cowboy doesn't know what he's getting into," Alderson said to himself.

Libs, from a farther distance, saw the young man riding down the sky through a hail of enemy bullets. "I'd like to shake that man's hand," Libs marveled.

Once Pitsenbarger was on the ground, Hammond at the side door of the Huskie reeled up the hoist cable, attached a litter basket for the wounded and relowered the cable down to the airman.

"Pits" Pitsenbarger patched up several wounded men and lifted one of them into the litter. Hammond hoisted up this wounded man, lowered the litter again to pick up another one. This first helicopter left the spot over the hole in the trees so it could fly the two wounded to the first aid station at Bien Hoa. The second Huskie found the same hole in the trees, retrieved two more wounded. Each Huskie made three trips to the battleground, rescuing twelve of the fifteen wounded.

The two Huskies returned in hopes of hoisting up the remaining three wounded and two dead. On the ground Pits was trying to get the wounded ready for the painful 200-foot trip up to the side door of the Huskie. He had run out of the splints he had brought down from the chopper and was feverishly fashioning make-do ones out of sticks and vines. But this time the Vietcong opened up on the hovering Huskie, ripping holes in its fuel and hydraulic lines. The Huskie lost power. Hammond motioned Pits to climb into the litter basket so he could be pulled back into the helicopter before it left the battleground. Pits waved off the chopper, electing to stay with Charlie Company. The Huskie struggled out of the hole in the trees under heavy fire. The basket caught on the treetops. Hammond cut the hoist cable, freeing the struggling helicopter. The Huskie made an emergency landing a few miles away.

Left by his own choice with the seemingly doomed men of Charlie Company, Pitsenbarger joined the fight. He gathered the idle rifles and ammunition off the killed and wounded and distributed them to the men still fighting. He used up all his dressings, picked up an M-16 discarded by a wounded soldier and helped a fire team fight the Vietcong.

An Army UH-1 Huey helicopter hovered over the company to kick cases of ammunition out the side door. The ammo was supposed to land within the company's perimeter. The helicopter pilot radioed down that the fire was so heavy he was going to leave without dropping all the ammunition on board. Kroah radioed back: "If we don't get it, you don't leave." The pilot could not be sure whether the beleaguered lieutenant would make good on his threat to shoot him down. He stayed until all the ammunition was kicked out. It was an accurate drop. The ammunition cases landed only 20 yards from where Nolen and Alderson were trying to organize their forces.

"We gotta get out of here," Nolen told Alderson. He told him to find a platoon and try to break out of the Vietcong's tightening circle. Nolen got wounded shortly after giving that order. He was already traumatized by his first big battle.

Alderson and Radio Telephone Operator Bash moved toward the perimeter to organize a breakout. Vietcong AK-47s opened up on them as they moved. One round smashed into Bash's helmet, knocking him to the jungle floor, face down. Alderson thought he was dead. He rolled the soldier's body over.

"What's wrong?" Bash asked as he stared back at the astonished Alderson. The bullet had bounced away or through the outer steel of the helmet without hitting Bash's head.

*Boom!*

Another Vietcong bullet knocked the helmet off Alderson's head. Again, the bullet ricocheted away from its target, Alderson's head.

Bash's radio was attracting so much fire that Alderson ordered him to stash it behind a tree rather than continue to wear it on his body. Alderson could communicate only if he stayed near the radio. This became impossible during the fluid fight. The radio was soon destroyed anyway.

Alderson was trying to reach the center of the perimeter when he encountered a sergeant from the 1st Platoon sitting against a tree with the blank stare of battle shock. The sergeant's rifle was lying unused on the jungle floor. Alderson talked to him, gently.

"The only way we're going to get out of this is to fight our way out," Alderson said. "If we can't do that, let's not make it easy for them. Most of our leadership is already gone. We need you."

The sergeant picked up his rifle and moved toward the perimeter to fight and die.

At 4 P.M., the Vietcong began marching 60mm mortar fire across the company. Most of the men escaped the mortar fragments by hugging the ground. A mortar bursts in a mushroom shape. It will get you if you are standing up. First Battalion of the Seventh Artillery, at a base a few miles behind Charlie Company, zeroed in on the mortars pinpointed by counter-radar, finally silencing the position by firing twenty rounds on top of it.

Lying flat protected the troopers against mortar fragments but not against the Vietcong snipers high in the trees ringing the company. The troopers kept getting shot in the back as they lay in the prone firing position. Many rolled over on their backs and shot into the trees. The Vietcong would send one of their soldiers running across a clear spot between trees to draw Charlie Company's fire. This would help pinpoint the defenders for the Vietcong snipers blasting away with AK-47 rifles from up in the trees.

Libs concluded the company had been drawn into a carefully prepared kill sack. He knew the company had to break out to survive. Marty could break the Vietcong's choke ring if anybody could. Libs decided to ask him to try. Libs, the most experienced jungle fighter, was out of sight and had no radio contact with his senior officers. He assumed it was up to him to try to save the company and went into action.

"We've got to break it, Marty," he told his buddy.

"Fucking A," Marty responded over the radio.

Kroah and his platoon made a stab at breaking through the enemy lines closing in on the company's spearhead pointing northwest. The Vietcong stopped them with a killing curtain of fire.

"Sorry, John," Marty radioed back. "Couldn't break it."

Libs and a group of riflemen then tried to break the noose in their southeast sector. They ran into another curtain of concentrated fire from the ground and up in the trees.

Vietcong riflemen under covering fire from the trees assaulted the lines of 3d and 4th platoons in a screaming attack. The Americans fought back fiercely. Artillery kept crashing down, preventing the Vietcong from staying massed against any one position.

At 5:45 P.M., Libs and others heard the heart-sinking *chung*,

*chung, chung* of two .50-caliber and *pat, pat, pat* of eight .30-caliber machine guns from outside the company perimeter.

D-800 had moved its heavy weapons out of the nearby base camp and placed them all around Charlie Company's steadily shrinking circle. Machine-gun bullets, especially .50 caliber, are lethal not only because they come in streams but also because they are heavy and cut through brush and branches without losing accuracy or killing power. Two .30 caliber and one .50 caliber were slamming rounds into 3d and 4th platoons on the company's northwest point; a second .50 caliber and a .30 caliber were firing into 2d Platoon holding the northeast quadrant of the perimeter, and two .30 calibers were raking 1st Platoon in the southeast quadrant.

"Damage Five," Libs radioed to Major Bibb Underwood, battalion executive officer, who was 1,000 feet above the raging battle calling in artillery from the back of a Huey helicopter. "Mike Six. Get something more in here. The motherfuckers are all over the place. Up in the trees. The sons of bitches have got .50s. We've lost a lot of people already. Where the fuck is Bravo Company?"

"Mike Six. Damage Five. Hang in here. We'll give you everything we've got. Bravo Company is still 1,000 meters away."

"Damage Five. Mike Six. They'll be too fucking late. We'll be rotting in the jungle by the time Bravo gets here."

Bravo Company was out on Charlie Company's far left flank. The jungle was so thick that Bravo could only move about 100 yards an hour by hacking out a single-file trail. There was no open area anywhere near outnumbered Charlie Company for helicopters with reinforcements to land. Charlie would live or die depending on what it could do all by itself.

At 6:30 PM. soldiers from the 4th Platoon charged the .50 caliber position on the northwest flank while their comrades shot up into the trees to suppress the deadly fire of the Vietcong snipers. The troopers who were not cut down knocked out the .50 with hand grenades.

The wounded, if they had the strength, crawled from the outer edge of the oval-shaped defensive ring to its center. When a man was killed, his buddies left their firing positions long enough to carry him to the center of the oval to lie there with the wounded. Casualties were leaving big holes in Charlie Company's outer perimeter. Libs feared the Vietcong would charge through one of these gaps and wipe out the whole company at any moment.

"Mike Six," Kroah called to his old buddy Libs. "November Six. I'm hit. Think Langston's dead." Fourth Platoon Sergeant Gene Langston, 27, of Leachville, Arkansas, was a company favorite. Everybody called him "The Round Man." He had taken Private First Class Gregory L. Bishop under his wing. The troopers taunted the religious Bishop because he called himself a conscientious objector and would not carry a rifle. He served as Langston's radioman. The beefy sergeant threatened to waste anybody who taunted Bishop. The two became as close as brothers. When Langston died from .50-caliber bullets, which almost cut him in two, Bishop's spirit died with him.

The Vietcong concentrated fire on Kroah and the two soldiers beside him, a medic on his left and Radioman Carpenter on his right. Bullets from snipers in the trees slammed into Kroah's right shoulder, calf and ankle. His medic received a burst in his back and lay helpless and bleeding alongside Kroah. One bullet cut the cord of Carpenter's radio. Another slammed through his helmet and went out the back without hitting his head. A third hit him in the shoulder.

"Help me," Carpenter cried to Kroah. "Help me! I've got a wife and kids. I want to go home and see them. I don't want to die here!"

"Shut the fuck up," Kroah rebuked. "Just lie still and you'll be all right."

A second medic crawled out to Kroah and stuffed a towel into his gushing shoulder. It slowed the bleeding. Another bullet slammed into the already crippled platoon leader.

Kroah heard a shout from First Lieutenant Steinberg, commander of 4th Platoon. "I need some help over here!"

"George, I can't help you," Kroah shouted back. "I've been hit five times."

"I've been hit seven," Steinberg replied.

"Always the bullshitter, huh, George?"

"No bullshit, man."

And it wasn't. Steinberg died with those words.

His 4th Platoon fought on with heroic abandon, even to grappling with the charging Vietcong with bare hands after ammunition ran out. The troopers also hurled their CS gas and smoke canisters at the attackers to stop one of the three waves, halting it long enough for the few troopers with any ammunition left to cut it down.

25

Sergeant James W. Robinson Jr., 25, of Annandale, Virginia, was fighting with the same abandon in 1st Platoon's southeast sector. A mountain of a man who had chafed during his years of ceremonial duty as a Marine, Robby was now undergoing the test by fire he had always sought. He picked up an M-79 grenade launcher, a thump gun, and fired grenades into the trees where the Vietcong snipers were shooting down on the platoon.

He shifted his attention to the woods just outside the perimeter. He saw a medic and a sergeant pinned down by enemy fire. He ran through bullets, locked one man in each arm, dragged them inside the perimeter, dressed their wounds, gave them shots of morphine and then assessed his fire team's situation. It was desperate. The pile of wounded and dead behind the platoon's defensive line was growing. Robinson collected all the serviceable rifles and ammunition, redistributing the small arsenal among the survivors. He kept the leftover rifles and grenades for his own one-man stand. He hosed through the trees again, killing more snipers.

One of his buddies had been cut down by machine-gun fire. Robinson ran to him. The same machine gun hit Robinson's leg as he ran. He reached his comrade, pushed him behind a tree, tied bandages around the worst wounds and patched himself as best he could under cover of the tree.

"I see the .50!" Robinson shouted to his men. "I'm going for it! Cover me!"

Robinson by this time had no ammunition left for his M-16. He placed the empty rifle beside the private he had just dragged behind the tree. Sitting beside the wounded man where the tree protected him from the machine-gun fire, Robinson pulled two grenades off his web belt. He yanked out the pins so they were ready to go off once he let his fingers off the spoon firing mechanism running down the side of the grenade. Taking a deep breath, Robinson struggled to his feet behind the tree and gathered his strength for the dash to the .50, about 20 yards outside the company perimeter.

With a Marine growl, Robinson ran toward the .50, one grenade in each hand. A tracer round hit him in the leg, setting his trousers on fire. He staggered to within 10 yards of the machine gun despite its withering fire, shifted his two grenades onto his one good arm and lofted them expertly smack into the machine-gun position. The two grenades went off in one giant blast, killing the crew and silencing the .50 for the rest of the battle. Robinson fell dead, his body riddled with the last burst of the machine gun. He would be awarded the Medal of Honor, the nation's highest military award.

Twilight approached. The Vietcong firing stopped except for a few shots here and there. D-800 was holding its fire to give their women employed as a support force time to shoot any wounded outside the perimeter, strip the bodies and report where the biggest gaps seemed to be in the company's ragged perimeter.

With the firing stilled, Libs could hear Vietcong jabbering all around him, both in the trees and on the ground. He noticed his company no longer had enough men in the line to form an unbroken protective ring of fire. He saw only tight pockets of two, three and four riflemen. There were big spaces between these small clusters. Libs knew it was only a matter of time before the Vietcong mounted their final charge and raced through one of the gaps. He also knew he was going to die. He could not think of anything he had not tried except one last do-or-die breakout attempt. He was puzzling out how best to make this suicide drive when he saw a green-yellow cloud of gas rolling toward him. He thought the Vietcong had launched a gas attack before moving in to annihilate Charlie Company. But the gas had been blown southward from the point where 3d and 4th platoons had made their valiant stands and wafted onto 2d Platoon.

"Gas!" Libs shouted, remembering his Fort Benning training. He instinctively reached into his gas-mask pouch to withdraw his mask. His hands felt catsup, mustard and an onion. "Oh shit, I don't have a mask." He dug a little hole in the ground and put his head in it to escape the CS gas choking him. "They're going to find my head in this hole with a bullet through it," he told himself, "and say, 'Libs was a coward.'" He allowed himself a giggle, saying, "Who gives a shit?"

The wind blew the gas away. The Vietcong had not made their final assault. Breakout was now or never. Libs gathered up the few men still firing and capable of running. They included his big horse with the shotgun, Phil Hall.

"Let's go, you guys! We're going to break through here. We're going to assault! Move! Move! Move! Get your ass out from behind that anthill," he commanded Hall, who was lying behind it firing.

"Jesus Christ!" Hall exclaimed as he stared death in the face again and prepared to charge. They raced forward a few yards before the Vietcong fusillade forced them to drop to the jungle floor. Private First Class Edward W. Reilly, 22, of Upper Darby, Pennsylvania, was killed. The clean-cut, redheaded young man died with his hands clasped together over a cross he wore around his neck. The survivors tried to crawl forward to blast away the enemy. Artillery and heavy firing had stripped much of the jungle away. Libs could see his small force was outmanned and outgunned. Nobody would live long enough to reach the .50-caliber machine gun causing so much havoc. A grenade exploded between Hall and Private First Class Jackie K. Lancaster. The hot fragments missed Hall but hit Lancaster. One fragment went clean through Lancaster's helmet without hitting his head.

"Get back in!" Libs shouted.

"Can you get me back?" the wounded Lancaster asked Hall.

"Yeah, I'll get you back."

Lancaster with painful effort got his arm over Hall's left shoulder as they lay on the ground. Kicking knees and digging with elbows, the two crawled back toward the perimeter together. They stopped inside the perimeter behind a big log that artillery had knocked down. Hall left the wounded Lancaster there and returned to his M-60 machine-gun position on the perimeter. Libs examined Lancaster's wounds. An AK-47 bullet had gone through his helmet and grenade fragments had caught him under his left arm but he did not seem to have broken any bones.

In other sectors Libs could not see, soldiers were still fighting and dying heroically.

Private First Class Marion F. Acton, 18, of Huntsville, Alabama, sneaked up on one machine-gun and wiped out the entire crew. He kept firing his M-16 at point-blank range, killing several more Vietcong before a sniper in the trees above him shot him dead.

Libs, having failed at attempts to break out of the ring of fire, knew Charlie Company could not hold the Vietcong at bay much longer with the small amount of firepower it had left. He had to call in artillery and keep it exploding right next to the few survivors of Charlie Company. He had lost Flake and his radio. Libs called Hall away from the M-60.

"I've got to have a radio to call in artillery or we're dead. Find me one!"

Hall ran and crawled among the dead and wounded lying in the smoke. He found a dying radioman from another platoon and told him: "Sorry. I've got to take this."

"No problem," the soldier rasped. He was lying on his back, bleeding to death. Hall looked into his eyes and saw the hurt and puzzlement of a boy about to die. Hall would see the boy's eyes for the rest of his life. The boy tried to turn his body to make it easier for Hall to take away his radio. Hall had no way to help the dying boy. He left him on the jungle floor to die alone. His radio, set on the same frequency being used by Underwood in the chopper overhead, was soon in Libs's hands.

Libs radioed up to Underwood, who kept over the battle hour after hour, taking time out only to fly back to the field at the headquarters named Bear Cat to jump into a fully fueled helicopter when his own ran low. "I wanted to let them know they had somebody up there in touch with the world," Underwood would say later.

"Damage Five. This is Libs. I've taken command. We've got to have artillery all night long."

Underwood noticed that Libs's voice had gone from frenzy to resignation. Libs sounded through the 1,000 feet of smoky jungle air like a man who knew he was going to die soon. "You've got it," Underwood answered in as reassuring a voice as he could summon up from his sickened soul.

Libs went from one cluster of Charlie Company survivors to another to say goodbye. Night was falling fast. Muzzle flashes showed up against the dark from all around the perimeter. The Vietcong seemed to have riflemen everywhere beyond the little circle that was Charlie Company. Libs heard the Vietcong women and children moving from body to body on the perimeter. He knew what they were doing and grimaced. His message to his men was brief.

"Hey, we ain't gonna make it. So whatever you see, kill it. Whatever moves, kill it."

Libs figured light would help keep the Vietcong jackals away from some of his dead and wounded and also make the attackers better targets. "We've got to have flares," he radioed to Underwood. "It's black down here."

Kroah, his radioman Jasper Carpenter, and a medic who had just joined the platoon—all three of them grievously wounded—lay helpless in that blackness outside the tightened perimeter. Kroah noticed that enemy fire in their forward sector had slackened. He allowed himself to hope the Vietcong were withdrawing and that he might make it out alive after all.

He raised his head to look for Vietcong. He saw bobbing dots of light off in the distant darkness. They were moving toward him. He realized the Vietcong were walking with candles inserted in cans held out in front of them with long poles. The poles were to keep the people holding them from being hit by bullets fired at the lights. Kroah heard the high-pitched sing-song of Vietnamese women. This told him D-800's scavengers were advancing toward 3d and 4th platoons to shoot wounded and strip bodies of rifles, ammunition—anything useful.

"Our only chance is to play dead when they get near us," Kroah told his medic and radioman. The three bleeding men reached for each other's hands, clasped them tight and said the Lord's Prayer in a whisper. Then they lay down as dead as they could manage.

Kroah heard the footsteps of somebody approaching, then heavy breathing. He felt his rifle being pulled away from his body so gently that he thought it must be a woman standing over him. His mind shouted this out while he struggled to lie quiet as a corpse. He felt Carpenter's body being rolled on top of him and could hear the scavengers pulling out the clips of M-16 bullets. The medic lying next to Kroah was stripped next but apparently made a lifelike movement. Kroah heard the deafening explosion of the medic's own .45. A scavenger had shot the medic through the head.

The Vietcong moved on to other bodies. Kroah and Carpenter opened their eyes. Carpenter slowly lifted his head in the inky darkness to look around. It was about 9 P.M.

"See any lights?" Kroah asked.

"No," Carpenter replied.

"Got a cigarette?"

"Christ, man, you're not going to light a cigarette, are you?"

"Give me a cigarette and then go back inside the perimeter and see if you can find me a radio."

Kroah never saw Carpenter again.

Underwood, in his helicopter, passed on Libs's request for Air Force flares. Soon they were drifting down from the sky, taking some of the terror out of the night.

The eerie light enabled Libs to see the South Vietnamese national policeman assigned to Charlie Company standing over his dead German shepherd. The dazed policeman was listening to the high-pitched exhortations of Vietcong commanders outside the perimeter.

"What are they saying?" Libs asked the bilingual policeman.

"They're getting ready for the final attack."

Vietcong commanders shouting through megaphones were ordering their snipers down from the trees. They massed troops for the charge. Libs knew most of his defenders were dead. There were gaps 30 yards wide in his circle. A well-directed Vietcong unit could probe Charlie Company's perimeter until it found one of these big openings and then signal the rest of the force to charge through it. The Charlie Company survivors were so few in their ragged oval that it would take the Vietcong only a few minutes to kill them all.

In the eerie quiet before the final storm, Libs heard the translator who had lied about what the dying Vietcong scout had said the previous afternoon. He was shouting to the Vietcong outside the company perimeter.

"Lieutenant," the national policeman yelled. "He's telling them where we are."

Somebody fired an M-16 burst into the traitor. He went down. The Vietcong held back from making their final charge. Libs felt release in the continuing quiet. He called up to Bibb Underwood to bring the artillery in even closer.

"I'm going to lay down this barrage," Underwood radioed back. "Tell me if that's where you want it."

A volley of shells came crashing down about 50 yards outside Charlie Company's perimeter.

"Goddamn it, Bibb! Bring it in closer! It's our only chance!"

Underwood, reading the map full of numbers on his lap in the chopper, radioed back new coordinates to the artillery battery. In less than thirty seconds it sounded to Charlie Company survivors as if freight trains were coming down on them from the sky. The artillery shells hurtling in whizzed, hissed and whooshed before plunging into the ground with explosions so powerful it seemed as if they would split the whole earth in two. Chunks of hot metal, branches and dirt filled the air over the heads of Charlie Company survivors. In the seconds of quiet between artillery bursts, Libs and the rest of the men heard screaming and crying from the Vietcong massing outside the perimeter. Artillery was decimating

31

the massed attackers. Whole minutes went by and still there was no charge.

"Closer! Closer!" Libs yelled up to Underwood.

"You've got it! You're on the ground. You're in control."

Artillery shells soon were exploding even closer to the edge of the Charlie Company perimeter. Soldiers hugged the vibrating ground. They pressed their faces into it, seeking refuge inside Mother Earth. When a shell hit real close, the ground came up and punched them in the gut. The shells kept coming, coming, coming. The ripping explosions turned the Vietcong's ground into a moonscape. The Army would say later that 1,100 artillery shells were fired to help save the company. Libs called in much of the fire. Alderson found a radio and got back in contact with Underwood to help bring other fire to the edge of the perimeter. The Vietcong rifle fire from outside the perimeter slackened. Underwood stayed up there in the chopper calling in the curtain of artillery fire.

"God bless you, Bibb Underwood," Libs said into the earth bouncing into his face. Air Force aircraft kept circling, dropping flares.

Acting Platoon Sergeant Charlie Urconis of 2d Platoon was one of the many who never gave up. He kept crawling from man to man, distributing ammunition. In one crawl to the ammunition crates piled up in the center of the circle, Urconis thought he had been hit. But it turned out to be the impact from a C-ration can exploding under him after a bullet pierced it.

Urconis winced at the cries of wounded he heard as he was crawling around in the dark. The company had run out of bandages, water, morphine—everything that could have eased the pain of the dying.

"Please, somebody shoot me," Urconis heard a bleeding sergeant cry out from the center of the perimeter. "Please, please somebody kill me."

"Somebody help me," begged another soldier.

"Water! Christ, somebody give me some water!"

"Oh! Oh! Oh!"

"Mother, I'm dying out here. Mother!"

"Somebody come and help me."

Groaning. Sobbing. Crying. All the horror of war was concentrated in a small spot nobody had ever heard of or cared about. And the jungle would reclaim it without ceremony.

No further fire came from the Vietcong. Libs and/or Alderson suspended the fire but told Underwood to be ready to resume it in a hurry. Kroah was still lying outside the perimeter. He was covered by branches that had been shot off trees. He heard a soldier call out: "Anybody here?"

Kroah answered and asked him to find a radio. Kroah did not know the trooper. He was from another platoon. But this unknown trooper obliged the bleeding lieutenant and returned with a radio. Kroah still had enough strength to check in with his old buddy, Johnny Libs.

"Mike Six. November Six here. Are you there?"

"Marty?" answered Libs incredulously, having dispensed with call signs long before to save time. It no longer mattered what the enemy heard.

"Yeah."

"I thought you were dead. I've been calling you for two hours."

"I'm out here."

"Hang on, Buddy. I'll send somebody out for you."

"Sergeant," Libs ordered Urconis around 1 A.M., "go out in the 3d Platoon area and get November Six. He's lying outside the perimeter."

Urconis crawled out to that area and started calling softly for Kroah.

"November Six. This is Oscar Five. Where you at?"

"We're over here," replied Kroah's new radioman, whose name was also Carpenter.

Urconis crawled toward the voice. He found Kroah and his radioman lying side by side. Kroah's back seemed to be bleeding the most. When Urconis went through the jungle, he carried two socks tied together around his waist to air them out. He untied this belt to bandage Kroah's wounds with them as best he could. The lieutenant was obviously bad off. His radioman appeared unscathed.

"Crawl back and get a tarp and some sticks so we can carry him out of here," Urconis told the radioman. The radioman would not move. He was frozen with fright.

Urconis could not prod the man to action. The sergeant crawled back to the perimeter by himself, got Specialist Four Noyce to help him, collected sticks and a tarpaulin and crawled back with his helper to Kroah and his radioman. With great difficulty they

33

rigged the tarp and sticks into a stretcher and slid it under Kroah.

"I'm only going to tell you this once, Private," Urconis warned. "You either crawl out of here with us now or we're going to leave you out here to die. Now get your ass moving, soldier, now!"

The wide-eyed radioman got his legs and elbows moving. He was soon performing the infantryman's low crawl and was making his way to the perimeter.

Urconis and Noyce struggled to slide Kroah along the jungle floor as gently as they could. As they bumped Kroah over one of the logs, the earthy lieutenant whose life was pouring out of five bullet holes warmed Urconis's heart and made him smile by saying: "Now look, if you bastards hurt me, I'm going to have your fucking ass!" Then the lieutenant laughed, right there at death's door.

"Pick up the cadence," Kroah ordered his rescuers. "Get in step you! Left, right; left, right; one two, three four."

"Gotta save this guy," Urconis said to himself.

Once in the middle of the company perimeter, Kroah felt comparatively safe. He managed to open a can of beef stew and suck in its juice with a vengeance. Then he lit a cigarette.

"Put out that cigarette," somebody hissed at him from the dark.

"Fuck off. I've been lying outside the perimeter."

Libs walked over to see his old friend. All of Kroah's clothes had been torn off except his undershorts and boots. Blood was all over his tattooed body.

"How ya doing?" Libs asked.

"Great now."

"Marty, you're some looking sight."

"Yeah, well, we're all going to die anyhow."

"I know, Marty. But we'll take 'em one more time because they're going to bring one more in on us."

"Do your thing, Johnny. Get the job done. Tie me up to a tree."

Libs pulled his dying friend over to a tree so he could lean against it while looking out into the dark. He placed Marty's rifle beside him and was about to say some final words to him. But Marty had passed out against the tree.

Libs counted the able-bodied men he had left in his sector to repulse the next Vietcong assault. He counted nine plus Marty, who might or might not regain consciousness and have the strength to fire his rifle or hurl grenades before the Vietcong attackers killed him. The oval-shaped perimeter by now was only 40 yards across, half its original width.

Alderson, whom Libs and Underwood had thought was dead, reunited with Libs. Alderson, Libs, Urconis, Hall and Noyce established a command post for their pathetically small force of survivors behind a big log that artillery had knocked to the jungle floor. They deployed their M-60 machine guns to cover as many avenues of approach as they could when the Vietcong launched the final annihilating attack. Alderson asked for a quick refresher course in firing the M-60 from Hall and Noyce.

"It's awful quiet," Libs told Urconis. "I don't hear them anymore."

"Yeah, even the monkeys aren't making any noise."

Nobody dared think they had won; that they would live; that the Vietcong had broken off the attack. Alderson feared the Vietcong were just waiting for Bravo Company to come to the rescue. Then they would surround that second American company and kill everyone in both of them.

The quiet persisted for more than three hours. Libs, Hall and Noyce agreed to take fifteen-minute catnaps in rotation. Each in turn lay face down behind the log. They were physically exhausted, but their minds would not turn off. The desperation that had fueled their movements while under heavy fire gave way to cold fear in the quiet of the pre-dawn hours. The man resting did not want to look over the log because he was afraid he would see the Vietcong coming out of the black shadows for the final attack. But life suddenly looked closer than death. This made the fear of dying more consuming. Not now, God. Not now. The artillery fire had not resumed. Birds started chirping in the distance. The jungle lightened. Dawn of April 12, 1966, was finally breaking over Charlie Company.

*Bang!* A shot rang out 40 yards outside the perimeter.

"Aw fuck!" Hall exclaimed to his comrades behind the log. "Here we go again. They're coming again."

Alderson, Libs, Hall and Noyce aimed two M-60s in the direction of the noise from the single shot. Jungle fatigues marched toward them from the bush. United States Army jungle fatigues! Bravo Company had hacked its way next to Charlie Company during the night and come into the perimeter at 7:15 A.M.

Some Charlie Company survivors would remain embittered for the rest of their lives that Bravo Company did not come to their aid when they were dying from Vietcong assaults. DePuy after the battle blamed himself and other top officers overseeing the deployment for not putting Charlie and Bravo companies closer together, given the thickness of the jungle. He also lamented that Charlie Company commanders pushed so much of their force into the Vietcong kill sack rather than holding back while small squads probed the terrain ahead more thoroughly. Battalion commander Hathaway countered that Bravo Company went into the jungle with the standard separation for such operations. He praised Captain Juris Plakans, Bravo Company commander, for pushing his men through the jungle all night, guiding themselves by the sound of the exploding artillery shells, to reach the edge of Charlie Company's perimeter before dawn. "If there's no fighting," he said he ordered Plakans, "stay outside the perimeter until first light. If the fighting starts up again, get your ass in there regardless." Hathaway said he did not want to risk Charlie Company defenders mistakenly shooting Bravo soldiers in the dark if the Vietcong had broken off its attack.

As the day of April 12, 1966, lightened, Charlie Company survivors heard helicopters overhead. Air Force Huskies and Army Chinooks hovered over the battle area. There still was no place big enough to land. Air Force para-rescuemen rode cables down from their choppers to the jungle floor. Rope ladders tumbled out from the rear doors of the Chinooks. Engineers descended down the swinging ladders. Chain saws and other gear were dropped down. Soon trees were falling. A patch of sunlight lit up the inside of Charlie Company's perimeter as the engineers hacked out a big clearing for the Air Force and Army rescue helicopters to land in.

Charlie Company survivors said little. Bravo Company eyed them with awe. Nobody had to tell the relief troopers what the men hanging onto life had been through in the long afternoon and even longer night. The survivors rummaged for food, bandages and medicines. They looked for buddies. Many of them were dead. They comforted the wounded as best they could. Medics with fresh supplies were finally on hand. Charlie Company troopers drank water by the gallon and peed a thousand nervous pees as the easing of tension loosened up a thousand little muscles that had been clenched like numb fists for more than sixteen hours.

Most of Charlie Company's survivors stood or sat in the now-secure perimeter and cried unashamedly. Urconis told a friend he felt like crying but knew once he started he could never stop. So much pain. So much death. So much being alone. Urconis raged inwardly at the stupidity of leaving Charlie Company out there at the end of such a long string. He was among those who felt Bravo Company should have been kept in much closer to Charlie Company. Urconis went from man to man looking for friends. He found Reilly dead with his hands still clasped in prayer. He found a dead trooper in clean fatigues. He could not figure it out until he noticed the Air Force insignia. It was Pits Pitsenbarger.

Urconis had to get away from so many dead friends. He wandered outside the perimeter where the Vietcong had been. He noticed blood on the bushes and in the trees. They had paid a heavy price, too. He also saw hundreds of little plastic bags. He could not figure out what they were. There were always rumors that the Vietcong were issued dope before making a charge. He doubted this was true. But what were all those empty bags? He never found out.

Phil Hall held off crying until he helped his buddies in Charlie Company put their dead comrades in green, rubberized body bags. Many of his old friends were now bloated bodies turning black. Flies swarmed over the bodies. Hall felt overcome with rage: "All these kids! All these guys! Dead! Dead! What a waste! What was this battle for? Why did everybody die? They're flying us out of here. What did we accomplish? Somebody explain this fucking war to me!"

Libs was also depressed. He did not cry. He sat inside the old perimeter, which Bravo Company was now holding down. He felt bitterness, anger and sadness watching his kids who had fought so hard being zipped into body bags. "They fucked us—fucked us all," Libs lamented to himself. "Bait. Fucking bait. That's all we were. So many great kids. Who will ever know what they did? Nobody. No-fucking-body."

General DePuy's helicopter settled into the freshly cut landing zone. Libs made no attempt to get up and greet him. He was burned out and did not give a damn about anything or anybody—even a general. Fuck it. The United States Army is getting no more out of Johnny Libs this day.

DePuy asked Alderson what had happened. "They trapped us. They ambushed us from the trees." Alderson was not bitter. He thought the company should have been sent out after D-800, that DePuy's plan had been sound.

37

DePuy's officious aide, a captain in the pressed uniform of the safe rear area, strode up to Libs still slumped against a tree.

"Lieutenant! The general is here. Get up!"

"Fuck you, Captain."

DePuy took in the scene. He had been in enough battles to know exactly how Lieutenant Libs felt. He knew the exhausted young man at his feet had beaten back D-800, which outnumbered Charlie Company three to one.

"You're excused, Captain!" DePuy snapped to his aide. The captain walked off. DePuy sat down on the ground next to Libs. "What happened?" the two-star general asked quietly.

"You fucked us, General! You put us out there as bait. And I want that fucking _____ fired," he said of the artillery commander whom Libs believed was responsible for the off-target artillery fire that had killed and wounded Libs's men. "He killed our men. I want him fired. It's either that or I'm going to kill him."

DePuy sat silent. Libs knew he had gotten through to the general. He suspected there would be action taken against _____, but DePuy let silence be his answer. Then he said, "I want to know exactly what happened."

Libs wearily went through every phase of the battle as the general sat beside him listening. He ended his debrief by saying, "You walked us into a goddamn holocaust, General."

"Yeah, but there's no other way to get a goddamn fight going," DePuy replied.

"Well you got one going here."

Word had spread through the press corps in Saigon that the Big Red One had been in one hell of a fight. The Army flew a group of reporters and cameramen to the scene. A CBS cameraman spotted DePuy talking to Libs and walked toward them.

"Will you talk to these guys?" DePuy asked Libs.

The television man asked DePuy and Libs a few questions and then took his camera away to record the gore in the clearing. Libs hated the ghouls of the press. He learned later that one good thing came out of the televised interview when it was shown in his hometown of Evansville: Libs's mother learned he was alive at the very time she was reading that everybody in Charlie Company had been killed.

"Here's a good one over here," a cameraman said to one of his buddies. The "good one" was a particularly grotesque body that had been a real live, loved soldier of Charlie Company the previous morning.

"Get the fuck out of here, you assholes!" one of the survivors yelled at the cameramen.

Few of the Charlie Company survivors would say anything to the reporters and cameramen. They stood silently waiting to get on the helicopter that would fly them out of this hell nobody who had not been there could ever feel. Phil Hall was among the survivors who could still stand. He made a count of how many of the 134 members of Charlie Company who fought in the battle could make formation at the base in the rear where the helicopter set them down. He counted twenty-eight enlisted men, including himself. He did not know how many officers besides Libs had made it. Hathaway in his after-action report listed thirty-five killed in the fierce battle, plus Airman Pitsenbarger, and seventy-one wounded. This would leave only twenty-eight unwounded or slightly wounded like Libs. With 106 out of 134 men killed or wounded, Charlie Company's casualty rate for the Easter battle was 80 percent, a rate that top commanders considered unacceptably high even if more Vietcong had been killed. Hathaway estimated in his after-action report that at least 150 of the crack D-800 troops had been killed in the battle. Unwritten in any of the after-action reports were the wounds this battle and others like it in Vietnam would inflict on the men who fought them and on their families.

Libs, Kroah, Urconis, Hall—all of whom I interviewed to reconstruct the Easter battle—were among those who told me the nightmares never stop. Libs could not adjust to civilian life nor talk about the battle to release its demons until we talked it out for hours around the dining room table in his home in Evansville, Indiana. I sat between Libs and Hall as the scenes charged back into their minds. They sweated, shook and fought back the tears as they relived the battle. I sent Libs my reconstruction of the battle after talking to other survivors. He wrote me back a moving letter which said, in part: "I cannot find the words to tell you how much 'Legacy' has affected me and Phil . . . God, George, you must have been there!

"I'll tell you something from my heart that I don't believe I've ever told any man before. Over the years I have agonized over Abilene to the point of damn near insanity.

"I ask the questions: Could I have saved more men? Did I move quick enough? Was I smart? Why, in God's name, am I alive? Am I a coward for being petrified during the battle?

"I know that these are not unique questions, nor particularly earthshaking, but by damn they are brutal and painful.

"I tell you this because, after all these years of sometimes debilitating thoughts comes a stranger who somehow has given Johnny Libs his pride and dignity back . . ."

Libs would leave Vietnam without knowing that the battle of Xa Cam My would not only shake him and other survivors but also top military commanders all the way up to General Harold K. Johnson, Army Chief of Staff, in 1966.

Johnson flew from the Pentagon to Vietnam shortly after the battle and visited DePuy at his headquarters in Lai Khe, not far from the scene of the battle.

"You know," DePuy told me Johnson warned him, "The American people won't support this war if we keep having the kind of casualties suffered by Charlie Company."

Casualties continued to mount in the rifle companies in Vietnam for no clear purpose. The American people stopped supporting the war. Protesters filled up Washington streets and shouted "Hell no! We won't go!" in regard to the draft. Young men agonized about whether to answer their summons to Army duty or go to jail or flee to Canada. Bearing the burden of this war was no longer a clear-cut obligation for the young men of the nation. A frustrated President Lyndon B. Johnson could not find a way to win the war. The Vietcong and North Vietnamese on January 31, 1968, launched their Tet offensive. They scored a stunning psychological victory, but not a military one, by penetrating all the way to the inside of the U.S. Embassy in Saigon. "From that point on," wrote Colonel Harry G. Summers Jr. in his history of the Vietnam War, "the problem was not how to win the war but how to disengage."

President Johnson shocked the world by announcing on March 31, 1968, that he would not seek re-election. Richard M. Nixon, seeking to replace Johnson in the White House, promised to end both the Vietnam War and the draft.

On March 27, 1969, shortly after his inauguration, President Nixon appointed a commission chaired by former Defense Secretary Thomas S. Gates Jr. "to develop a comprehensive plan for eliminating conscription and moving toward an all-volunteer armed force."

Less than one year later—on February 20, 1970—Gates, in submitting the commission's report to Nixon, said: "We unanimously believe that the nation's interests will be better served by an all-volunteer force, supported by an effective standby draft, than by a mixed force of volunteers and conscripts; that steps should be taken promptly to move in this direction; and that the first indispensable step is to remove the present inequity in the pay of men serving their first term in the armed forces. We have satisfied ourselves that a volunteer force will not jeopardize national security, and we believe it will have a beneficial effect on the military as well as the rest of our society. . . ."

Expounding on those conclusions within its 211-page report, the commission said:

> In recent years military service has been scorned and condemned by some Americans. No doubt, the Vietnam War is partly responsible, but the draft has also contributed to the military's unpopularity.
>
> Young men are inevitably skeptical about a career in an organization which has to use compulsion to obtain recruits. Moreover, the low pay implies that society places little value on a soldier. The termination of the draft should immediately enhance the prestige of enlisted service. The knowledge that those in the armed forces have freely chosen to serve their country cannot but improve their image—in their own eyes as well as in the eyes of society . . .
>
> The return to an all-volunteer armed force should improve the quality of military life. Conscription enables the military to ignore individual dignity and desire, secure in the knowledge that the draft will replace those who do not like the military system. The entire military "atmosphere"—the approach to training, discipline and treatment of individuals—must be re-examined . . .
>
> Members of both the white and Negro communities have expressed concern that the all-volunteer force might fill its enlisted ranks with the poor and the black . . . We have concluded that the racial composition of the armed forces cannot be fundamentally changed by ending the draft. Even if higher pay appealed only to the poor, twice as many whites as blacks would be attracted . . . The best estimate of the proportion of blacks in the all-volunteer

force is 14.9 percent, compared with 14.1 percent in a mixed force of conscripts and volunteers . . . Even if higher estimates [of blacks] were realized [in an all-volunteer military] we would not consider asking the government—including the military—to cut back on hiring blacks or to set quotas . . .

Congress at Nixon's urging allowed the authority to draft young men to end on July 1, 1973. The Army struggled to fill its ranks with volunteers. Some Army recruiters in their desperate effort to fill their quotas for volunteers faked credentials and broke other rules to get warm bodies for the ranks. Not until the 1980s did the tide change. Vietnam was ancient history to the new generation. Higher pay and benefits made soldiering look better than working at McDonald's to many young people.

The size of the Army shrunk from its Vietnam high of 1.57 million men and women to 781,000 by 1987, enabling it to be more choosy in accepting volunteers. After years of sending out its message on the wrong wavelength for America's young people, the Army in the 1980s got through with the slogan: "Be all you can be, join the Army."

Today the United States is gambling its safety on this new, small, all-volunteer, post-Vietnam Army. The biggest gamble is whether the Charlie companies of this Army will fight and hold like the old one that fought the Vietcong D-800 Battalion.

Who are these men volunteering to risk dying in terror-filled battles like the one Johnny Libs fought, for a chance at a better life? What are they like? Why do they do it with nobody saluting? Will the new Charlie Company fight and die and win like the old one if the bell tolls?

# 2. The New Volunteers

"You've got just sixty seconds to get off my fucking bus, and fifty-nine of them are already gone," the Army drill sergeant screamed from under his Smokey-the-Bear hat, the symbol of authority and pain for fresh recruits like 18-year-old Kristian C. Selvester reporting to Fort Benning, Georgia, for basic infantry training in July 1987.

Selvester, freshly shorn of his shoulder-length blond hair and gold necklaces, was destined to become part of the new generation filling the ranks of the same Charlie Company that was almost wiped out, three years before he was born, in some distant place called Vietnam. Selvester knew there had been a war there. But that ancient event had nothing to do with him joining the Army. At Benning, he and other recruits would train together as Delta Company but fill the ranks of Charlie Company later.

Selvester joined the Army to get the hell out of Lincoln, California, and all the problems that threatened to drown him there—problems at home, at school and in the bars and dance halls around his small hometown, 40 miles north of Sacramento. He had chosen the infantry because it sounded exciting and offered a $5,000 bonus for signing up. But on this hot July morning in 1987 he found himself wondering if in jumping from Lincoln to the Army he had jumped from bad to worse.

"You better not be the last one off this bus, Yo-Yo," one of the sergeants screamed at Selvester. The 6 foot, 4 inch, 245-pound Selvester stood up in Fort Benning's "cattle car" and tried to push his bulging belly toward the door. He hoisted the Army duffel bag full of uniforms over his left shoulder, grabbed his own flimsy suitcase stuffed with civilian clothes in his right hand and plowed like a supertanker through the other recruits standing between him and the side exit of the cattle car.

"Shit!" Selvester exclaimed as his suitcase caught the upright rail on the right side of the bus door. The case sprung open. His jeans, sportshirt, underwear and other vestiges of civilian life ejected from his suitcase, landing around the feet of another glowering drill sergeant standing on the sidewalk beside the cattle car.

"Whatsamatter, Fat Boy, lose something?" the sergeant sneered. "Move!"

Selvester jammed as many clothes as he could back into the sprung suitcase and carried the rest of them in the crook of one arm while holding the duffel bag with the other. He knew rushing down the sidewalk with such a sloppy load was asking for trouble from the drill sergeants standing all along the route. But he felt compelled to keep moving. He inserted himself in the stream of recruits half trotting along the sidewalk. He saw a big blue sign, DELTA DAWGS, arched over the entrance to an open courtyard. He passed under the sign and stood awkwardly in the ragged formation of soldiers the drill sergeants were putting together with obvious disgust. A match-thin drill sergeant sauntered up to Selvester, planted himself smack in front of the trembling teenager, looked him up and down and shouted: "On your face!"

"Pardon me, Drill Sergeant?"

"Down, Fat Boy!" answered the drill sergeant, pointing to the cement. "Give me fifty."

Selvester fell to the prone position and started doing push-ups, deducing this was what "on your face" meant. But he was not strong enough to do fifty. After struggling through about a dozen push-ups he lay exhausted on the cement.

"On your feet!" commanded the drill sergeant. "Run in place, Fat Boy."

Selvester tried. But he was too tired and scared to bring his knees up as high as the drill sergeant was demanding.

"Look at that! You can't even run in place. I hate fat people."

"So do I, Drill Sergeant," huffed Selvester in a feeble attempt to please his tormentor. Selvester felt the angry men in the Smokey-the-Bear hats closing in on him. Dear God, he asked silently, how am I ever going to survive thirteen weeks of this?

At last the drill sergeants turned away from Selvester and gave concentrated doses of "Shock Treatment" to other recruits who struck them as misfit or defiant. Those with "an attitude" had to be changed in a hurry.

"Hey, I got one over here who wants to hit me," exulted Drill Sergeant Randy Stover. Stover, a hotshot paratrooper and Ranger who had been in on the invasion of Grenada, stood staring down Aaron Henson, 20, of Tyler, Texas, a short, muscular black man.

Like Selvester, Aaron Henson had joined the Army in hopes of breaking out of his dead end at home. Also like Selvester, he was destined to become one of the new generation of mud soldiers in Charlie Company. But he was discovering he could not handle the torment of Army life. He wanted to slug one of his tormentors in the Smokey-the-Bear hat. He had clenched his fists. Stover had spotted them, calling over the other drill sergeants who ganged up on Henson to excoriate his anger or make it explode.

"You're a momma's boy," taunted one of them. "You can't take it. Get the fuck out."

Henson, to the astonishment of the drill sergeants, grabbed his civilian suitcase and headed for the highway at a trot. Stover ran him down before he had reached the blacktop road outside the barracks.

"You come back," Stover warned, "or I'm going to send you to Fort Leavenworth," the Army's prison in Kansas.

Disoriented, afraid and confused, Henson returned. Stover led him past the formation of recruits he had just left and into the comparative privacy of the orderly room, the training company's office.

"Here's what the law says," Second Lieutenant Keith Raines, Delta's executive officer, told Henson gravely as he looked in a thick book on his desk containing part of the Uniform Code of Military Justice. Raines convinced Henson the Army would indeed send him to jail if he failed to carry out his enlistment contract, a threat Raines could not have carried out. Drill Sergeant Stover suddenly turned brotherly, telling Henson the Army was not

45

going to be as bad as the Shock Treatment he had just experienced out there on the cement. Henson did not believe him. He wanted to go home. He would convince himself over the next two days that suicide was the only way out of the Army—and attempt it by drinking down a can of glass-cleaning fluid.

But he could not escape the rest of Shock Treatment. He rejoined the formation standing at attention on the plaza under the three-story brick barracks. The drill sergeants left Henson alone but kept on Selvester, probably because he was so big.

"Dump all your gear from both bags on the floor," a drill sergeant ordered the now-terrified recruits. "We're going to search for contraband."

Selvester had not hidden any dope or liquor or other forbidden items among his civilian or military clothes. Even so, his stomach churned as Drill Sergeant Raul Rodriguez pawed through his two mounds of clothing dumped on the cement.

"What's this?" taunted Rodriguez as he held aloft two packages of Trojan condoms that Selvester's crying mother had given him during their farewell embrace "because I don't want you to get in trouble."

"Are you queer or something?" asked Rodriguez. "We ain't going to let you into town where there're women. What do you plan to do with these, use them on your buddies?"

"No sir, Drill Sergeant," Selvester struggled. "My mother gave them to me."

Selvester's answer broke the grip of terror on the teenagers. It made the recruits believe for an instant that they were back in the high school classroom. Almost everyone smirked. A few recruits even giggled. Selvester saw laughter in Rodriguez's eyes and told himself he would get out of this Shock Treatment alive after all.

The drill sergeants struck more gold in searching the civilian clothing of James E. Proctor II, 20, of Indianapolis. They had found the silky, sexy red-and-black negligee top and panties that the handsome black man's girlfriend had given him during their last night together to remember her by.

"Put these on!" commanded Drill Sergeant Rodriguez in handing Proctor the stringy top. Proctor got the top around his shoulders. Rodriguez handed him the red-and-black panties.

"Now put these on your head, Lover Boy."

Proctor, repressing a grin, obeyed and tried to stand at attention without laughing. Four drill sergeants gathered around him.

"Sure that's your come in there?" one of them asked.

"Yes, Drill Sergeant!" Proctor responded in the loud voice all recruits were ordered to use.

John P. Brooks, 19, a college boy who had run out of money while attending the University of Maryland and decided the Army not only would enable him to put away money to continue his education but give him the discipline he needed to make something of himself, quaked as he watched the drill sergeants gang up on the fat and the weak. Brooks doubted he could lift his barracks bag up one more time, as the fresh arrivals were being ordered to do. His exhausted arms failed him as he bought the bag down from over his head. The bag went off course, hitting Drill Sergeant Rodriguez on the head, knocking off his Smokey-the Bear hat.

"Did you do that on purpose, boy?"

"No, Drill Sergeant!"

"Beat your face!"

Brooks starting beating his face with one hand after another.

"Not that!" Rodriguez screamed. "Down there!" corrected the drill sergeant, pointed to the cement floor.

Brooks finally figured out he was supposed to do push-ups. He did as many as he could and then staggered to his feet. He dared look around because no drill sergeant was near him. He saw the tough guys who had swaggered around the reception station and intimidated him were having as much trouble as he was. Derrick Brevard, one of the swaggerers at the reception station, was struggling. Brooks decided Shock Treatment was a great leveler. Everyone was starting out at the bottom. The drill sergeants seemed to hate them all.

Shock Treatment, the process drill sergeants use to assert authority in the first few minutes of basic training, had lasted only twenty minutes. It seemed like an eternity to the boy-men trying to live through it. I interviewed the recruits afterward to reconstruct their experiences and feelings. Selvester told me he thought Shock Treatment was damaging. Brooks and others said it was a good way to put all the recruits in their place at the beginning. Benning commanders were moving to phase out Shock Treatment in the summer of 1987.

The drill sergeants organized the training company of 200 men into platoons one, two, three and four alphabetically. They ordered them to stow their civilian suitcases in the storeroom off the plaza and then go upstairs with their military gear to find their bunks on the second and third floors of Albanese Barracks. They were told to store their military gear neatly in their lockers, return to the plaza where they would form up again by platoons and march off to the chow hall on the first floor of Albanese Barracks.

The shaken Selvester left the plaza, climbed to the third floor of the barracks with the other frantically rushing recruits, found his bunk and locker—only to run into a new set of problems. He could not get the hang of stowing his gear. He also took so much time trying to button his Army blouse and rolling up its sleeves that he found himself standing all alone in the eerie sleeping bay. His fellow trainees had left to form up by platoons and march into the chow hall for lunch.

Looking like an unmade bed, Selvester rushed down the stairs in hopes of catching up to his buddies and slipping into their formation. He encountered a deserted plaza except for the fearsome-looking first sergeant working on papers at a card table he had set up outside where the new trainees had just gone through Shock Treatment.

"Excuse me, First Sergeant. Where do I go?"

First Sergeant E. D. Williams looked up from his paperwork, took one glance at Selvester's twisted Army clothes and bellowed: "Get the hell out of here, Private! You look like a fat sewer rat!"

Selvester was lost and scared. He did not know where the chow hall was or what the drill sergeants would do to him if he found it and entered late. He retreated back up the stairs to his platoon bay. He opened his locker door and hid behind it until the other trainees returned from lunch. His platoon mates by now had sized up Selvester as big but not dangerous, a klutz they could safely tease. They named him Tweety, the little bird that goes with Sylvester the Cat.

I had traveled to Fort Benning to learn what the post-Vietnam Army was like from the inside. Army leaders had agreed to give me full access. I could talk to whomever I wished with no escort officer present and watch the troops be trained with no restrictions.

To assess this all-volunteer Army that the nation is counting on to protect it, I decided I had to get with the soldiers who would take the point in any next war, the infantrymen. I went home with

48

a cross-section of these new volunteers to find out the worlds they had known growing up. I discovered that the worlds of these post-Vietnam volunteers resembled the worlds of the draftees I had known in Vietnam. The old and new Charlie Company were non-Establishment. The kids who became soldiers had no automatic up-escalator to step onto that would whisk them painlessly to colleges, to high-paying jobs, to homes in the suburbs with cars in the driveway. They had to risk their lives to get a chance at sharing the American dream. I saw the world and attitude of machine gunner Phil Hall from the 1966 Charlie Company in most of the recruits. They, like him, felt trapped by circumstances and saw the Army as a way up and a chance to have some adventure. If it meant risking your life to get that, so be it.

Partly because he seemed so ill-suited for Army life but tried so hard to adapt to it, I went to Lincoln to learn about Selvester's world. His past struggles, I reasoned, would help me understand and portray the new ones I would chronicle in the months ahead when I watched him and others of this new generation try to negotiate the difficult passages from boy to man, from man to soldier in the new United States Army of the 1980s. The first part of the world Selvester left behind was downtown Lincoln, California, his hometown of 4,100 people 40 miles north of Sacramento.

Standing at Lincoln's main intersection at 5th and G streets, I saw and felt depression. An abandoned gas station occupied one corner; a feed store and tool shop a second; a liquor store and shabby department store a third; faceless low buildings the fourth. I talked to teenagers in the soda shop and on the main street. They complained that there was no movie house or skating rink in Lincoln. Unless you had a car, they told me, "The bowling alley and Round Table pizza parlor are it."

Up the street, a new teenage center run by Lincoln's churches was just getting underway. The director told me his biggest problem was dealing with the emotional trauma many fathers were inflicting on their daughters by sexually assaulting them. It was one of the dirty little secrets in the blue-collar town of Lincoln, he and others in the town told me. The teenage center's director said drugs were plentiful in Lincoln but good jobs for the young people were not.

From downtown Lincoln, I drove to the little ranch on which

Selvester had grown up with his stepfather, Harold, a hot-tempered cabinetmaker who often blew up at the irresponsible teenager, and Karen, his anguished mother and best friend. Selvester had told me that his stepfather's shouts of "goddamn stupid idiot" assaulted him so continually that he began to believe that was exactly what he was.

A dirt road wound away from the paved road, turned a hard right and took me past the outbuildings announcing that a little ranching was done on this small piece of ground. A horse looked at me unconcernedly. No other humans were on the property at the time. I noticed that Selvester's stepfather had started and then abandoned a porch alongside the trailer. Only the framing was completed. Selvester had told me that most of his hours inside the trailer had been unhappy ones when he was in high school.

"Even when I did something like play football for the school, my father made me quit because he said I wasn't doing the work at the farm. I've never had a chance to do anything."

Yet this troubled teenager did not condemn his stepfather, despite all the verbal and physical abuse Selvester said he got from him.

"That's just the way he was brought up," Selvester said forgivingly. "He didn't know any better. We're good friends now that I'm in the Army."

I looked up Selvester's girlfriend, Teresa Muna, to see another dimension of this innocent-looking infantryman who would soon be carrying an M-16 rifle for Charlie Company. She lived in Auburn, the suburban town adjacent to Lincoln. She struck me as a wisp of a girl, not a woman, until she started talking. It turned out that she had seen more of the dark side of life in her fifteen years than most women see in fifty.

Teresa said life brightened for her the very first time she spotted this gentle giant named Kristian Selvester playing pool in The Sportsman, a bar off Auburn's Route 49. She recounted the scene for me as we visited The Sportsman during the tour she gave me of Kris's world. He was Kristian to Teresa most of the time, or Kris. Almost nobody back in Lincoln and Auburn called him the Army's "Selvester!" His male friends called him Bird after Tweety Bird.

Kris's father was sitting on a bar stool, drinking, Teresa said in recalling her first encounter with Kristian. Teresa's mother was tending the bar. Teresa herself was sitting alone at a back table doing homework. She decided to make her play while Kris was folded over the pool table lining up a shot. She slid out from behind her table, sneaked up behind him, jiggled his cue at the crucial second.

"Hey!" Kris barked. "Quit playing with my stick!"

"I wouldn't play with your stick in a million years!" Teresa retorted. She flounced back to the table and stared into her schoolbook.

Teresa's mother broke the standoff several days later by relaying Kris's message from the bar that he would like to see her again. "He really likes you," her mother said. "Why don't you ask him to go dancing?"

Their first date was at Dance Connections in Auburn. She brought along a long-stemmed rose for him. He brought along nothing for her. But he did bring along joints for himself. His eyes were bloodshot. He was giggling.

"You got high, didn't you?" she accused.

"No, I'm fine," he lied.

They got through that first date somehow and made a second. Kris was high again in this second meeting.

"Look," she scolded. "I don't need this shit. You can just forget this relationship if you're going to keep getting stoned."

Teresa said Kris finally admitted he was into drugs big-time but would change now that he had met her. She said she had heard that promise over and over again, along with promises to go back to school, to get a job. Kris attended school off and on, filled out job applications but seldom handed them to prospective employers. He continued to fight with his stepfather. Teresa remembered his periodic moves out of the trailer home and into the homes of relatives until they tired of him eating up their groceries and filling up their living room watching television hour after hour.

Teresa told me Kris's flaws made her love him all the more. She felt she had to stand by him. Besides, his touch electrified her. Nothing else mattered when they were together. She told me of how, when she was 15 with no access to a car, she would walk from her home to The Sportsman in hopes of finding the 16-year-old "Teddy Bear" there. "You know," she laughed after we drove the distance together that she had walked, "it's 11 miles!"

With her parents' blessing, Teresa took Kris into her own home off and on. When the sun was out, they would seek out their special hiding places in the Kingdom of Camelot they had made for themselves around Auburn. Teresa led me behind The Sportsman, to what looked to my old eyes like a drainage ditch lined with bushes. She said that to her and Kris, it was a shining stream where they could sit together and share big dreams without anybody watching or listening. She took me to another part of their Camelot: a ribbon of a brook across from her rental home in Auburn, spanned by a cement bridge and walled by bushes and trees. She told of how she and Kris sat on the bridge hidden by the foliage, arms around each other's shoulders, and confided their ambitions for the life ahead.

"This is where Kris told me, 'As soon as I'm 18 I'm going to own my own house.'

" 'Oh B,' I told him, 'You can't buy a house with no money. Where are you going to get the money?' " They called each other B in such private moments.

"He said, 'I'll get a job. I can do a lot of things.' "

Kris did hold a carpenter's job for a while after moving in with Teresa. But she said he often stayed home from work so they could make love until she had to leave for school. He would watch television after that. Kristian lost the job. Teresa's mother became fearful.

"My mother kept warning me, 'He's using you. You're too easy. You're going too fast.' "

"I knew she was being logical," Teresa told me in one of our long chats. I understood after a while that this child-woman could not be logical because this boy-man was the only one who could light up her life, make her feel needed emotionally, fulfilled sexually. She could not give him up. She forgave him a thousand hurts and letdowns as she tried to be counselor, lover and savior for this wild, irresponsible, tractionless light of her life. She showed me passages from her diary in hopes I would understand.

Today was kind of a good day. Went back to school. Saw Kristian in the morning. He was higher than a kite. He went to all his classes but got drunk after school, then came to my house. He risked a lot coming over, but I was glad he did. I enjoyed myself tremendously. Went for a round, then played volleyball. Then his mom came and got him and he was BUSTED [restricted to his home by his parents]. He said it was worth it though. I love him soooo much. Waiting and wondering . . .

Kristian was supposed to come over tonight after school but never showed up. I cried so hard because I'm sick of getting my hopes raised up and then being dropped so fucking low. I can't handle this anymore. It's pure torture. I love him and can't live without him and I miss him. I love My Beautiful Bright Eyes Baby. Got to go to sleep with my Krissy Bear. Love you baby.
  Good night.

Love Always,<br>Teresa

P.S. He's also supposed to spend the night tomorrow night but I am not counting on it.

The night before Halloween. Kind of bored. Kristian is over but he is asleep. Oh well, life's a bitch!

I've got to see him because I need him more than he will ever know . . .

Teresa told me about the day Kristian stunned her by suddenly turning serious and declaring fervently that he had to stop his slide into nothingness.

"He said, 'I've got to get hold of something. Else I'm just going to be another ding-a-ling hanging around on the corner. What would you think if I went into the service? I was thinking about the Navy.'

"What! Go away rather than stay home with me? Leave me here? I wouldn't like it at all. What are you talking about?"

Despite her screams and tears, Teresa said Kristian went to see the Navy recruiter in Sacramento. The recruiter was not in his office. The Army recruiter in the adjoining office was. Kristian entered. He saw the sergeant's Army greens and wished he had something like that to wear around Lincoln where he had failed to graduate from high school. Kristian had told me that the recruiter suggested he go into the infantry because it was the most exciting branch and offered the fastest promotions. Karen, with tears, signed the consent form so her only child could join the Army at age 17. He turned 18 on June 18, 1987—two weeks before the Army paid for him to fly from Sacramento to Atlanta en route to his transformation at Fort Benning. The airplane ride—like so many adventures to come—was a first for Kristian Selvester, volunteer Mud Soldier.

Again, to see where these new volunteers came from and what they hope to get from serving in the post-Vietnam military, I studied the home ground of the other recruit who had so much trouble during Shock Treatment, the troubled young black, Aaron Henson. His world revolved around Tyler, Texas, 100 miles southeast of Dallas, where young blacks and whites of an evening leave the rows of suburban homes to congregate on separate sides of the town square, eyeing each other apprehensively.

Henson had told me a lot about his life in Tyler before I visited there. He described high school days as carefree as Selvester's had been troubled. Thanks to a doting mother and a part-time job stocking shelves at the Tom Thumb-Page supermarket in town, Aaron drove to John Tyler High School in a black 1979 Pinto; played football and ran track; had more girlfriends than he could handle; was the popular, always smiling party boy at the black teenage hangout in Tyler called the TXA Club; was voted most likely to succeed by fellow seniors.

Aaron told me the bottom started falling out of his life after he graduated from high school in 1985. First, he found young blacks did not get the good jobs around Tyler—a town run by the white Establishment. He had set his heart on becoming a fireman in Tyler. He saw himself whizzing around corners hanging onto the side of a long red fire truck, manning a thick black hose while wearing a fireman's hat and slicker. He took the fireman courses in Tyler and passed them easily. After Aaron had completed the courses, Tyler officials suddenly decided he was too young to become a fireman—something they could have told him before he started the courses. He felt he had been smacked in the face with racial prejudice for the first time in the town that had felt so comfortable during high school. Yet he needed a better job than stocking groceries. His younger high school girlfriend, Mar-Shawn, had given birth to their son, Jeremy. They decided she should stay in high school and live with her mother and the baby. Aaron would continue to live a few miles away in the white-frame, two-family house his divorced mother owned in Tyler. Aaron and MarShawn agreed each could date if they tired of each other. But he would send her as much money as he could for Jeremy. This was not much, given the few jobs available to him around Tyler.

I called on Aaron's uncle, Dan Key, a former Air Force sergeant, who was a big influence on his nephew. Key was the family success story. He lived in a big brick rambler in Tyler, was married to a lovely woman and had worked his way up to supervisor at the Carrier air-conditioning plant in Tyler. We sat in his family room, dominated by a mantel crowded with athletic trophies Key had won. This big, handsome, black pillar of a man repeated for me the advice he had given his young nephew, Aaron, when the boy was trying to find a way to make it in Tyler: "There ain't nothing out here for you. Go in the Army and get a little education and be a man. Then you'll be ready to do something. The sky is the limit in what you can do for yourself. But you've got to take the first step. You can be a bum or a doctor. I know. I've done it. I went from shooting screws on an assembly line to being a supervisor."

Aaron doubted he could leave everything he loved in Tyler, particularly his baby son, and try to be a soldier in places he had never heard of where sergeants and officers might beat him up without anybody outside the military finding out. Yet he agreed there was no way he could provide decently for MarShawn and their son in Tyler. He ventured into the office of the Army recruiter in Tyler several times but did not sign up. He even went into Dallas to take a physical in the military processing center. He still could not take the final step. He anguished. He talked to brothers in the Church of the Living God in Tyler about whether to go into the Army. Aaron summoned up his nerve and revealed his thoughts to MarShawn, a petite girl only 5 feet tall with big, trusting eyes:

"I'm thinking of going in the Army."

"Why?" MarShawn shrieked, and started crying.

"So I can make a better life for you and Jeremy. I also want to build my character and get some discipline. I'm slipping into bad habits. Whenever we need something, I get it from my mother. I've got to get out of Tyler and make something of myself."

"Don't go. I don't want you to go. I'd miss you too much. Don't leave. I can't raise Jeremy all by myself. You know that, Aaron."

"I'll help by coming home as often as I can. My family will help you. Your family will help you."

"But I'll miss you. I want you here. I don't want to talk about this anymore."

Aaron hugged her tight. She blubbered into his shirt. She seemed like a baby herself at that moment, not the mother of his son.

Aaron said the wise old women in MarShawn's family agreed with his Uncle Dan that going in the Army was the best way to reverse his slide and become somebody. He could come back to Tyler as a man, they said, who had something more to offer employers than a naked high school diploma. MarShawn's family worked on her, too. One night, Aaron told me, MarShawn bit her trembling lip and told him, "Maybe it's for the best for you to go into the Army."

With tears rolling out of his eyes and homesickness coursing through him, Aaron watched the brown expanses around Dallas fade as his airliner took him toward his rendezvous with a new life at Fort Benning. He was not at all sure he had done the right thing. Aaron told me his Army recruiter had assured him he could get out of the infantry he had signed up for right after basic training at Benning. The recruiter also promised him—but of course did not put it in writing—that he would be sent to Fort Hood, Texas, only about 200 miles from Tyler, to study mechanics. Recruiters are not supposed to deceive, but they are under pressure to sign up volunteers for combat branches like the infantry. All this made Aaron Henson particularly vulnerable to Shock Treatment and the traumatic days of basic training to follow.

James E. Proctor II, a handsome black, told me that he fell in love with the Army during Shock Treatment even though the drill sergeants had ridiculed him by making him wear his girl's red-and-black lingerie. "I told myself, 'Now this is the military.' I was enjoying their teasing but couldn't show it. I use to do that crazy stuff in high school. I streaked the senior breakfast wearing nothing but sneakers and a paper bag over my head. I got all my buddies to wear miniskirts and combat boots with no laces to school one day."

Proctor's world was one where he saw a black person could make it if he tried hard enough. His mother—teenaged, pregnant with Proctor and unwed—had fought her way out of the ghetto where his life started. She worked, went to school and reared her two babies with little help from anyone except her mother, Constance Proctor, wife of an Air Force sergeant. She finally found steady work on the night shift in the admitting office of the Army hospital at Fort Dix. Proctor told me the income enabled the family of three—his mother, baby sister three years younger than he, and himself—to move from ghetto apartments in Pemberton, New Jersey, and rent a two-bedroom house in a better neighborhood.

"We lived in Pemberton from the time I was 4 until I was 12," Proctor told me. "Once I got to be 8 or 9, my mother stopped working the midnight to 8 A.M. shift, switched to the 4 P.M. to midnight shift and cut out my babysitter. I would rarely see her except on the weekends. I'd come home from school, pick up my baby sister from the house two doors down, cook dinner for me and my baby sister and fix another meal which I'd put in the oven for my mother. I'd go to bed before she came home from work and leave for school before she got up. I'd sometimes find a note from her in the morning saying 'nice dinner' or something like that."

Proctor said he was enjoying the role of being the 9-year-old man of the house. He bitterly resented the Army medic his mother started dating and eventually married. An Army family, they moved to Augsburg, West Germany.

The rivalry between Proctor and his stepfather often erupted into fist fights. After one particularly severe fight which he lost because "I was small," the jealous, disoriented teenager said he warned his stepfather: " 'Don't go to sleep.' I carried around a baseball bat and a blanket for two days. He would not go to sleep in those two days. After that, we never got along, would never talk to each other.

"My mother sat me down and said, 'Look. This is the man I married. He's not your real father, but give him the same respect you'd give your real father.' I just couldn't accept that. This conflict went on for the whole three years we were in Germany. I started going with the wrong people, the hoodlums in Germany. They were still in the military, but they were hoodlums. I started getting Cs and Ds in junior high. I was hanging around with the wrong people and got arrested for shoplifting. My dad was in the field at the time. When he came home, he started beating me and all and I said, 'Forget this. I don't want nothing to do with him.' I was 12 going on 13. I totally rebelled. Then my mother started getting into it. I had helped her out and all, but we started arguing. She would hit me. I would never hit my mother back. But I started rebelling against her."

Proctor told me Grandmother Constance Proctor persuaded him to change the way he acted in the house and on the street. He and his stepfather established an uneasy relationship by the time the Army transferred the family to Indianapolis, where Proctor entered John Marshall High School. Proctor said he found himself in a new and better world. He broke out of the bad crowd, made new friends with students and teachers, earned the highest grades of any black male in the high school, won an appointment to the Air Force Academy.

"After my senior year I went to the Academy prep school in Colorado Springs and went crazy. I had money coming in, knew I was going to go to the Academy, sent for two credit cards and got them. I bought so much stuff on my credit cards that I couldn't pay the bills. I was in debt for $3,500. I decided to quit the Academy and work until I paid off my debts. The Air Force didn't seem like the military I always wanted while I was on the ROTC drill team in high school. They were too laid-back. When I quit, my stepfather told me, 'You made a dumb decision but I can understand why you made it.'"

After paying off his debts, Proctor joined the infantry "because it looked like it would be real military and provide a chance to travel and meet females to get some trim [sex]." He was 20 years old when Drill Sergeant Rodriguez handed him the red-and-black panties to wear on his head. But he told me that first hour was a start toward fulfilling his dream. "I'm going to be a helicopter pilot. I believe my grandmother. She told me: 'If you work for it, you can get it, no matter what.'"

I asked this optimistic young black man whether he realized infantrymen like himself usually die first in war. "Are you ready to do that?"

"It's the best country in the world," he answered. "I believe what it stands for—democracy and freedom. That idea in itself, to keep everybody free, I would die for. Even the slaves if they had had a chance to die for this country back then, they would have."

I traveled to the coal country of West Virginia to acquaint myself with the world of Norman L. Adkins Jr., an 18-year-old who typified the nation's young men who not only sought adventure in the American military but felt an obligation to serve. His house is what West Virginians call a double-wide, a pre-fab that can be hauled in halves along the highway. The house sits in Seth, outside Charleston, along a winding blacktop road that follows the Coal River through the valley. Adkins, a short, chunky youth with strong enough legs to play fullback in high school and earn the nickname "Stormin' Norman," told me as we rode around his world in the family pickup that he used to catch smallmouth bass in the river right across the street from the house.

Inside that house, Rosalee Adkins, Norman's mother, had fixed a mountain of sandwiches and a pot of coffee for the visitor from a place they had only read about, Washington, D.C. Norman chuckled in telling me that he had to argue hard to keep his mother from getting all dressed up for the visit. " 'Mom,' I told her, 'he wants to see us as we really are.' "

Norman L. Adkins Sr., Norman's father, moved slowly around the house. He was cursed with the miner's disease, black lung. He talked proudly of his son, saying: "Norman always wanted to be a soldier."

Mother and father led me into their son's room. Its walls were covered with posters of military men doing daring deeds, such as parachuting out of transport planes in full combat gear.

Norman had told me that he had been offered a full wrestling scholarship to a number of colleges but figured "that would have meant sitting in my room at night studying. I wanted to go and do something, become a Ranger."

I visited the Burger King in the vast shopping center in Charleston where Norman had worked as an order taker for $3.35 an hour. I learned that at night the shopping center metamorphosed into a teenage night club. Young boys and girls would visit each other in parked cars, promenade across the blacktop, congregate in the Burger King and other fast-food spots at ringside of this improvised night spot in the heart of Appalachia's hard-times coal country. Norman had told me at Benning that he longed for the day he would stride around the center in his Army dress greens with the Ranger tab on his shoulder.

Mrs. Adkins said it was a bittersweet day when she, her husband and their daughter, Tina, 13, drove to the Charleston airport to see Norman off to the Army to chase his dream. Shortly after he arrived at Benning he sent back to his mother a letter saying he was not so tough that he could not bring himself to tell her how much he loved her. She handed me the poem he had written to her shortly after he had gone through Shock Treatment at Albanese Barracks:

> *My Mom's a good Mom; she loves me a lot;*
> *And now that I'm gone in the Army to stay,*
> *I wrote this poem 'cause I wanted to say:*
> *I love you, Mom. You know it's true;*
> *Can't you tell by the things I say and do*
> *That of all the moms I've met*
> *You're the best one I've seen yet?*

Steven Henson, also black but no relation to Aaron, felt like a young man on a mission when he volunteered for the infantry at the recruiting station in Baltimore. He had grown up in one of the city's ghettos. The family apartment was often cold in the winter because there was not enough money to buy oil for the space heater. Henson told me his father, a cook, sometimes turned violent. One time in his boyhood, Henson said, he saw his father punch his mother so hard that she vomited blood in the kitchen sink. Young Steve called the police. They seemed to take forever to respond. When the police finally arrived at the apartment house, they refused to enter unless his mother agreed to sign a complaint against her husband. Steven told me that he vowed then and there to become a cop in his native Baltimore "so I can do good; so I can separate the good from the bad." He reasoned that if he went through infantry training he would learn skills that would make him a better policeman in Baltimore.

I drove there to meet the center of Steven Henson's world, his mother, Betty A. Henson, who by his account "spoiled me to the teeth." This woman who had supported her four children after her husband had left the household projected no gloom or bitterness as we talked about her son, the apprentice mud soldier. She exhibited a verve, laughed easily and showed none of the scars of being battered by a violent husband; of struggling to keep a family together with almost no money; of going to school at night so she could be somebody; of scrimping until she could buy a house for her children in a safe neighborhood.

"I told Steven if I could do it, he could do it. I told him to make something of himself. When he said he wanted to go into the Army after he had done so well in high school with the ROTC, I said, 'You can do it.' "

Steven took two buses each way to the school that had an ROTC unit he could join. The bus trip was usually an hour long. He persevered and became commander of the ROTC unit. The military looked like a way up. He left for Fort Benning full of hope. He believed he was taking the road to the top of the hill.

After her lanky Steven had left for the Army to begin his passage, Betty Henson told me she called up his father and had this conversation:

Mother:    Your baby son is gone now.
Father:    Where?
Mother:    In the Army.
Father:    I don't want to hear that!

I was to learn from long talks with the green, lonely soldiers at Benning who had put their lives in the Army's hands that the worlds of Selvester of California, Little Henson of Texas, Proctor of Everywhere, Adkins of West Virginia and Big Henson of Baltimore were typical of the new breed of soldiers in the post-Vietnam, all-volunteer Army of the 1980s. They were non-Establishment kids willing to risk dying for the chance of living better lives than they could have around home. Adventure, security, patriotism, self-improvement, desperation—these were all forces pushing the young Americans to volunteer.

Christopher S. Cashman, 26, and Ty J. Barker, 20, were among the married men who had volunteered. They had broken their picks trying to scratch out a living in the civilian world and figured the Army could not be any worse.

Cashman told me he had spent his youth playing rugby in Australia; met Kerry there and married her; came home to Santa Rosa, California, with their baby only to find his credentials of high school graduate and star rugby player could command no better job than bagging groceries in a supermarket. Kerry was pregnant with their second child. They could not afford their food and rent. They were not making it no matter how hard Cashman worked. Cashman had no home, car, college degree or good job like the old friends he had grown up with in California had obtained while he and his schoolteacher parents were in Australia for their own fresh start.

"I felt as if the world had passed me by," Cashman told me. "The Army looked like a place I could make a fresh start. And they would pay for our baby. They held out a $5,000 bonus for signing up for infantry. We were desperate. I just said, 'Where do I sign?' "

Barker of Fremont, California, had worked in the family restaurant, Barker's Lunch, landed a boring $6.75 an-hour job in a warehouse after the eatery folded. He married Rhonda, his home-town sweetheart, who also worked at a low-paying job in Fremont. Like the Cashmans, the Barkers were not making it. Barker, fat and down on himself, told me he figured joining the Army "would allow me to prove I could be something more than a little fat kid." He had the open, freckled face of Spanky in the comedy show *Our Gang,* and picked up that nickname as soon as his fellow volunteers in Albanese Barracks spotted him.

David Shawn Murray, 21, of New Cumberland, West Virginia, loved the outdoors. He could have gone to college on a wrestling scholarship but wanted something more exciting. The brick factory in his home area had closed down. There was nothing out there for him. His $3.35-an-hour busboy job sucked. He signed up for the infantry in the belief it would be an exciting life for twenty years when he could retire with an Army pension and return to West Virginia to resume his fishing and hunting. Soldiering, he figured, would pay enough money to support his high school sweetheart, Ruth, and their children. They would put enough money away during his twenty years in uniform to build a cabin in the West Virginia woods and live happily ever after. That was Murray's dream.

Michael A. Austerman of Elizabethtown, Indiana, at 23 was, like Cashman, older than most of the young men signing up for the infantry in 1987. He had found civilian life boring in comparison to the four years he had spent in the Navy. He regaled me with sea stories, including jumping into Naples harbor at the end of liberty when the shore patrol dared suggest he was drunk and tried to restrain him at the dockside. After leaving the Navy, Austerman worked long hours for $9.40 an hour in a factory where life's highlight had become the next cigarette. "My uncle loved the infantry," "Chief" Austerman told me with a grin, "so I thought I'd try it. What the hell?"

I asked the trainees at Benning to fill out questionnaires so I could determine the statistical profile and determine if the company was representative of the whole Army racially. The 182 responses (the rest of the 209 trainees in the company were either hospitalized or away for other reasons) showed:

• Delta Company, whose graduates would fill billets in the new Charlie Company that fought in Vietnam, was 78 percent white, 13.7 percent black and 8.3 percent Hispanic, American Indian and Guamanian.

The percentage of blacks in Delta Company, 13.7, was close to the 14.9 percent the Gates Commission predicted for the whole Army in recommending switching to an all-volunteer Army in 1970 and under the 17.8 percent of black males who comprised the American civilian population aged 18 to 21 in fiscal 1987.

However, the 13.7 percent in Delta Company was less than half the 29.3 percentage of black males who joined the Army's enlisted ranks for the first time in fiscal 1987 in all the specialties, not just combat branches like infantry. Army leaders at Benning told me that by 1987 the blacks were showing preference for the noncombat branches such as clerical and hospital slots, which could lead to jobs in the same field in the civilian economy when they left the military. An expert rifleman is great for the infantry but not especially attractive to General Motors.

• Eighty-five percent had graduated from high school compared to 91 percent Army-wide of those who volunteered in 1987.

• More than half, 54 percent, of the volunteers were 18 years old or younger. Eighteen was also the median age compared to 20 for all those who volunteered in 1987.

• Nine percent were married, but dozens of trainees said they intended to get married soon now that they had steady jobs. The married percentage among first-time enlistees Army-wide in 1987 was 12.4 percent.

• More than one third, 38 percent, came from broken homes as a result of divorce.

• Their parents' combined incomes totaled $50,000 a year or less for about half the 113 recruits who said they knew what the figures were. Only seven said the family income was over $100,000

• Fifty-seven percent of the trainees said they intended to make the Army a career, 37 percent said they would get out after finishing their enlistments and the remaining 6 percent were undecided.

• The volunteers came from thirty-seven states and Guam, with the largest contingents from Texas (21), California (18) and New York (14).

I asked the volunteers to check which of the nine reasons I wrote on the questionnaire best described why they had joined the Army infantry in 1987, a year free of any pressure from the draft. The results, with the most compelling reason listed first, were:

1. I saw it as the best way for me to put away money for college (50).
2. Life at home was boring; I wanted to try something more adventuresome (29).
3. I just always wanted to be a soldier and love the idea of charging up hills and firing rifles (28).
4. I want to be a paratrooper and decided the infantry was the best way to start on this path (28).
5. I was sick of the jobs I could get and figured the Army offered better ones (14).
6. I was slipping into bad habits and wanted to get some discipline (14).
7. I was unemployed and decided the Army was one job that would be steady (10).
8. I wanted that $5,000 bonus for joining the infantry (4).
9. My parents kicked me out of the house so I did not have any other place to go. (No trainee listed this as the number one reason for joining, but four said it was among the reasons for joining the Army.)

Their responses on the questionnaires underscored what the young American males had told me in interviews in their homes and in the barracks: they joined the Army in the belief that it would get them somewhere in life and provide them with some fun and adventure along the way. Many came from the dark dead ends of towns and circumstances. The Army looked like a crack of daylight and they ran for it. In their backgrounds, hopes and dedication, the volunteers I came to know at Benning typified the volunteers the whole Army was attracting in the 1980s. They were looking for a sliver of America's good life and would risk their lives for a chance to get it.

Statistics compiled by the William T. Grant Foundation Commission on Work, Family and Citizenship in its 1988 report, "The Forgotten Half," shed further light on why the Army and the other military services looked more attractive in the 1980s to young people without college degrees than the jobs they could find around home. These young people have been left behind economically. In comparative 1986 dollars, the commission discovered, males aged 20 to 24 with a high school diploma earned $15,221 in 1973 but only $10,924 in 1986, or 28.2 percent less. The federal government's General Accounting Office calculated that the total compensation of a 19-year-old soldier with a high school diploma in 1986 came to $22,000, counting not only basic pay but the worth of his free hospital coverage, food and housing allowances and other benefits. In dollars and cents, then, the Army in 1987 was in a favorable position to compete with the local McDonald's restaurant, lumber yard or brick factory for young men who had high school diplomas but could find no place around home to use them as poles to vault over the walls hemming them in.

Noting this trend, Charles C. Moskos, professor of sociology at Northwestern University and chairman of the Inter-University Seminar on Armed Forces and Society, wrote in his 1988 book, *A Call to Civic Service:* "What characterizes American society today is that both good and bad economic times coexist to an extent not found since the abolition of slavery. A seemingly permanent underclass of youth has become restlessly juxtaposed with youth enjoying unprecedented material affluence.

"The cause of the youth underclass is hard-core unemployment," Moskos wrote. "On top of general trends working against youth employability: increased participation of adult women and old people in the labor force, increasing mechanization of unskilled and semiskilled labor and increasing movement of jobs outside the United States entirely, there are factors that weigh especially heavily on minority youth, namely, a pattern of racism . . ."

Compounding these difficulties for young men and women in search of work but with no connections to members of the Establishment class who run much of the the civilian marketplace, Moskos said, "many of the young poor lack the basic capacities—literacy, knowledge of workplace expectations and basic job skills—needed to obtain and keep almost any job."

I knew from talking to the young trainees at Benning and their parents, studying the questionnaires and observing these new soldiers day and night that I was immersed in the flesh and blood of the national problem called the youth underclass. The U.S. military in 1987 could provide the money and benefits that most of these volunteers in the post-Vietnam Army could not find at home. But I wondered if the leaders of this new American Army realized that they had to make good on their promise to enable these new, high-quality employees to "be all you can be." If the leaders did not provide these volunteers with job satisfaction, I feared they would become disillusioned, quit the Army at their first opportunity, and advise their friends back home not to join. The employers whom the volunteers at Benning would come to know first, and remember the longest, were their drill sergeants. As "the drills" took over the shaping of these scared, scalped, desperate but determined teenagers in Benning's woodsy outback, I would be there to watch the great national experiment in action—the attempt to build the post–Vietnam Army with volunteers who expected more than the old "three hots and a cot" the draftees had to settle for, like it or not.

# 3. The Drills

"Hey, Mr. Wilson! You gonna camp out with us? Over here! Sleep over here. We'll give you our tent."

"Don't sleep with those weirdos! Come over here with us, Mr. Wilson. We're the guys you want to write about. I'll tell you my life story."

The exchange came as I walked through Delta Company's tiny village of two-man tents pitched under the pine trees at the bivouac site called A. O. Eagle. I often slept out with the boys of Delta rather than retreat to the shower and soft bed available in the quarters I was renting on the main base at Fort Benning. The trainees could tell this was one of the nights I was going to stay with them because my sleeping bag hung underneath my backpack.

Even though it was 6 P.M., the heat was holding onto the day. I could smell the tar still being cooked out of the Georgia pines. I wondered if it ever got cool in the piney woods of Fort Benning. They felt hotter to me than either the Vietnam jungle or the Sinai Desert. In these first weeks of basic training, the only time the troops and I felt cool was when it rained on the ranges or when we were inside an air-conditioned barracks, classroom or church.

Fort Benning was laid out something like a national park. The main part of the base was really a miniature town that the trainees never got to see. They were kept miles away in Sand Hill, which had barracks, a few related buildings and stores but mostly pine woods. Blacktop roads snaked through the woodsy part of

Sand Hill. Dirt roads ran from the blacktop into big campsites like A. O. Eagle and firing ranges. The campsites and ranges had buildings with toilets inside, called latrines, and grandstands where trainees would sit to listen to lectures from sergeants before carrying out their instructions in the fields and ranges.

Trainees would usually ride in the big silver buses called cattle cars from their brick barracks to the A. O. Eagle campsite about 7 miles away in the pine woods. They would either ride or march to ranges and classrooms for instruction, depending on the distance. Saturday mornings were often the times they rode from the campsite back to their brick barracks. The return to the hot showers, flush toilets and bugless beds of the barracks rejuvenated the trainees after a week of camping out among the fire ants and mosquitoes and lying on hard ground.

My walk this August twilight was the unhurried one of the parish priest. I felt the heat coming out of the sand through the pine needles and into my boots, heating up my feet. I had no place to go and nobody to talk to except my newly adopted parishioners who were isolated from everything familiar and supportive. Their only family right now was themselves during days that started at 5 A.M. and ended at 9 P.M. I went from tent to tent listening, laughing and consoling these trainees who were still more kids than soldiers. Only one drill sergeant was on duty to harass and harangue them. It was the closest thing to quiet time during the long training weeks. Drill sergeants took turns sleeping out with the trainees.

I noticed a few of the trainees were lying on their stomachs on the pine needles, trying to write a legible letter home. Others were talking. But most of the young trainees were just staring off into the darkness gathering in the distant woods. I knew from one-on-one chats that this quiet time at the end of the day was when homesickness and second thoughts about their decision to join the Army took over their minds. The harassing and haranguing and hurry up and wait of basic training pushed down those feelings during the day. But right now, I knew, the suppressed homesickness was taking over. To lift their spirits in this vulnerable twilight time, I hoped the water truck would hurry up and come to A. O. Eagle to plug into the crude showers rigged over the parking area beside the campsite.

The grinding noise from the approaching water truck broke the quiet of A. O. Eagle. My parishioners ran from under the trees toward the showers, towels and soap in hand. They were soon under the water soaping up and throwing verbal jabs to their buddies, the kind of punching and counterpunching that makes soldiering fun for those who can adjust to the close-quarters environment where survival depends on making friends out of strangers without at the same time revealing chinks in your armor, which everybody would stab if they detected them.

"Look at that little worm," one soldier said, pointing belittlingly to his buddy's drooped penis. "What do you expect to do with that?"

"More than you'll ever do, Fat Ass!"

"Hey, Adkins," called a soldier to the fireplug of a man from West Virginia. "No short people wanted around here."

"Yeah. Well this short people is going to save your ass some day."

After showering, the trainees slipped on their gray shorts and T-shirts for sleeping. They would wear that gear plus running sneakers they had bought in the base post exchange for the morning run and calisthenics.

I visited with the youngest man in Delta Company, a black named Wayne T. Hewlett who had just turned 17. He knew I was on leave from *The Washington Post* and asked me what was going on in the world outside Sand Hill. The trainees received no newspapers in the field or barracks on the theory that this would distract them. I told Hewlett I had been confined to Benning, too, and knew little more than he did about doings in the world outside it. We fell to talking about why he had joined the Army as we sat together on the pine needles in front of his two-man tent.

"I wanted to be like my dad. He'd been in the Army. There was one point in high school where I didn't care. My father told me, 'You're going to have to make it into the service. You're going to be nothing in life unless you straighten up.'

"And here I am in the Army. I joined to get away from home, for adventure, to get money for college. In high school I always wanted to be a leader but was scared of it. Now I'm platoon guide [the trainee responsible for running the platoon in the drill sergeant's absence]. It's the biggest thing I've ever done. It's me. It's my passage to manhood. I'm going airborne!" he exclaimed with a smile that lit up the twilight dimming the encampment under the pines.

Although Hewlett and his fellow trainees of Delta Company had only been soldiering a month, he said the Army had already changed him, challenged him, given him a sense of obligation to others. "I used to live in the ghetto in northeast Washington, D.C., on Georgia Avenue. It was rough. Full of crime. Drugs. Very rough. If more of the people I knew back then came into the Army, D.C. would be a nicer place."

I moved off from Hewlett and stopped to talk with a white suburbanite from Burke, Virginia, 18-year-old James "Dallas" Henderson. He pulled a picture out of his pack showing what he looked like in his former life as a rock musician. His hair was down to his shoulders. He looked spaced out. We both laughed as I rubbed my hand over the blond stubble barely covering his scalp now that he had had his Army haircut.

"I get homesick once in a while," Henderson confided. "I called my mother when we were back at the barracks and told her about it. She sent me back a whole mess of pictures of my friends right away. That helped a lot. She's great. She's more like a sister to me than a mother.

"My parents aren't exactly rich," Henderson said in explaining why he went from party-boy musician to motivated mud soldier. "I don't want to go to a two-bit college, and I don't want to bankrupt my dad. He's a carpenter. My mom is a legal secretary. They're divorced. The Army gives me a chance to grow up a little bit, save money for college. I'm into art. I want to be a photographer."

I heard a similar explanation when I stopped by the tent of John Brooks, who had accidentally hit Drill Sergeant Rodriguez in the head during Shock Treatment. "I joined the Army to get disciplined. I had no incentive in college. My grades were slipping. I wanted discipline, and I wanted to save money so I wouldn't have to borrow money to finish college. I'm still glad I joined."

In August 1987, when these trainees were sharing their dreams, the all-volunteer Army was offering to put away for college $25,200 for qualified young men who would sign up for infantry or another combat branch for four years. Only $1,200 of that college fund total came out of their paychecks. On top of that, they could receive a $5,000 bonus after completing basic training for a combat branch like infantry. Congress also had extended the GI bill in hopes of attracting enough volunteers to fill military billets. Most of Delta Company would collect their bonuses.

As I continued walking slowly around the campsite, Marcus D.

Foreman, 18, of Southlake, Texas, told me about a problem that demonstrated that some things in the military never change. He had lost his glasses. "I'm blind as a bat without them." Yet he waited day after day for the Army bureaucracy, which was spending all this time and money to teach him to shoot straight, to come up with a replacement pair. Foreman was taking the foul-up with good grace, laughing about it and telling me the Army was still better than his last job as a $5-an-hour janitor. "I've always wanted to be a soldier," he told me.

Kenneth D. Ray, 23, of Hayden, Alabama, told me he had already done four years in the Army, tried civilian life and gratefully rejoined the Army. "After doing my four, I did wheel alignments at Lincoln-Mercury in Irondale, Alabama, for $5.50 an hour. Went to Firestone for $7 an hour. What a rip-off. The alignment machine didn't work, and we still charged people.

"When I got out of the Army in January 1987, I found my friends on drugs. Mostly marijuana. Some doing acid. The Army's a better atmosphere. I'm going to stick this time."

Robert Perry, another old man at 24, said he, too, did four years in the Army and went home to Carlisle, Ohio, with high expectations. "Only job I could get was dishwasher in the Ponderosa. I did it for six months and decided the Army had more to offer me. My wife told me, 'It's either me or the military.' I chose the military. It was a friendly parting of the ways. You make more in the military and get respect from people higher than you."

So many dreams out here in the pines, I thought to myself. Would the Army ever be able to fulfill them? I would chronicle the passage of these young men for a year. Before the end of it I would see much of this bright hope turn to dark despair. But the dream would stay alive in some of these unsure apprentice soldiers around me.

I heard some shouting at a nearby tent and walked over to it. A young, red-faced recruit was pacing up and down yelling, "I'm not going to take any more of this shit!" His friends told me the drill sergeants had been dropping him [disciplinary push-ups] all day long.

"Sit down, asshole!" a friend told the rebellious recruit. "You haven't done nothing yet." The tableau froze as the booming voice of the on-duty drill sergeant bounced through the pines. "Get to bed you little motherfuckers or I'll drop your ass!"

It was a little before 9 P.M. Light at last was being defeated by

71

the darkness invading the Georgia sky. I moved to the outer edge of the tents and spread my poncho out under a big tree. I unrolled my sleeping bag, spread it on the poncho for a mattress and lay on my back watching the clouds drift along. Soon a million stars began staring down at me. I have always liked sleeping out under the stars, even in Vietnam where mortars were sometimes a threat. One summer our whole family—wife Joan, daughter Kathy, son Jim and I—backpacked through Yellowstone National Park where the stars seemed close enough to grab by the point. Sleeping out at A. O. Eagle was less unifying. As much as I liked the kids lying all around me in the pine grove, I still felt alone in the crowd. But I realized it was a lot tougher for them than for me. I had all kinds of escape hatches and support systems during this basic training. They did not.

Sleep came easily as long as I stayed on the poncho. But every time I rolled off it, fire ants would wake me up with their quick bites. Fire ants seemed to be everywhere on Sand Hill. They would find you whenever you sat or lay on the ground. This night I had forgotten to pack the bug repellent. Slipping into the sleeping bag was my defense. But then the recruits who had been assigned to walk around the campsite all night looking for fires would believe I was a private who was supposed to be in his tent and wake me up. "Oh, it's you, Mr. Wilson. Sorry."

At 3:30 A.M., while I was sleeping fitfully at A. O. Eagle, alarm clocks went off in little houses in and around Fort Benning to summon the drill sergeants to another day of struggling with the trainees they called Yo-Yo, Hardhead, Knucklehead, Little Motherfucker, Legs, Hero and Asshole. On a good day a recruit might hear "Private!" On a better day he would hear himself called "Son." On the best day he would not hear himself called anything at all.

Joyce Williams was used to her husband, Ted, a nickname inspired by his first name of Edward and lanky resemblance to the baseball star, sliding out of bed in the pre-dawn dark. He had been doing it since they were married in 1971. She knew First Sergeant E. D. "Ted" Williams was in love with the Army as well as with her. She tolerated the competition. She realized he was truly happy only when he was with soldiers. She might see him for supper this day or she might not. She never knew. Her husband considered a workday stretching from 4:30 A.M. to 9 P.M. ordinary. Ted Williams was a workaholic. But unlike many workaholics, he was efficient. He got an enormous amount of work done during his extraordinarily long days at Delta Company.

As First Sergeant, Ted Williams was like the blue-collar foreman of a factory manufacturing soldiers. His job was to make sure the orders of the white-collar executives in the front office— Captain Jim Fleenor, Delta Company commander, and his executive officer, Second Lieutenant Keith Raines—were carried out by the drill sergeants running four separate production lines, the 1st, 2d, 3d and 4th platoons comprising Delta Company.

As the senior enlisted man sitting outside Fleenor's office on the ground floor of Albanese Barracks at Sand Hill, Williams was physically and spiritually the buffer between officer and enlisted—between white and blue collar in the industry sense. Because he was one of their own, drills could bitch to Williams without being insubordinate to the officers. Williams had to walk the tightrope between officer and enlisted without leaning too far one way or the other. He impressed me after several weeks of close observation as an enormously accomplished tightrope walker. As Top Sergeant—the senior enlisted man in the company—he could boom out commands, lead recruits on 5-mile runs with his long strides, schmooze with the drill sergeants out in the field, laugh at their tales of how officers had fucked up the detail—without being disrespectful to either side.

Williams's wry humor was a delight. One day Second Lieutenant Raines, a West Pointer whose youthful appearance and manner made him the favorite target of the drills, had mistakenly put on a sergeant's helmet instead of his own. The sergeant's helmet had the marking of his rank and pay grade (E-5 with E for enlisted and 5 for the fifth rung up the pay ladder) on its cover. At the same time the baby-faced lieutenant was unknowingly asking the drills to do something contrary to what Captain Fleenor had ordered.

"What do we do, First Sergeant?" one of the drills asked Williams when they were standing with me out of Raines's hearing.

"Well," Williams answered with a smile, "the Captain is the one with the railroad tracks [the double bars signifying his rank]. We'll go with him. The lieutenant," he continued, pointing to

Raines's helmet with the sergeant markings, "is already down to an E-5. We could always do what he says and get him down to an E-2."

Back in the office, Williams raced through paperwork and met with sergeants and soldiers to dispose of the hundreds of problems generated by green, mixed-up, lost, homesick and sometimes violent recruits. The 209 recruits in Delta Company were like walking time bombs that could go off any second on the rifle range, at A. O. Eagle campsite or in their barracks. How wisely Williams answered the questions pressing in on him could determine whether a trainee succeeded or failed, whether his platoon kept or lost its motivation, whether Delta Company rose or fell in the eyes of the brass at Benning:

"Is that character faking or should we let him out of PT [physical training] and send him to the hospital? Should we send this other clown who stole a little plastic folder from the PX [post exchange] to the stockade or give him another chance? What are we going to do about this letter from this asshole congressman who says we are abusing Mrs. Smith's little boy? Has anybody arranged for the water truck to get out to A. O. Eagle? Brigade wants a sign. Who can paint it? That little motherfucker Jones has been selling cigarettes to his buddies for $2 each. He looks like a criminal. Should we process his ass out of here? Green lost part of his M-60. How are we going to get a new part without brigade finding out? Somebody stole two of our bunks while we were out in the field. Company X must have come up short in its inventory and stolen ours. Should we send some guys over there to steal them back?"

When I was with Williams in 1987, he was making $23,000 a year. I figured what he got done in a day would be worth twice that to any civilian business of Delta Company's size. Williams no doubt could have gotten such a job. He was smart, articulate, industrious. So what the hell was he doing at age 37 still working seventeen-hour days and living in a crackerbox house with his wife and two children in hot and muggy Columbus, Georgia, for God's sake? I knew as a long-time student of the military that the generals and colonels at Benning would notice Williams only if one of his privates committed suicide, raped a girl in town, shot himself or somebody else at the rifle range or went AWOL. So why does this Army have such a hold on you, Ted Williams? I asked him one day.

He d          robably thought I was stupid
and in        e bobbed and weaved with a
verba        cian would envy. I also sensed
that W       stled with that same question
as the      st to post where they took their
turn      e houses they were assigned;
mak     er set of curtains while trying to
get     new surroundings—again. The
sim    I realized after listening to Wil-
lia    is one sentence in his response:
"N    e Army."

H    money to send him to college after
h    High School, Long Island, in 1968.
I    Associated Press in New York City.
"    it more studying. I had a low lottery
number [for     y. So I figured I might as well go join
the Army."

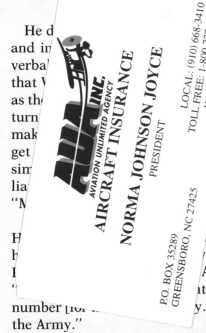

AUI, INC.
AVIATION UNLIMITED AGENCY
AIRCRAFT INSURANCE
NORMA JOHNSON JOYCE
PRESIDENT

LOCAL: (910) 668-3410
TOLL FREE: 1-800-727-3823
HOME: (910) 784-5487

P.O. BOX 35289
GREENSBORO, NC 27425

He signed up in January 1969, and was leading a fire team in an American Division rifle platoon in Vietnam by that fall. He survived the year in Vietnam, went to West Germany with the First Infantry Division and then was selected for the job he would always love the most: drill sergeant.

"Being a drill sergeant at Fort Dix from 1975 to 1978 was the most satisfying part of my career. I'd stay with my soldiers from 4 in the morning until 11 at night. I knew if they turned out good, it was because I had been good. I knew if they turned out to be shit, it was because I had been shit. I knew what they were was because of me. I had total control. A lot of people writing these new regulations which restrict the drill sergeants have never been down here dealing with it." [Army rules forbid drill sergeants from swearing at or putting their hands on recruits, among other restrictions.]

I pondered Williams's answer as I watched the drills interact with their troops day after day, week after week, month after month in the field and in the barracks. I saw that it was an intimate, taxing relationship. Neither could escape the other. The drill father, unlike the civilian father, could not go off to work and leave his wife, school teachers or cops to deal with his sons. The drill had his Army sons day and night whether he wanted them or not.

I viewed the drills with deep suspicion at first, partly because I had covered trials of Marine drill instructors who had abused their charges, including Private Bubba McClure of Lufkin, Texas, who had been beaten to death with pugil sticks [poles with pads on the end used for close-up, one-on-one fighting] at the San Diego Marine Recruit Depot while his drill instructor watched. A few privates told me that they had been kicked and punched by their drill sergeants at Benning when they were out of sight of everyone in the company, including me. But I came to believe this was the exception rather than the rule in Delta Company. Otherwise the recruits I came to know well and interviewed constantly would have told me. My mistrust of drills evolved into sympathy for their plight. They were given too much to do by commanders at Benning, by Army leaders at the Pentagon, by us civilians at home who leave it to the drills to train soldiers to protect us. No foreman, no father, I concluded, with such power over his workers or children and constant exposure to them could keep his perspective and temper if he had to work the crushing hours of a drill in the dangerous, demanding environment of an infantry training center. The drills' dawn-to-dark workdays explained to me why so many of them had been divorced and became estranged from their natural children.

I came to admire many of the drills and marvel at how much they were able to transform often aimless, surly recruits into disciplined soldiers with a desire to become something in life at last. The drills forced unformed teenagers to relate to something bigger than themselves—their platoon, their do-or-die team where each man had to carry his load or lose the battle for his buddies. Platoon-vs.-platoon competition was fierce during basic training. But I think the most successful technique, the one that came naturally to the most successful drills of Delta Company, was to show their soldiers every day that they cared about them; wanted them to do well; would do their best to keep them alive in battle. One soldier told me: "This is the first time anybody gave a shit about me."

Each drill had his own style of imposing discipline and teaching what had to be learned. There were coaxers, shouters, demonstrators and needlers—differences also found in high school coaches and state troopers. Sergeant First Class Raul Rodriguez was one of the most successful drills. And he seemed to enjoy talking to me about his job, about his soldiers, about the Army, about himself. I discovered that many officers and sergeants believed civilians like me were not interested in their work and appreciated it less. I defrosted the drills just by showing interest and listening. I asked Rodriguez in one of our many chats on the rifle ranges at Sand Hill how he saw his role as the drill in charge of 2d Platoon.

"It's almost impossible to fulfill everything that's expected of you," he told me. He said that he had to be bad guy, good guy, teacher, leader, listener, psychiatrist, medic, coach, athlete during sixteen-hour days with kids who could have been anything from class sissy to hardened criminal in civilian life. The platoon sergeant was the first suspect if one of his recruits got hurt, failed tests or misbehaved. Deep down, Rodriguez, like First Sergeant Williams, loved being the drill in charge of a platoon of young soldiers. He glowed with the satisfaction of saving kids whom parents, teachers, priests, cops, psychiatrists and judges all had written off as hopeless losers. Rodriguez's experience in the non-Establishment world of the have-nots gave him credibility with the soldiers who had just come from it.

As a small Mexican boy growing up in the New Mexico town of Las Cruces, 42 miles north of the Mexican border, Rodriguez knew the hurt of prejudice and the dispiritedness of a teenager looking at dead ends ahead. He joined the Army as a medic in 1967, did his three years and then reentered civilian life in the belief his training would get him somewhere. The best job he could find was service manager at the Toyota dealership in Las Cruces. "I found it boring." He tried to reenter the Army at his old rank of E-5 sergeant in 1975. "No way," the recruiter told him. "Only way to get back in is to come in as a private in the infantry," which Rodriguez did. He had worked himself up to sergeant first class, E-7, by the time we met at Benning.

One night at A. O. Eagle, I had watched Rodriguez extend himself after his regular long workday to recharge the recruits he sensed were restless, bored and snarly from too many days of doing the same thing. He organized an attack against snipers he had hidden in the woods around A. O. Eagle. It was too early in the training cycle to give the recruits blank cartridges for their M-16 rifles. No matter. Rodriguez told them to yell *"bang-bang"* or *"pow-pow"* when they fired. Pine cones would be their grenades.

Tensions mounted in the young soldiers advancing toward the woods where they knew the snipers were waiting to kill them.

Rodriguez and I walked behind them. A sniper shouted, *"Bang!"* The advancing troops dropped to the floor of the woods. They tried to tell each other what was going on by whispering across the space of ground separating them.

"Once you come under fire," Rodriguez corrected, "there's no sense keeping up this whispering. The enemy knows you're here. Communicate, communicate. If you get a malfunction, you've got to let your buddy know so he can reduce his rate of fire to save ammo."

"Cover me while I move," shouted one recruit to his buddy a few yards to his right.

"Got you covered. *Pow! Pow!"*

The trooper ran a few steps, dropped to the ground and struggled along in the infantryman's low crawl he had just been taught.

"If you're going to stick your ass up there like that," Rodriguez scolded, "it's going to be shot off. Then we'll have to ship it home with a Band-Aid on it."

He asked slow-moving Ty "Spank" Barker: "What are you doing, Spank, waiting for a train? Get your ticket out; it'll be here in a minute."

To another slow mover: "You've got a case of mucosis: iron in the blood that turns to lead in the butt."

Rodriguez could also be the father many of the recruits never had, calling them into his office to talk softly and earnestly one on one. He believed the Army had more to offer than his recruits realized. Rodriguez had to quit the Army to learn why he missed it. I heard him preach this sermon to the whole company assembled before him one day on an expanse of rolling sand:

"There's only two kinds of people in the military, men: the professional soldier and the slug.

"I'm telling you right now, the military service is one of the best things going. It's one of the best paying. It's the only job in the world where they give you thirty days' leave the first year. That's paid vacation. You tell me where you can go find a job that does that for you, and I'll kiss your foot.

"So what is the problem with your motivation? Let's face it, men. The only time you get in trouble is when you fail to do what you're supposed to do. Am I not correct in that?"

"Yes, Drill Sergeant," the soldiers shouted back in unison.

"Why do we drop you for push-ups?"

"Motivation! To be better soldiers!" the assemblage answered, having been told week after week that this was the proper answer and they damn well better shout it out when asked.

"Now, you've been taught the proper position of attention. Where's Munchies at?" ["Munchies" was the nickname given to Private Harold Hudson, 18, of Omaha, Nebraska, after he had been caught sneaking cornflakes into his mouth while he was supposed to be standing at attention. He had been dogged for his offense by performing dozens of punitive push-ups.]

Munchies, dressed like his comrades in fatigue pants and brown T-shirt, stood up from among the soldiers sitting on the sand and came to attention.

"Explain to everybody, Munchies, what the proper position of attention is," Rodriguez ordered.

"The position of attention," Munchies began in the loud voice he had been taught to use, "is feet on the line; feet out at a 45-degree angle; legs straight, not locked; knees slightly bent; back straight; chest slightly out."

"That's good, Munchies. Outstanding. You know that you could be a drill sergeant, couldn't you?"

"No, Drill Sergeant."

"Yes, you could. Not only that, but tell us what your IQ is."

"About 150."

"Very outstanding. You're a good man, Munchies. Now tell everybody why you got dogged out."

"Because I ate cereal while we were in formation, while we were supposed to be at attention."

"Now, was that the proper position of attention?"

"No, Drill Sergeant."

"Now, was the drill sergeant wrong to chew you out?"

"No, Drill Sergeant."

"Thank you very much, Munchies. Now have a seat." Then with his voice rising, Rodriguez came to his summation before this jury of teenagers trying to decide whether they should take basic training seriously or not.

"Listen up, men. Listen up. You think it's funny. But the main ingredient of a successful military unit is the discipline of its soldiers. I'm not picking on you, Munchies there. I'm not picking on you; you just give a good example, right?

"If you're in a combat situation, and you have to depend on this guy next to you, and instead of watching the perimeter he's munching down on some cereal, next thing you know you've got a bayonet up your ass, and you'll want to know where your buddy was. He was off getting some milk for his cereal. See what I'm trying to tell you men?"

"Yes, Drill Sergeant," the men sitting on the sand answered with growing restlessness. The fire ants had crawled down the pants of many, including mine, and were biting fiercely.

"You have one of the hardest jobs in the United States Army: The infantry. The hours are long. The gratitude is nothing. You're going to be out there twenty-four to thirty-eight hours without sleep on missions. You're going to be out there in subzero weather. And you're going to have to guard that perimeter. There's none of this, 'I'm going in to get warm.'

"You're also going to be in 110-to-120-degree temperature, and they're not going to haul you off to cool you down. You're going to be thirsty. You're not going to have somebody following you around with lister bags of water. You're going to have water in your canteen, and that's all. You're going to have to learn to conserve it.

"It all boils down to one thing: discipline.

"That's the last thing I'm going to say about discipline.

"I'll tell you what. If I don't see this company motivated a little more than you have been, we're going to have some plans for you. We're going to train. If we have to train until 11 o'clock at night on where you're screwing up, that's what we're going to do."

Rodriguez paused for effect. Then he shifted down from the senior drill sergeant out in the field addressing the whole company to the competitive leader of 2d Platoon. With a smile he concluded his sermon on the sand with: "If you can beat 2d Platoon, I congratulate you. But no way."

Rodriguez, like many other sergeants I met at Benning, had discovered too late that he had put the Army too far ahead of his wife and child. One day he found a note on the kitchen table and an empty house. He was still trying to reestablish communication with his daughter when we talked in 1987. Here was the best communicator of all the drill sergeants of Delta Company, unable to communicate with his own daughter. It hurt him. He had gone into an emotional tailspin when his wife left him. "I used to blame her," he told me. "Now I realize it was my fault. I don't blame her for leaving me." He had since remarried a supportive woman, Ruth. After years of trying, hoping and waiting, they succeeded in adopting a baby girl, Sara.

Raul Rodriguez made me see how the Army can become bigger and dearer than life itself for the sergeants who feel they actually run the institution down on the ground where soldiers are made or not made, where battles are won or lost, where men live or die. These senior enlisted people who work in the field with soldiers, as opposed to the sergeants who shuffle papers back in headquarters and take delight in being obstructive and officious, are the pillars of the American Army. They know it. Most civilians do not. They do not hear about the sergeants in the woods leading rifle squads through enemy fire by hand signals. They hear about the generals in headquarters directing divisions by tapping a pointer on a map.

Rodriguez's deputy in running 2d Platoon was Staff Sergeant (E-6) Randall Nelson Stover, 29, who had lived the hard-scrabble life of the West Virginia coal country. Born in a hollow in Oak Hill, he was seven when the family moved to Beckley, West Virginia, where he went to Woodrow Wilson High School. His father was in the merchant marine, was seldom home. His mother, a nurse, struggled alone but was overextended trying to work and rear three children. In high school, Randy drank a little, chased the girls a lot. His reddish brown hair, flashing blue eyes and ready smile projected the image of a devil-may-care hell-raiser. He had no master plan for his life after high school. He went into the coal fields for lack of better options. He soon found himself standing in a foot of water lifting heavy batteries in and out of the little locomotives that pulled cars of coal out of the mine.

"I told myself there had to be something better than this," Stover recalled in one of our many conversations in the bush. "I always wanted to be in the military. I wanted to be a paratrooper. I couldn't think of anything more exciting in life than jumping out of an airplane with a rifle ready to fire when I hit the ground."

Stover joined the Army in 1979, too late for Vietnam but just right for Grenada. He had led a fire team of the Third Battalion of the Eighty-second Airborne Division's 325th Airborne Infantry during the Grenada invasion of 1983. Somehow all the kids in training at Benning knew this. It made Drill Sergeant Stover their war hero. I had to remind myself that most of these soldiers I was with were born in 1969, one year after the Tet offensive and three years after Johnny Libs's battle in Vietnam. Grenada was their war. And Sergeant Stover had fought in it. Wow!

"When Drill Sergeant Stover tells you, 'Outstanding,' after you do something," Spank Barker told me one day, "you feel great."

One broiling afternoon Stover took off his Smokey-the-Bear drill sergeant hat, grabbed a soldier's M-16 and rolled in the sand, saying: "Like this, son." He got up, brushed the sand off his fatigues and told me, "I don't mind doing that for a kid trying to learn. It's the ones who don't care that get me."

I saw Stover bring listless soldiers to life time after time. I asked him his secret. He smiled that wide-open smile of his and answered: "The man who's down on himself, I say: 'I know you can do it.' Then he does it. Then he smiles and says, 'I did it, Drill Sergeant.' I smile back and say, 'Outstanding.'

"These soldiers are the finest Americans—the finest men in the world. If they've got someone leading them, they'll do whatever needs doing."

I decided after watching Stover in action for months at Benning that he succeeded because he felt grateful to the Army for pulling him out of the mines and wanted to do all he could do to pay the Army back. He knew if it were not for the United States Army, he would be stuck in Beckley working for Batteries Inc. for $5.50 an hour and getting his blood tested over and over for lead poisoning from the batteries he was wrestling with day after day.

"One of the great things about the Army," he told me, "is seeing different places, meeting people. Some really outstanding people. I can learn something from all of them. And I know they'd give their life for me anytime. I want to die with paratroopers."

One day the trainees were bitching to him about their assignments, such as learning how to fire mortars or antitank weapons rather than be allowed to remain as an 11 Bravo [Army military occupational specialty] rifleman charging through the woods. Stover listened for a while, shook his head negatively so vigorously I thought his hat would fall off.

"Listen up! Listen up! You can learn something from anything the Army tells you to do. And if you do it well, you'll eventually get to do what you want. Now they gave me the radio to hump when I was a paratrooper. I didn't want to carry the damn thing. But I humped it all over. Whenever they called for me, I went running.

I was the hardest charging RTO [radio telephone operator] they had. I wasn't supposed to have to carry it as long as I did. But I didn't complain. I did it. I finally got to do what I wanted. You got to do what the Army gives you. If you learn somebody else's job and he gets killed, you can do it. You're better. You see what I'm saying?"

I came to regard Rodriguez as the professor of the drills because of all his long lectures; Stover as the John Wayne because of his hard-charging style; Drill Sergeant Mario A. Zuniga, 29, as the wild man because of his temper that erupted like a volcano, terrifying the recruits in their first weeks of basic. I could sense Zuniga's frustration as he ached to hit or kick a miscreant rather than just yell at him. He gritted his teeth but kept hands off—at least while I was watching. Yet once his troops got over their fear of Zuniga, they came to love him. They figured out he wanted them to break with their pasts as he had done with his when he was their age. "Goddamn it," he was trying to say with fire and brimstone because he did not have Rodriguez's subtle verbal weapons, "I know you can do it because I did it, you Yo-Yo." Frequently he would ask his platoon, "Are you motivated?" They would roar back the answer they had been taught: "Motivated! Motivated! Hell yes! Motivated!"

The oldest of nine children, Zuniga had grown up in Honduras. He was a bad-ass member of the Red Devils gang in the Honduran capital of Tegucigalpa. He told me with a laugh that he was one of the long-haired Red Devils who had hung U.S. GO HOME signs on the walls and fences of the U.S. Embassy compound in Tegucigalpa that he now was sworn to protect as a soldier.

"I became a hoodlum. I painted OAS [Organization of American States] on the side of donkeys. I didn't mean anything by it. We were just kids raising hell. I quit school at 13. My father sent me to military school where, whenever I did something wrong, they punched me in the stomach. They stripped me of everything. I was there from age 13 to 15, when I moved to a little town of 150 people, Choluteca. I was having a lot of fun there when my father decided to move to the States. I raised my right hand in that same American Embassy I used to hang signs on and became an American citizen. We moved to Queens, New York, where my father became a kitchen designer for Sears, Roebuck. I went to the Spanish American Institute to learn English. I signed up for its typing class because I knew there would be lots of girls there. I fell in love with a Spanish girl in the Bronx. The parents of the two families got together, and I never saw the girl again.

"My father wanted me to join him in the kitchen business. I didn't want to. I went to an Army recruiter in 1977. I said, 'I don't care what you put me in as long as I can jump out of airplanes.' "

Zuniga reported to basic training and saw the U.S. Army had the same aluminum trays he had known in the brutal Honduran military school. He thought everything else was going to be the same. "I was scared shitless." But his fears were unfounded. He thrived in the American Army, becoming an enthusiastic paratrooper with the Eighty-second Airborne. He got married, had two daughters but, like Rodriguez, worried more about the Army than his family. He came home one day to find everyone gone. "I got married to the Army. Now I know better."

I asked Zuniga what he liked about being a drill sergeant when the frustrations were many and the hours endless. He smiled his devilish smile, dark eyes flashing, and answered: "I like the power!" But then, as so much else with Mario Zuniga, came the contradiction revealing his thoughtful side. I asked him who was the best drill sergeant in Delta Company. He reflected for a moment and then named his arch-rival, Rodriguez: "He's got more patience. I'm learning that from him."

The smallest drill in Delta Company was Sergeant Norman K. Williams, 27, 5 feet 6 inches tall and 135 pounds. He gave me this rationale for starting out tough with his trainees and staying that way until they graduated: "I'm the smallest guy out here. You've got to have a power base. If I get off them for one minute, I lose it. From Day One, I show them I'm an asshole and stay that way."

The drills delighted in scaring the recruits with gimmicks. Williams, for example, told me about the time he brought a pit bull with him to the training field. "Sergeant Williams is going to sick a pit bull on us," the recruits whispered with a shudder until Williams could not hold his stern look any longer and broke into a laugh.

Drill Sergeant Charlie Butler was the biggest of the drills, standing well over six feet with the build of a football tackle and a voice to match. He had taken recruits through three basic training cycles by the time we met. He symbolized to me the struggle the drills were having in obeying the Army's rule to move from raging dictator to restrained mentor who did not even swear.

"I'm a man, Mr. Wilson," he said. "I've just got to swear at some of these knuckleheads. You've seen how it is out here." And how Charlie could yell, "Get out of my face, Private!" would send whiners running. The big black man could use this shout like a cattle prod on lagging recruits: "Earn that dollar bill!"

Because he was so big and good-hearted, the other drills loved to kid Charlie Butler. Stover one day at A. O. Eagle hid the keys of Butler's new car. He let Charlie look all over the car and out under the trees before he fessed up. Butler lit up in a million-dollar smile rather than take a swing at Stover. His defense against such kidding was often, "I've got more time in the shithouse than you've got in the Army."

I got the feeling from Charlie Butler's initial standoffishness that he could not figure out why the Army was putting me in his face—yet another knucklehead to deal with. We eventually bridged the gap. I found him a warm leader who cared about his recruits but had been worn down by too many training cycles.

Drill Sergeant Gerry Acuna was the opposite of Butler. He was just starting out as a drill. He was not trained as an infantryman but had decided to change his military occupational specialty to win the blue cord of infantryman. The older drills kidded Acuna, too. On his birthday they ordered the whole company to sing happy birthday to him. Acuna's response was to order a recruit to come before the company, drop his pants and moon the formation of well-wishers. In the field with the infantry, the humor is all homemade.

I asked the senior drill sergeant, William Glenn Sutphin, 30, who was First Sergeant Ted Williams's eyes and ears in the field but did not run a platoon, what made a successful drill. "He's got to be a teacher. If Joe's got a problem, he's got to feel he can come to you." He agreed Stover was exceptional. "He keeps it high and tight. He leads the way. The soldiers—they eat that shit up."

The ever-nervous recruits often called their drill sergeants, "Sir," the deference that is supposed to be reserved for officers in the Army. "I'm no Sir," Sutphin would always scold, "I work for a living."

The worst thing a girlfriend of one of the recruits could do was to send him a perfumed letter. The drill passing out the mail might hold back the perfumed letter and open it himself or order the recruit to read it out loud to the whole company standing around him. One of the drills told me how he had hit pay dirt in the last training cycle when he opened up a perfumed letter and found a big picture of a girlfriend's naked rear end inside. The picture was inscribed with a tribute to Big Rocky, the recruit's apparently large organ: "I want Big Rocky to ride me and ride me. I can't wait to make Big Rocky soft and nice." The drill told me "I was getting a hard-on reading the stuff so I passed the picture around the platoon. The guy told me at first that his father had taken the picture of his girl's ass. But you could see the car mirror and everything. He took it. I wouldn't give the picture back to him until graduation. I'd keep asking him, 'Hey, is your girl coming to graduation? I want to meet her.' He'd say no. We all called him Big Rocky. He was a good kid. He laughed, didn't get upset. I told him this was the infantry where you shared everything with your buddies."

Making fun of officers, especially the junior ones, was a favorite pastime of the drills. One day I sat with a group of them while one of their number regaled us with tales of "Messy Marvin," a young officer in West Germany.

"He could never use a map. He would take the map out of the plastic case and tape it on top of the case. Then he would smear the map up with grease pencil rather than just marking the plastic cover. Afterwards he'd mash the map into a ball and throw it in the back of the vehicle. The sergeants wouldn't follow him because they knew he didn't know where he was going. The troops knew about him, too. He was a Parkay lieutenant [a second lieutenant with the single gold bar resembling a stick of margarine]. The troops would say, 'Parkay! Parkay!' whenever Messy Marvin walked through their mess. And he made captain, too!"

I also heard about the recruit who came to his drill sergeant's little office in front of the barracks, claimed to be a homosexual and requested to be discharged from the Army on that ground.

"Son," the drill thundered, "I don't know if you're queer or not. But if you weren't a homo when you got here, you're going to be one when you leave. Drop your pants!"

The recruit fled the room.

I winced once in a while at what some of the drills did. I spotted one kick the arm out from under a kid while he doing punitive push-ups. The drill's occasional screams into the faces of teenagers hit them like an ax, immobilizing the victim. I say again, though, that these violations were the exception rather than the rule in Delta Company. And some of the recruits were indeed

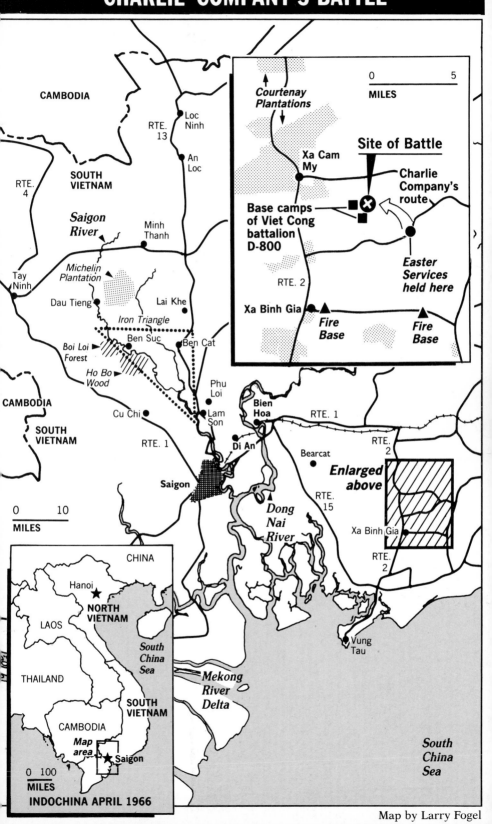

# CHARLIE COMPANY'S BATTLE

CAMBODIA

RTE. 13

Loc Ninh

An Loc

SOUTH VIETNAM

RTE. 4

*Saigon River*

Minh Thanh

*Michelin Plantation*

Tay Ninh

Dau Tieng

Lai Khe

*Iron Triangle*

*Boi Loi Forest*

Ben Suc

Ben Cat

*Ho Bo Wood*

CAMBODIA

SOUTH VIETNAM

Cu Chi

Phu Loi

RTE. 1

Lam Son

Bien Hoa

RTE. 1

RTE. 2

Di An

Bearcat

*Enlarged above*

RTE. 15

Saigon

RTE. 1

*Dong Nai River*

Xa Binh Gia

RTE. 2

0    10
MILES

CHINA

Hanoi ★

**NORTH VIETNAM**

LAOS

*South China Sea*

THAILAND

**SOUTH VIETNAM**

CAMBODIA

*Map area*

★ Saigon

0   100
MILES

**INDOCHINA APRIL 1966**

*Mekong River Delta*

Vung Tau

*South China Sea*

## Enlarged inset

*Courtenay Plantations*

0        5
MILES

Xa Cam My

**Site of Battle**

Charlie Company's route

**Base camps of Viet Cong battalion D-800**

⊗

*Easter Services held here*

RTE. 2

Xa Binh Gia

*Fire Base*

*Fire Base*

Map by Larry Fogel

# AMONG THE HEROES

Lieutenant John W. Libs on patrol near Bien Hoa, Vietnam, in 1965.
(U.S. Army photograph by SP5 Allen K. Holm)

Major General William E. DePuy pins ver Star on Staff Sergeant Charles Urco at Bearcat base camp on April 14, 1966 (U.S. Army photograph)

Sergeant James W. Robinson Jr., Medal of Honor winner.
(Family photograph)

Former machine gunn Phillip Hall finds nam of Charlie Company de on Vietnam Veterans M morial in Washingto D.C.

# TRANSITION

Kristian "Tweety" Selvester before.
(Photo by Karen Selvester)

Kristian "Tweety" Selvester after.

ian Trotter before.   (Family photograph)

Brian Trotter after.

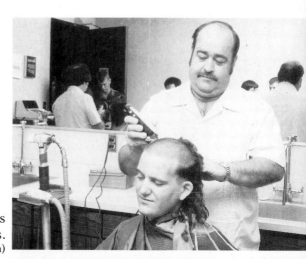

ymond N. McDaniel Jr. loses his
civilian locks.
S. Army photograph by Bill C. Walton)

# SHOCK TREATMENT

New trainees rush off bus for first formation.  (U.S. Army photograph by Bill C. Walton)

"On your face!" Rafael Castro gets the
treatment.
(U.S. Army photograph by Bill C. Walton)

"Louder!" Drill Sergeant Mario Zuni
orders Dallas Knox.
(U.S. Army photograph by Bill C. Walton)

"Higher!"
(U.S. Army photograph by Bill C. Walton)

# THE DRILLS

Drill Sergeant Randy Stover.

Drill Sergeant Raul Rodriguez.

Drill Sergeant Randy Stover.

Drill Sergeant Mario Zuniga.

rnabout as trainee Frederick E. Waddell
hews out" Drill Sergeant Lee Cocks in skit.

# LEARNING HOW

Under the wire.

War paint.

On the march.

James Gordon mastering the M-16 rifle.

# RESPITE

"Mail Call!"

e T. Hewlett tries on first dress
s.

"Hi, Mom!"

# THE MANAGEMENT

Colonel Richard S. Siegfried, Commander of U.S. Army Infantry Training Center, Fort Benning.

Captain James R. Fleenor II.

Second Lieutenant Keith Raines.

First Sergeant Ted Williams counsels recruit.

infuriating. One had no regard for anyone but himself. He pulled his platoon down by dropping out of exercises when he could not fake doing them. He sold cigarettes to fellow recruits at $2 each. He smoked in the barracks and got caught several times, meaning his whole platoon got punished under the one-for-all, all-for-one psychology practiced by the drills. He bragged about selling drugs before he came into the Army. He picked his nose and held up the result for all to see. He lied. He faked injuries, often winning a soft couple of days in the hospital. No amount of shouting or punishment motivated him to do better. He was what the military calls a training risk because an exasperated drill might hit him. He was discharged from the Army during basic training. His presence had been a colossal waste of time and effort for everyone who dealt with him. But at least he was not carried along as he might well have been in the early years of the all-volunteer force when the Army struggled to fill its billets.

The drills did more disciplining and baby-sitting than training during basic training. They got the troops up in the morning, led them in calisthenics, supervised their feeding and then marched them to firing ranges where other sergeants at Sand Hill would do the training. There was a time in the Army when the platoon drill sergeants taught their recruits soldiering skills. But the new Army leaves most of these to specialists who work at the ranges, teaching one platoon after another. Falling asleep in a grandstand while the obviously bored training sergeant droned through his lecture for the 1,000th time was a common occurrence. The dozer was yelled at and ordered to stand up.

I sympathized with the young soldiers who did fall asleep. I often left the grandstand to sit with the platoon sergeants under a tree while the range sergeant lectured the trainees. I was impressed with how rarely the drills talked about anything but the Army or the people in it. I was so used to hearing government bureaucrats in Washington talk about the previous night's TV show, their new car, or the latest problems with their kids. The drills talked shop as much as we reporters, I discovered.

The drills in passing each other in the field would often cross their wrists to protest silently the strictness of the rules on what they could and could not do to recruits.

"The drill sergeants are going through an identity crisis," Captain Fleenor explained. "They have this image of themselves as being the tough guy. But the Army is into mentoring. The drill sergeants don't know where they fit nowadays, especially since they do so little of the actual training."

Not all drills at Benning were as skilled as the ones at Delta Company whom I got to know well. Just as not everyone in civilian life has the temperament, maturity and skill to be a teacher or a policeman, so it is with Army drill sergeants. Major B. R. Deal, chief of community mental health services at Benning when I was there in the summer and fall of 1987, dealt with the youths who had been abused by sergeants miscast as drills who could not distinguish between bullying and teaching. These drill sergeants had made emotional cripples out of too many trainees in Deal's view.

Deal was no softie. He told me he had gone through Army basic training himself twice, once in 1958 at Fort Knox, Kentucky, and again in 1967 at Fort Polk, Louisiana. He had seen the days when it was common for drills to smack recruits with fists and rifle butts. Since his enlisted service, Deal had earned a degree, specializing in psychology. When we talked long into the afternoon at his office in Benning he acknowledged that drills had become more enlightened in their treatment of their charges but lamented the fact that too many still were not willing to treat recruits as confused teenagers trying to find their way in life.

"The image of the DI [drill instructor] is that I've got to yell and scream and be a son of a bitch," Deal told me as we chatted on the second floor of one of those wooden temporary buildings at Benning that will probably stand forever. "A guy who tends to be understanding, cares about the trainees and does not fit the norm is sometimes ostracized himself because he doesn't fit the mold. And there is a mold. And there is an image of a DI. You are Lou Gossett [who played the tough Marine DI in the movie, *An Officer and a Gentleman*]. If you don't fit that mold, you tend to become an outcast."

I realized Deal saw the trainees who had tried to commit suicide to escape their drill sergeants; who had been immobilized with fear by all the yelling and screaming; who had lost their bearings and did not know what was right, what was wrong, which foot was right, which was left. Yet Deal spoke as the soldier who had been there and knew that there were better ways to turn teenagers into soldiers than many of the drill sergeants at Benning were practicing. He warmed to the subject as I listened with fascination and, most of the time, with agreement.

"You have young men here who, in some cases, are very immature and emotionally fragile; away from home for the first time; away from girlfriend or wife—the mother. They haven't adapted to society, in some cases anyway; have had trouble with discipline throughout their life. Then you put them in an environment that is totally authoritarian, threatening with a lot of yelling, plus fear."

Some of the trainees told Deal they had been physically beaten and mentally tortured by their drill sergeants. Deal was not an investigator, he was a counselor. But many of the terrified trainees told him stories so detailed and realistic that he knew some drill sergeants were breaking the rules and handling the kids in their charge the old way.

"There's a fine line between abuse and forcing a kid to train. The majority of the DIs who place hands on trainees do it with the intent of, 'Maybe I can scare him through this adjustment period and force him to train.' I don't think the intent from the majority who do this is to abuse the trainee. It's trying to use fear to motivate. The training environment is a stressful environment. There's nothing wrong with adding a little stress to the environment as long as you understand there are people who are different and will act differently than others. But what some of the DIs do is home in on the ones who are different as weaklings. I'm not sure that those who go at these trainees this way are not saying, 'I'm going to make you break' rather than 'I'm going to make you train.' When they home in on that guy and call him a weakling or wimp, piss-poor protoplasm—I'm not sure the attempt is not to use him as a focal point. This kind of humiliation is lowering the trainee's self-esteem; creating an onset of depression. What you're doing is setting up the scene for the guy to end up in mental health for threatening suicide to get out of the Army."

Of the 25,000 young men going through basic training at Benning every year in the late 1980s, between 2 and 4 percent of them became so desperate that they tried to kill themselves to get out from under the pressure of training, or made what was called "suicidal gestures."

"If I had to put my finger on one thing" as the cause for making life not seem worth living to these teenagers, Deal told me, "I think it's the fear and shock of the yelling and screaming, especially by two or three DIs yelling in a kid's face all at once. When you do that to a kid who is very immature and emotionally unstable, what you're really doing is pushing him beyond what he can cope with. This past week we had a kid who had been immobilized by fear. We placed him in the hospital. He couldn't concentrate; he couldn't think; he was frightened of everything that was going on around him.

"Having gone through basic training twice myself and being subjected to screaming twice and watching it during my seventeen years in the military as enlisted and officer, I'm not sure screaming adds much to the training environment. If you could get through to these guys by yelling at them, their parents would have been more successful because a majority of these folks here have been yelled and screamed at all their lives. I think that 99 percent of the kids who are trained with yelling and screaming could be trained without it. We wouldn't be seeing some of these suicidal guys here if the DIs could do that. But that's not the image of the DI."

Deal had evidently talked longer and more feelingly than he had planned. I had not interrupted this concerned officer sharing his frustration with me—someone outside the command who was not asking for reports, figures or successes. I was just asking him to tell what he felt inside. I had seen enough victims of harassment to relate to what he was saying. I agreed with this sensitive major and asked what he thought could be done to reduce the risk of drill sergeants, usually unwittingly, inflicting psychological wounds on their charges.

"You'd have to change the standards for DIs, the education level and the hours. You can't work a man sixteen hours a day and expect him to function under the current rules through the whole training cycle. There's going to be a letting off somewhere. If he's married, and goes home to more difficulties, you've magnified the pressure. And he's going to let it go. Displacement seems to be a good way of doing that. Trainees are handy; they're vulnerable; they're like a good dog. You can kick them and get away with it. I'm not saying all DIs do that, but I dare say some do."

I was awakened from my sleep in the pre-dawn dark of 5 A.M. at A. O. Eagle by the 1980s version of reveille: a private going from tent to tent shouting: "Get up, people!"

90

The sleepy recruits knew that their tormenting drills would be on them if they did not hurry through their wake-up routine of shaving without water and reporting to the cleared area to form into platoons for the morning calisthenics and run.

"Hey, Legs!" Drill Sergeant Zuniga bellowed to a slow-moving recruit. "I'm going to drop your ass!"

"What are you waiting for?" he asked another stumbler who was left behind by fellow recruits running out of the pines and into the clearing. "A private invitation?"

Rodriguez was standing on the platform in front of the clearing to lead the recruits in calisthenics. First came stretching exercises, then jumping, then push-ups. After each set of exercises the recruits would shout back the chant they had been taught in their first week of basic training:

"We like it! We love it! We want more of it! Make it hurt, Drill Sergeant, make it hurt! Ahhhhhhhhhhhhhh!"

Calisthenics concluded, the trainees and their drill sergeants marched into the driveway one platoon after another. It was still dark. They broke into a run as soon as they reached the road. I jogged behind them for a while but did not try to make the whole five miles. I was a 50-year-old-plus-has-been-cross-country-runner who had jogged in such formations long ago as part of Navy pilot training. At least that was my rationalization this hot August morning when I stopped on the blacktop outside the encampment to watch Delta Company wind up the steep hill. The runners carried flashlights, making them look from my distance like a flight of low-flying fireflies. A truck eased along behind the running formation to pick up anyone who passed out. I felt uplifted by the scene. The Army at that moment seemed cured of its post-Vietnam diseases. This new generation of soldiers running up the hill was full of hope, enthusiasm and pride. I noticed that even little things had changed for the better, like the Army's decision to allow recruits to run in running shoes rather than the old boots with the seam down the inside heel, which raised crippling blisters. I also felt grateful standing there in the purple light for the absence of the folded green body bags I had seen following Army companies in Vietnam. These charged-up replacements for Johnny Libs's Charlie Company had not yet suffered their first casualties. But this was about to change. An enemy they had always regarded as a friend was about to strike many of them down.

# 4. First Casualties

Delta Company left its A. O. Eagle encampment in the pine boonies of Sand Hill for the central part of Fort Benning to see what was supposed to be an inspiring demonstration of what trained Army troopers could do with guns, knives and bare hands. As we filed into the grandstand overlooking the open-air stage with a pond behind it, the sun speared us. It shot its rays down from the cloudless August sky and sunk them into our heads. There was no roof on the grandstand. I worried about the trainees suffering heat stroke. I could escape to the shade behind the stand without any drill sergeant stopping me; they could not. They would have to stay impaled by these piercing rays of sun until the demonstration concluded. Mercifully, the drills had let the trainees keep their helmets on their laps. A helmet traps heat like an upside down frying pan. But a colonel looking over the row upon row of shaved heads decided this white nakedness looked unmilitary. He ordered the helmets put back on. "It felt as if my helmet was cooking my brains out," Chris Cashman would tell me after Delta Company suffered its first casualties.

The record 98-degree ferocity of the sun on this day, August 10, 1987, reminded me of the sun that injured several riflemen and myself in another Army company in 1968. We were walking leisurely out of Fire Base Stud near the demilitarized zone dividing North and South Vietnam. Our mission was to relieve the Marines in Khesanh. Suddenly, North Vietnamese ambushers crouching in spider holes alongside the trail opened up a crossfire on the front of the column. The ambushers' squad kept us pinned down on flat ground from midday until twilight. We were wearing helmets and the old-fashioned, heavy, hot flak jackets. I was out of range of the ambushers in the thick woods at the head of the column but not of the sun's rays. Several troopers lying in the sun near me and I became dizzy and nauseous. I remembered as I sat in the grandstand in Benning how helpless we felt against the sun. Doctors told me later that such overheating can kill as well as disable. I wished the colonel who had ordered the helmets put on these young trainees knew that.

The Army troopers on the stage demonstrated hand-to-hand combat, sniper fire and a long slide from a high tower down into water by cable. I could not tell whether the show excited the privates in the stands or not. I figured all they were thinking was, "When the hell are we getting out of this sun?" The demonstration finally ended, freeing Delta Company to leave the stand and board buses for a map-reading class. The sweating trainees sought the shade, gulped from their canteens before boarding the cattle cars.

I broke off from the company as it rolled off to map-reading class. I rejoined it late in the afternoon at the A. O. Eagle encampment. I sensed as soon as I arrived there that something had gone terribly wrong. Captain Fleenor, Lieutenant Raines and the drills were all milling around in a highly agitated fashion during what was usually a quiet time. The trainees told me that Drill Sergeant Rodriguez just before I arrived had ordered them to do push-ups and flutter kicks and to run in place when they returned to A. O. Eagle from map-reading class. The calisthenics were punishment for not paying attention in class. Rodriguez, the senior drill on the scene, left the formation and turned it over to Drill Sergeant Lee Cocks. Cocks ordered the hot troopers to do another set of punishment exercises, including the dreaded NBC (nuclear, biological, chemical) drill. It consists of falling to the ground on your stomach, rifle under you, and pressing your face into the dirt to shield your eyes from the nuclear flash. Cocks left the formation, leaving Drill Sergeant Keith Owens in charge. Owens was the least senior of the drills and seemed to relate best to young trainees having trouble coping with the demands of Army life. His shell had not hardened. Owens could see the recruits had been overheated. He called off the exercises as soon as the more senior drills were out of sight. He ordered the recruits to drink water, put on their shorts and prepare to shower. But it was too late, said the trainees in reconstructing the episode for me.

One overheated recruit fell right off a grandstand at A. O. Eagle where he had been resting after the two sets of punitive exercises. About a dozen more fainted under the pines near their tents.

"You're trying to hurt us!" shouted one recruit at Owens as he saw his buddies fall. He raised his fist to hit Owens, the only drill in sight.

"Hey, asshole!" Owens responded. "I'm not the one who fucked you guys up."

No blows were struck.

The Benning ambulance rushed to A. O. Eagle, picked up the trainees who had passed out and took them to the base hospital emergency room. Doctors considered six of the stricken troopers to be injured seriously enough to be hospitalized. I heard bitter talk as I moved among the clots of shocked trainees sitting and standing under the pines. They had come to trust their drill sergeants with their lives. They knew the drills would exhaust them but had confidence they would not maim them. This confidence had just been broken.

I felt both rage and sympathy. Rage that a drill sergeant might have killed one of these trainees who could be my own son. I was already regarding these young soldiers as sons, not anonymous troops. Sympathy for Rodriguez and Cocks who were supposed to keep troops motivated in hot weather and in cold and who did not have the medical training needed to detect the first signs of heat injury. Fleenor regarded Rodriguez as the best drill in the company. This one bad decision could eclipse the thousand good ones Rodriguez had made in his years on the trail. Should Fleenor recommend that Rodriguez and Cocks be court-martialed for abusing troops? Or should he urge battalion and brigade to view this stepping over the thin line between discipline and abuse as an honest mistake warranting no more than letters of reprimand?

Everything in the infantry is personal because everything you do as a private, sergeant, lieutenant, captain, colonel or general affects people's lives. Corporate executives usually only lose money when they make mistakes. Fleenor knew whatever he did about this excess of discipline would affect the people he was supposed to inspire and lead. They would judge him by how he handled this case where loyalty, responsibility, accountability, discipline, reward, punishment, sympathy and toughness all ran together. He knew he would be credited or blamed for whatever decision his superiors at battalion and brigade reached in regard to Rodriguez and Cocks, even if it turned out to be the opposite of what he recommended.

I had the luxury of being the chronicler in the heat-injury case, not the defendant, prosecutor or judge. But I wanted to talk to a wide spectrum of Delta Company before I reached my own silent judgment. I went to one of the brightest trainees in the company for testimony.

"Absolutely foolish dropping us like that when it was so hot," he told me. Other soldiers with the same kind of savvy and smarts told me the same thing.

I chatted with Lieutenant Raines. We agreed the heat injuries probably would not have felled trainees at A. O. Eagle if the colonel at the demonstration had not ordered the troops to put on their helmets under the blazing sun. Raines surprised me by standing up in front of the company shortly after our chat and confessing error. It was a no-bullshit statement which had a healing effect: "We all made mistakes today. The command made mistakes. If you're really feeling bad, that's when you want to talk to us."

Right on, lieutenant, I said to myself. It takes a big man to admit error to subordinates who have no power at all. I felt Raines could not have gone much further in his attempt to bring the company back together without intruding into the command's formal investigation.

I studied Captain Fleenor from a distance. Devastation darkened his face. He knew everything that happened to his company was his fault. He was the captain of this little ship. I decided against asking him at this painful moment what had gone wrong. Later, I joined him at the company compound to ride to the hospital to visit his men. He put on a smile as he went from soldier to soldier, bed by bed.

"Now, you're not going to miss any training," he assured one trooper, explaining that he would be given makeup instruction so he would not be recycled back to another company where he would be a stranger. I smiled to myself. Missing training was probably the last thing the kid lying on the bed before us was worrying about.

I let Fleenor finish his rounds before I talked to the trainees by myself. A captain is a captain to privates, even if he is as nice as

Jim Fleenor. The privates would hold back if he were at my side when I talked to them. As I went from bed to bed by myself, I was impressed all over again by the rough nobility of these knocked-around kids who asked for so little from their country and gave so much. I thought as I looked down on one teenager with a catheter inserted in his penis that I would want to kill the drill sergeants who put me in this position. I heard no such threats. I heard instead teenagers telling me how shocked they were to discover the sun could be their enemy; to learn that they were vulnerable to the point that the sun could kill them without warning. These young men had thought themselves invincible, only to be raped without ever seeing the rapist. As I listened, I realized they had shared the faith of warriors through the ages: it will be the other guy who gets killed, not me.

"It scares me," said Christopher "Hollywood" Sticco, 18, of Richmond, Indiana, son of a fire captain, as I sat on the edge of his bed. "Something hit me and I couldn't do anything about it." Doctors at Benning's Martin Army Community Hospital had already told him he was going to be discharged from the Army because he had proved too vulnerable to heat, aborting his dream.

"I'm leaving just as 4th Platoon is starting to get to be a big family," Hollywood told me, with sadness weighing down every word. "The Army can teach you that. It's neat. Best thing was that it taught you how to depend on each other. The worst was the hassle."

Frank Logan, 18, of Medford, Massachusetts, son of a factory worker, said he felt woozy during the exercises but told himself, "I'm going to put up with it." Despite his pain, including a catheter, Logan did not assail Rodriguez and Cocks. "I have no hard feelings about anyone. It was just bad judgment."

William Best, 20, of Camp Hill, Pennsylvania, joined the Army because "I wasn't making it" at the jobs he could get around home, like selling auto parts. He thought the military would provide a better life for him, his wife and the child they were expecting. His sudden vulnerability had shocked him. He had been voted an all-conference basketball forward back home and figured his body could handle any challenge.

"If it hadn't been for Sergeant Owens," Best told me as I sat at his bedside, "the whole thing would have been much worse. He told us, 'Secure your gear, get in the shade and get your PT uniform on.' I went over to the bleachers and passed out. They showered me, and I passed out again. I played a lot of basketball and football. It was the first time ever I was a heat victim. If they were going to give us remedial PT, they should have waited till later when it was cooler. Poor judgment."

"Are you pissed off at Rodriguez?" I asked Best.

"No. I had a lot of personal problems, and he helped me. He and Stover were a great combination."

Rodriguez and Cocks continued on duty while commanders weighed their fate. I could tell Rodriguez and Cocks were uneasy. "You do your best every day," Rodriguez told me one day while waiting for command's verdict, "and then you make one mistake. You'd think a person would be allowed one mistake."

Fleenor told me he saw it that way, too, especially in Rodriguez's case. He recommended to his battalion commander that the punishment be letters of reprimand, which would be taken out of the drills' files after they left Benning. These local letters of reprimands are slaps on the wrist.

After several weeks of tense waiting, Rodriguez and Cocks were summoned into the office of Colonel Jose R. Feliciano, commander of First Brigade. Feliciano told me later that this was what he told Rodriguez and Cocks: "My strength lies in my NCOs [noncommissioned officers]. My center of gravity is my officers because there are so few of them. You're my lieutenants.

"This was a leadership problem on your part. You're the individuals who I must count on. It was a failure in judgment to punish them that way in that environment. If there was a problem in map reading, perhaps it was a failure in instruction. It comes back to judgment. A failure in judgment."

In the end, Feliciano went along with Fleenor's recommendation and issued local letters of reprimand. Most of the drills thought that was about right. One drill disagreed, telling me: "They should have at least gotten Article 15s for the way they fucked those guys up."

Feliciano's words kept doing laps inside my head: "It comes back to judgment. A failure in judgment." My mind pondered his words as they went round and round. Yes, it was clearly a failure in judgment. But whose? Not just Rodriguez's and Cocks's but, when you looked at the big picture of cause and effect, the whole Army command from Fort Benning all the way up to the Army Chief of Staff. The generals at the training command and in the Pentagon

97

decide who gets what. The drills have to make do with what they get. Delta Company's first casualties raised these questions in my mind:

Why does the Army high command shortchange the places where soldiers are trained, especially in comparison to the U.S. Military Academy at West Point, New York, where future officers are indulged? The officers and drill sergeants responsible for turning teenagers into soldiers at Benning obviously had too much to do. They were bound to make mistakes. The training center needed more officers and sergeants to spread the load. I think everyone would have learned more and suffered less if each platoon was run by an experienced lieutenant, as is the case in combat, rather than a drill sergeant with too much to do.

Whose "failure in judgment" is it that the Army has only hit-and-miss procedures and equipment for treating peacetime casualties, like heat stroke victims? Is it fair to expect drill sergeants to be doctors and nurses along with everything else? Why doesn't the Army give every drill sergeant a small radio, like policemen carry, so they can call for medical help whenever a trainee goes down? Where are the medics? Why not have one assigned to every training company where there are so many accidents waiting to happen?

In visiting Delta's heat casualties in the hospital, I learned that a few rooms away, another trainee lay in bed unable to see or speak after having almost died in the field from heat stroke. He was Stephen M. Granoth, 17, of Morris, Connecticut. He had been going through basic training with the 3d Platoon of Charlie Company, Ninth Battalion, Second Infantry Training Regiment. I met his mother, Irene Granoth, at the hospital. She only knew the broad outlines of what had happened to her son. She felt the Army officers taking her from the guest quarters to the hospital day after day were not telling her the full story. Her suspicions were confirmed when she hired R. Christopher Blake, a Litchfield, Connecticut, lawyer and former Army officer who employed the Freedom of Information Act to obtain Army records on her son's case. In sworn statements I read, soldiers said the following:

• Granoth on August 4, 1987, told a drill sergeant he was not feeling well and requested permission to seek medical help by going on sick call. The sergeant denied his request. The private did the morning exercises, including a 1.5-mile run.

• The private, suffering from a cold which made breathing difficult, started marching the 3 miles from the company barracks at the area of Sand Hill called Harmony Church to the training range in the pines called Duke. He collapsed on the way and was pulled out of 3d Platoon's formation until the truck easing along behind the marching company stopped to pick him up. He was driven the rest of the way to Duke Range.

These excerpts from sworn statements taken by Army investigators reconstruct the rest of Granoth's tragic day:

"Private Granoth arrived at Duke Range at approximately 1050 (10:50 A.M.). He seemed to be extremely dehydrated when we fell into formation. About two to three minutes later, Private Granoth said: 'I think I'm going to pass out. Does anybody have any water?'

"I personally did not have any water left at that time because I drank my two canteens before we arrived. I proceeded to ask about four other soldiers for water. One of them had about one-quarter [of a canteen] left of water and gave that water to me. I then proceeded to give Private Granoth the remainder of the water. He still seemed to be depleted. He then dropped to the ground and started to panic . . ." —Private Christopher W. Cooper.

"His fellow soldiers started to help him out. Staff Sergeant [Leon] Smith told us to clear out. Then Staff Sergeant Smith told Granoth he would be all right and should act like an infantry soldier. He said this in a smart way. He said we were the weakest troops he had ever seen . . ." —Private Todd R. Bellavance.

"At that time, one of the range instructors, I believe it was Staff Sergeant Smith, instructed Private Granoth to 'get up and stick it out. You're an infantryman now.'" —Private Cooper.

Granoth struggled to his feet and walked to the first class of the day. Trainees said that the men still had not been allowed to refill their canteens. The range sergeant had forgotten to allow them to do so before sending them to hear a lecture on the LAW [light antitank weapon].

"The NCO who taught our class was on us 'cause we were acting tired and sick and weren't motivated. We told him we still hadn't gotten any water. And he told us to fall out to the lister bag and get water, as much as he hated for us to go during his class." —Private Jody K. Callahan.

Although soldiers in sworn statements said Granoth looked better, he was in grave trouble physically. Doctors would learn later that his temperature had risen to dangerously high levels. No medic was on hand to take his temperature or check his vital signs, steps which almost certainly would have warned he was on the edge of disaster. At 5 P.M., Steve managed to form up with his platoon and start the 3-mile march from Duke Range back to the company compound at Harmony Church. Apparently dizzy and nauseous, the 17-year-old kid fighting to be a tough American soldier again tried to gut it out.

"At 1700 hours [5 P.M.] I proceeded to walk back to the company area. Along the way I encountered two soldiers with possible heat injuries. The first soldier [Granoth] complained of side pains. I informed him to drink some water. I had the individual get out of the formation and walk beside me. He was sweating quite a bit. The soldier was breathing a little fast. I asked if he was dizzy, and he said, 'Yes.' I signaled for Sergeant [Wilmer] Hill to come forward, and I had the soldier kneel and wait for the truck . . ." —Staff Sergeant Eddie L. McKinley.

Drill Sergeant Walter E. Saffold, according to sworn statements, put Granoth in the back of his pickup truck which had a fiberglass top, affording little ventilation. Rather than call for a helicopter to evacuate the stricken private or drive his truck directly to the hospital, Saffold drove at a leisurely pace and stopped to unload gear at the company compound before taking Granoth to the hospital.

When the doctors and nurses at Benning's Martin Army Community Hospital finally got Granoth, they saw he was near death. He was in a coma. Army doctors told me his temperature pushed the mercury to the last mark on the scale, 108 degrees, and would have kept going if the thermometer had more room at its top. Such overheating is usually fatal, the doctors at Benning told me. Dr. Robert E. Laham, who attended Granoth, told me he felt Granoth had no better than a 50–50 chance of surviving the heat stroke. He called Mrs. Granoth at her home in Morris, Connecticut, to urge her to come to the hospital.

Irene Granoth is a warm, gutsy, no-nonsense, give-it-to-me-straight widow who was working two jobs when she got the call. She told me later that this was the exchange at 9:45 P.M. on August 4, 1987:

"Is he going to die?"

"Mrs. Granoth, all I want to tell you is to get here as quickly as you can. I suggest you call your local Red Cross. They'll help you get down here."

Irene Granoth called her daughter, Susan, who lived in Morris with her husband, and asked her to come right over. Mrs. Granoth told me she immediately called the Red Cross to get help with transportation to Benning and received nothing but "can't do" bureaucratese. She failed in her attempts to get on a commercial plane or charter a private one. She feared her 17-year-old son would die alone in Columbus, Georgia. A friend gave her the name of a man she had never met who might help her: Joseph Tringali, president of Executive Flight Service, of Oxford, Connecticut. Tringali not only booked her on the earliest commercial flight from La Guardia Airport to Atlanta, with a connection to Columbus, but drove her to the airport himself early the next morning.

Lieutenant Colonel Paul E. Cullinane Jr., commander of the Ninth Battalion to which Steve's Charlie Company was attached, met Mrs. Granoth and Susan at the Columbus airport outside Fort Benning. Mrs. Granoth asked him straight out as they were riding from the airport to the hospital whether Stephen would live. He shook his head negatively, she recalled, adding: "There's not much hope."

Mrs. Granoth told me her heart froze when she looked down at her son lying still as death under a white sheet at the Benning hospital. Tubes had been inserted in his nose and side. He was in a coma. This was the rambunctious teenager who only weeks ago laughed at his mother's ignorance about the surplus Army gear he used to prepare himself for a career of soldiering.

"I couldn't have asked for a better kid," Mrs. Granoth told me at the hospital in between her visits to Stephen. "All he ever wanted was to be was a soldier in the Army. He pasted Army pictures all over his room, bought guns and belts and stuff. I signed to let him go into the National Guard on March 19, 1987, the day after his seventeenth birthday. Before he came down here for basic training, he filled a knapsack with rocks and marched around the woods to toughen himself up. He did forty push-ups every day."

Stephen, at a chunky 5 feet 8 inches, had reported to Benning on July 2, 1987, to start basic training. It was the summer of his junior year at Morris Town High School. He planned to return to Morris in the fall to finish school and then join the Army for a career.

101

"His main dream was his dress greens," Mrs. Granoth told me, somehow keeping her voice steady.

Back at Stephen Granoth's company, the sergeants' mutual protection society mobilized to cover up the mistakes they made, according to the soldiers' sworn statements:

"The morning following the incident, Drill Sergeant Saffold called several of us down to the orderly room around 0600 hours. He instructed us to write out what happened, but saying that there was only one person in the back of the truck instead of the three that were present, and saying that the truck [from] there on went in front of the formation. After completing the statement, the drill sergeant overlooked the statement and released me." —Corporal John M. Karic.

"Drill Sergeant Saffold called all profiles [soldiers excused from full duties because of injuries or illness] to come see him at the orderly room. He singled out the people that witnessed or had anything to do with the incident concerning Private Granoth. He told us to write a statement, and told us that it needn't be mentioned that he went up to the company area to drop off Private Henry and some equipment. He also said for us to stick to what we write . . ." —Private Wrexford C. Johnson.

"At about 6 A.M. 5 August 1987, Drill Sergeant Saffold told us to write a statement for him. He instructed us not to mention anything about coming back to the company area; that there was no other heat casualties; that the truck went straight to the front of the company formation, and then went on to the hospital. Also he [Sergeant Saffold] told us to say that there was only one person in the back of the truck." —Private Maithy Van Huynh.

Army investigators zeroed in on Sergeant First Class Leon Smith and Drill Sergeant Walter E. Saffold as they tried to fix responsibility. Neither acknowledged error in their written statements.

Smith: ". . . I observed a soldier on the ground with a drill sergeant stand[ing] up over the soldier. I ask[ed] the drill sergeant if the soldier was OK, and the drill sergeant said and indicate[d] he was OK. As he [drill sergeant] walk[ed] away from the formation, I ask[ed] the soldier if he was feel[ing] OK. The soldier said, 'I will make it sergeant,' or words to that effect. When I observed the soldier, he had water pour[ed] over his head and look tired but in no bad condition than anyone else in the formation. I march the soldier over to the class area and start to

102

give the class. During the instruction, I said drink water, possible after a soldier said I do not have any water . . ."

In his first sworn statement, Saffold did not mention that he had kept several soldiers in the back of his truck, not just Granoth and a second soldier who tended him; that he took a detour to the company compound rather than take Granoth directly to the hospital. In a later statement, dated August 11, 1987, Saffold acknowledged he had poked along behind the formation as trail vehicle rather than rush Granoth to the hospital.

These questions asked by the Army investigator and Saffold's answers were at the bottom of Saffold's sworn statement:

"Q: Upon picking up Private Granoth, why did you not proceed directly to the hospital?"

"A: Because when I reach the intersection of Jamestown Road there were soldiers back there. One could not walk on his own. Other stragglers was there. I was the only NCO there. Plus I wanted to get some of the profiles [injured soldiers] off the truck before I got on a main road. And there were no other evacuation vehicle there if something else had happen[ed]."

"Q: Do you know any reason or why some of the trainee profiles would state that you gave them instructions to limit or modify their statements?"

"A: I don't know any reason why the soldiers would limit or alter their statements. The instructions were short and understandable. I told them to write what they knew about Private Granoth from the time he was picked up until they were off the truck or until he got to the hospital . . ."

In a separate sworn statement Saffold said he had previously observed the evacuation of an injured soldier by helicopter. He said the process took an hour. "I felt it would be faster to take him to the hospital" by truck. "It took about 20–25 minutes. When I pick up Private Granoth he didn't show any symptoms of a heat stroke casualty. So I didn't call for a medevac . . ."

On August 12, 1987, Lieutenant Colonel James C. Crowley, the investigating officer, warned Sergeant First Class Leon Smith in writing that he was suspected of "dereliction of duty." Crowley warned Drill Sergeant Walter E. Saffold in the same manner that he was suspected of "dereliction of duty, failure to follow policy, obstruction of justice."

Captain Stephen Lee Potts, Charlie Company commander, defended Saffold, declaring in his written statement that "Sergeant

103

First Class Saffold simply answered the questions in general terms and did not intentionally leave out the actual location where he turned the truck around at the head of the column to head for the hospital. At the time of incident, Sergeant First Class Saffold was probably unaware of the seriousness of Private Granoth's injuries and was also concerned about his mission as the trail vehicle in the column responsible for following the company to pick up any other injured personnel during the movement. Sergeant First Class Saffold is a very dedicated and professional NCO . . ."

Lieutenant Colonel Cullinane wrote in his sworn statement that Saffold did not tell him during initial interviews that he had driven all the way back to the company compound before taking Granoth to the hospital. "I was led by my emotion to believe that Sergeant First Class Saffold had deceived me into thinking he had taken timely and appropriate action, recognizing that he had made the wrong judgment. I am torn between this reaction and the possibility that Sergeant First Class Saffold believed, at the time, that he took the appropriate action . . . He clearly understood his responsibility to get the soldier to the hospital but did not recognize the severity of Private Granoth's medical condition. In my opinion, we placed responsibility on a noncommissioned officer who honestly thought he was carrying it out, but we failed to clearly establish the priorities which would allow him, as the trail vehicle driver, to desert the company."

Lieutenant Colonel Crowley, the investigating officer, was more direct and less charitable in his findings, declaring: "Private Granoth was not promptly evacuated to a medical facility." [Saffold picked him up at 5:30 P.M. and delivered him to the hospital at 6:08 P.M., thirty-eight minutes later.] "The hospital was within fifteen minutes (5.3 miles) travel time from location of the casualty. The delay by not moving to the hospital was at least fifteen minutes. This delay probably worsened his injury. The truck was a small, one-half ton pickup. Private Granoth was in the rear under a fiberglass top. It was not well enough ventilated to adequately cool him down. There was no ice available. If not a heat stroke victim on entering the vehicle, he became one en route to the hospital."

Saffold's stated reasons for not taking Granoth directly to the hospital "are not adequate," Crowley wrote. Benning's rules and policies "call for prompt evacuation of all heat casualties to medical facilities . . . The condition of Private Granoth was such that immediate evacuation was clearly warranted and necessary. When I questioned the road guides and Sergeant First Class Saffold, all said he [Granoth] could not respond to questions. The trainees in the truck also said he was not fully conscious. He could only mumble or moan . . .

"The company had no provisions for backup in the event of a need for medical evacuation. This put Sergeant First Class Saffold in a position of having to continue his trail duties or evacuate the casualty. This was clearly a shortfall, but the fact that the road march was less than 3 miles and Heat Category II [weather less than the most dangerous] would not generate the need for a second evacuation vehicle. However, better procedures were possible (e.g. dismounted radio with a capability to call for backup assistance, stop the road march, etc.) . . .

"Taken as whole, I believe that Sergeant First Class Saffold attempted to cover up facts that would disclose his lack of prompt reaction, but do not believe that this is provable beyond a reasonable doubt."

While the Army brass at Benning was deciding what punishment, if any, to impose on Saffold and Smith, the trainees from Granoth's 3d Platoon were trying to rally him from his paralysis, speechlessness and other ills. They visited him at the hospital frequently and sent him a giant get-well card from "The Third Herd" which included these handwritten notes:

"Pvt. Richard Carr #312—If I knew that you were sick, I would have told a drill sgt. You better get better. We all miss you. You get well. The Mad Guamanian."

"Pvt. Fuller—I know you're the type of person who never quit anything in your life. Even though you went around worrying about all of us, I am not going to worrie about you because with God's love and your strength, you're going to be OK."

"Pvt. Wm. 'Reverend' Mooney—3rd Herd is behind you all the way. We really do care for you."

"Pvt. Glenn Maraspin—Your guts and motivation are well respected in my heart."

"Jay Ghahhar #330—It's been great fun and you are one of the most motivated persons I have ever seen. I hope you get well soon. Your War Buddy."

"Pvt. Francis Hathaway—You are always a 3rd Herd and part of the Herd. We're pulling for you."

"Pvt. James E. Beach—Hope to see you on the obstacle course Saturday."

The Army command at Benning ultimately decided against court-martialing Saffold, Smith or anyone else involved in the Granoth tragedy. The only punishment was termed "non-judicial" by the Army, which usually means letters of reprimand. Mrs. Granoth went home to Morris, Connecticut, devastated but determined to do what she could to cure her paralyzed, speechless son.

# 5. First Pass

The heat casualties generated a new sense of caution among officers and drills. The trainees drank more water, often under orders. Bitterness among trainees who had seen their buddies fall from being overexercised in the heat became diluted. The transformation of unfocused teenagers into disciplined infantrymen continued apace. Much of the training was boring because the Army gears it to the slowest learners. There is no two-track system in basic training. And the people who write the Army instruction placards that are posted at Benning's training ranges could never pass Plain English One.

Even in the latrine the obfuscation holds forth. A poster in the latrine on the range where the troops learn how to use the claymore anti-soldier mine is entitled: "The Five Steps to Install and Fire the M18A1 Claymore Mine." Step One could have said, "Make sure you have everything in your claymore bag while you're still lying down." But the poster states: "Conduct inventory from prone position." At Malone firing range the training sergeant who was supposed to teach the recruits how to shoot straight said: "For those of you with a college education, you can understand these civilians who put these words on us: 'Lead the target for the same distance as the perceived width of the front sight post.'" If that rule were written in English, it would say: "Lead your target by the width of your front sight."

The best sergeant-teachers assigned to the ranges used humor, sarcasm and horse sense to pass on their knowledge in spite of the cumbersome teaching aids the Army gave them. "Hey, son," joshed Sergeant Terlin Kois, instructor in claymore mines, in his Alabama twang, "what are you going to do, kill moles?" The private was being instructed in how to set a claymore mine on the ground. The mine looks like a curved bar of laundry soap with thin metal legs attached. The claymore must stand level for its blast of 700 killing pellets to fly out of its curved surface in a deadly spread, cutting down anybody in its path. The private had pushed the front legs of the claymore too far into the ground, tilting the mine earthward. "All you'd do is put a hole in the ground," Kois chided in his effective counseling.

Another private trying to master the intricacies of the dummy claymore had forgotten to take the detonating switch with him when he walked down the range to place his mine. Drill Sergeant Cocks employed humor to make his point. Picking up the switch attached to a long wire, Cocks shouted to the trainee with the claymore in his hand: "Did you forget something? Stay there, I'm going to blow you away." He pressed the firing button on the switch and smiled at the abashed private.

"Lay down," said Kois to another trainee who had done the same thing, "you're not real."

To a trainee who kept making mistakes with his claymore, Drill Sergeant Zuniga cracked: "Now when you get to your unit, make sure to ask them to make you the point man." The message was to get himself killed in a hurry so he would not endanger others in his platoon.

"Takes one of them to get killed in combat, then they'll learn," agreed Kois.

Kois showed his brotherly side when he saw the privates wilting under the Georgia summer sun, hot as ever. The kids were fumbling through their claymore drills. I figured all they could concentrate on was how hot it was and the danger of passing out on the sandy range like many of their buddies had done at A. O. Eagle.

"Pull out your canteen and take a good drink of water," Kois ordered. "Talk to that man beside you when you do this training. Help each other."

At one point in his instruction, Kois held the dummy claymore against his chest, curved side inward. He told the privates to do this at night when they were on an operation to make sure they were setting the claymore to explode toward the enemy, not themselves. "If it won't rock, you got it in the right position."

As I listened to the range sergeants lecture while we went from one range to another in the first seven weeks of basic training and watched the apprentice soldiers try out what they were taught, I saw that this intensive, one-level instruction, despite its flaws, does indeed work. The teenagers who had gotten off the buses less than two months ago with long hair and no sense of direction for their lives were indeed shaping up into soldiers who knew how to prevent themselves from getting killed in the first hours of combat.

The key to Army training, and one reason it was boring to the fast learners, was breaking down each job into bite-size pieces and slowly feeding each piece to the trainees in hopes they would chew and digest it. Since nothing is more important than teaching an infantryman to shoot straight, to kill before he is killed, marksmanship was the most intensive part of infantry training. I had a low opinion of the M-16 rifle in Vietnam because I saw it jam so often even when it was kept as clean as dusty field conditions allowed. An American infantryman must stake his life on whatever rifle his country issues him. The M-16 is that rifle. Sergeants at the rifle range and platoon drill sergeants went all out to make tomorrow's infantrymen lethal with the M-16 by employing the bite-size approach to mastering the rifle.

Long before a trainee was allowed to shoot real bullets out of his M-16, he practiced taking the rifle apart, putting it together, cleaning it, aiming it, pulling its trigger in a steady motion, lying down and sitting with it in prescribed ways, positioning his chin on the stock at the right place, breathing and not breathing. It was like having a golf pro teach you how to swing a club by going through the backswing and downswing inch by inch for two solid weeks before hitting the ball. When firing day came, the drills as well as the range instructors hammered on the importance of hitting enough targets on the range when firing day came "to qualify." "Otherwise," they warned, "you're going home, Yo-Yo."

I did not go through the two weeks of instruction but figured I could qualify anyway from having done a lot of shooting with a .22 rifle as a boy and becoming familiar with the M-16 in Vietnam, although I did not carry the rifle on the patrols I went on as a reporter. You were either a reporter or a rifleman, as I saw it, and carrying a rifle would strip away any consideration captured reporters might receive from the enemy if you tried to be both at once. Besides, in a life-or-death firefight, I knew I could join it by picking up a dead man's rifle. Captain Fleenor gave me a crash course with the M-16 and let me at the targets. I got on the range only to find out I had a hell of a time seeing the pop-up targets out in the hazy distance and was far from rock steady in the prone position. I did not hit enough targets in this first attempt to qualify. I was the Yo-Yo, but luckily did not affect the standing of any of the highly competitive platoons. Nor could they send me home.

After Delta Company's trainees qualified with the M-16, they were at last sent into the woods to learn how to advance upon the enemy and kill him before he killed them. The training session began with the privates applying dark and light green camouflage grease on each other's faces from tubes that looked like lipsticks. I mused about how these future infantrymen standing all around me took on the look of warriors once their makeup was on. Only their giggling and grab-assing as the warpaint went on reminded me that they were still teenagers, virgins when it came to the terror of real battle. Sergeants told them over and over how to advance through the woods in combat:

Run for no more than five seconds; fall forward with the rifle in front of you so its butt hits the ground first, absorbing the shock; let your knees hit the earth and fall forward as flat as a snake. Never go into a high or low crawl from that position without doing a combat roll first to keep any enemy gunner from getting a bead on you. When you rise to rush, stay up three seconds but no more than five or else automatic fire will find and kill you.

"Keep your head down, son!" Drill Sergeant Stover shouted to a recruit trying to master the low crawl. "Sideways! Sideways!"

"Something's holding me back, sergeant."

"Your mind is holding you back. Use that rear drive," meaning the leg pressed hardest against the ground as he pushed himself across the sand like a two-legged crab.

The sweating trooper, despite sand in his eyes and resistance from the front edge of his helmet digging into the ground, low-crawled to the end of his lane.

"Was that so hard?" Stover asked.

"I did that?" the astonished recruit asked with a gritty smile.

"Looks like Lane 4 has an attitude," Stover called out to fellow

110

sergeants watching a private quit trying during his low crawl in his assigned lane. "He may have to do that again." The trainee dug his leg into the sand and pushed himself to the finish line of his lane.

After the troopers had mastered these fundamentals for staying alive under fire, the fun part began. They were issued clips of blanks and instructed how to advance through the woods to kill the enemy. They had to crawl under barbed wire and over log walls.

"Give me an extra clip," said one trooper to his buddy. "I want to shoot and shoot. I'll give you my cake for the next three nights if you give me an extra clip."

One trainee got stuck on top of the log wall as he tried to scale it.

"You're dead!" the sergeant told him.

"Well, how 'bout putting my rifle on top of the logs and firing it?" the frustrated infantryman asked once he had slid off the log wall onto the ground.

"You've been watching too much television."

Most of the troopers were exultant at day's end. They had practiced real fighting after boyhoods of playing soldier in hundreds of backyards and wood patches all across America. Private Richard "Alphabet" Florczyk, 18, of Horseheads, New York, broke into a huge smile and gushed to me and others standing in the woods, declaring: "That was fun, goddamn. Shit! That was some shit! Best day so far."

By the end of the sixth week of basic, the days had definitely gotten better for almost everyone in Delta Company. The survivors knew they were making it. They had contained their homesickness, controlled their behavior, swallowed their pride without losing it altogether and mastered at the least the fundamentals of being an infantryman. Best of all, they were to get off the base for the first time after one more week of training. Mid-cycle tests would culminate the seven weeks of basic training. Captain Fleenor had said their families were welcome to come down for this first weekend pass. The troopers had written or telephoned parents, girlfriends, long-haired buddies from back home and brothers and sisters to reserve rooms in the strips of motels outside the base. It was time to party! Sleep late! Eat greasy junk food! Drink cold beer! Show off those Army greens! Maybe light up a joint, although that might foul everything up if Fleenor ordered piss tests for everybody after this first weekend pass. Zuniga caught the spirit of anticipation by marching his 3d Platoon to this cadenced chant:

> *Here we go again,*
> *Same old stuff again;*
> *Marching down the avenue;*
> *One more week and we'll be through;*
> *I'll be glad and so will you.*

Parents and girlfriends started arriving on Friday, August 28, for this first pass. They were supposed to wait until after the next day's parade to embrace on the cement courtyard beneath Albanese Barracks. But many could not wait. I saw quick embraces throughout Friday afternoon and evening as parents and girlfriends snatched the trainees for a few seconds as they marched from barracks to chow hall. One trooper cried the whole time his parents stood with him. Fleenor was a humanitarian. He bent the rules when it came to choosing between the humanitarian way and the Army way during these emotional reunions. Saturday finally came with its obligatory morning parade. At noontime, Fleenor assembled all four platoons on the courtyard under the barracks and prepared to address his soldiers and their loved ones. The soldiers had dressed in their greens and looked great. I looked at fathers, mothers, girlfriends, sisters, brothers, grandfathers and babies crowded around the edge of the formation. Many of them were crying with pride. I felt teary myself. It was as if my own kids had suddenly grown up on me. I was immensely proud of these guys for gutting it out. Fleenor realized the shorter his speech the sooner soldiers and the loved ones they ached to touch could get together for the rest of the weekend.

"We care about these soldiers here," Fleenor began.

"These guys are important to us. That's what we're really all about.

"We're going to put them out whether they have parents or not. This is their first pass.

"You know that basic training is a very tough environment.

"We want you to get them back to us safe and sound.

"Enjoy the time you have with them. They're growing up on you; definitely growing up on you. I imagine a lot of you don't recognize them. Some of you will see that some of them lost a little weight. Some of them gained a little. Each and every one of the individuals we have here—there have been a lot of changes taking place in them while they've been here. Take the time to enjoy them.

"Now to you soldiers. I'm proud of you. You did well on your mid-cycle test yesterday. You did good.

"This is the first time you've been out for a while.

"I want you to take care of yourselves.

"Remember! You're now in the military, responsible for the uniform you wear. Represent it well when you're out there. Represent it well. This means you wear it properly. You display it proudly.

"Some of you I hope to see tonight at the run [which Fleenor had arranged in cooperation with his favorite restaurant in Columbus, Country's Bar-B-Q]. Drink some tea.

"I've told you a lot of the horror stories about what happened to some of my other troops on pass. Remember when you go out there, every female is not actually a female. It happens, men. It happens.

"I'm not telling you where to go while you're on pass, but I've told you before that Victory Drive is a military rip-off center. That's where people get into trouble. It's designed like those outside any other military post. It's designed to take your money.

"I've had men get a pistol stuck in their head because they didn't use good sense. Don't flash your money around. Don't flash your money around," he repeated to underscore the point. "Use good common sense and take care of yourselves.

"For those of you who aren't with your families, make sure you get in buddy teams. Take care of each other.

"Now the legal drinking age in Georgia, for those of you who take on some alcohol out there, is 21. Particularly, better take care of yourself if you're going to take on some alcohol. Don't drink and drive and the whole bit.

"I know some of you are talking about renting some cars. Take care of yourselves, men. Take care of yourselves, men," he repeated feelingly. "I want to see you back here, ready to train.

"Like I say, I'm proud of you.

"We'll be getting what's traditionally been called AIT [advanced individual training], now called Phase 3 OSUT [One Station Unit Training].

"You've done a good job."

The troopers broke in with a series of *"whoof-whoof"* self-congratulatory barks. Fleenor smiled.

"You have to be back here at 1700 hours tomorrow. Any questions about that?"

"No sir!" the troopers responded with a roar.

"Company! Attention!"

The happy soldiers snapped to attention and—after each platoon yelled out its nickname in order, 1st Platoon through 4th Platoon—were dismissed and ran to embrace moms, dads, girlfriends, sisters, brothers. Free at last! For a few hours anyway.

I drove off the base and checked in on my boys celebrating their first pass at motels around Columbus. The white soldiers in the pools were easy to spot. They had tan on their faces and tan on their arms up to where their shirts stopped and then everything else was stark white. The scenes were sedate at most of the motels: soldiers swimming, lounging at poolside or drinking beer in their rooms with buddies and/or parents. Many of the privates had filled their motel bathtubs with ice to keep the beer cold. At Days Inn at Exit Four the privates were furthest along in their partying.

"Hey, Mr. Wilson! Have a beer!"

Two frosty ones came at me at once.

Drill Sergeant Zuniga, dressed in a flowery Hawaiian shirt and white pants, climbed out of his sports car, big dark glasses covering his eyes. The troops could not have been happier to see their tormentor from basic training. They surrounded him, handed him beers and dragged him off to one motel room after another to meet girlfriends and parents. This drill sergeant nicknamed "Z Monster" had become a hero to many of the young soldiers.

A former bad boy from Roanoke, Virginia, Brian Trotter, 17, drew gasps when he showed up at the Days Inn pool sporting a still-bloody tattoo just below his shoulder.

"Where'd you get it?"

"Fast Freddie's on Victory Drive."

"How much?"

"Eighty-five dollars."

"I'm going to get me one."

I associated tattoos with dark, dirty parlors where drunk sailors got mermaids scratched into their skin by quick-buck artists. I was not prepared for Fast Freddie and his emporium.

"If you get a Salvador Dali," Freddie told me with deadly seriousness when I went into his place to talk about his trade, "you have to put it over your fireplace and have people come into your house and look at it. But if you get a body tattoo, people ooh and ah at you wherever you go."

"How much would you charge me to put a Salvador Dali on my back?"

"I don't even know what he painted."

"The Last Supper."

"Oh, The Last Supper. That would be $2,500."

Apparently satisfied I was not a cop or some kind of inspector, Freddie Fahs's daughter, Tracy, emerged from a back room. She was a lovely blonde who wore a net blouse over a sexy, very full black bra.

"I don't see any tattoos on you," I kidded.

She hiked up her skirt to reveal a tiny tattoo far up on her hip. I figured that was to keep daddy off her back, literally and figuratively.

"I don't know why women go for tattoos on their arms," Freddie said when I told him I had seen many tattooed women sitting at the Officers' Club bar at Benning. "I think it looks manly myself. But I don't argue with them. I give them what they want. West Coast women put their tattoos on sexier places, like their breasts and hips.

"For the young soldiers who come in here, getting a tattoo is the passage to manhood. Or maybe dad had a tattoo. Most of the guys are here only long enough for one tattoo. Probably get one on the left shoulder and later get one on the other one. We won't do drunks. Something about drinking thins the blood. They bleed. No smoking, either. Makes them move around."

I left Fast Freddie's with its walls lined with pictures of tattoos he would prick onto your skin, drove past the seedy-looking bars on Victory Drive advertising such featured performers as Chocolate Delight and Lacey Satin, revisited my boys at Days Inn and other motels off the highway. One prostitute working her way through a motel of Delta Company's half-drunk, sex-starved soldiers was making big money. She was giving blow jobs to a long line of soldiers, with the highest bidders above the $20 minimum going first. Seventeen stood in line at one point. She did not care whether her services were performed in private or before a crowd. All through the night, the halls resounded with running feet and shouts of both celebration and frustration. The prostitute continued to do a brisk business, going from room to room.

"I'll give anybody $25 for a rubber," some private anxious for relief but afraid of disease yelled out late in the night. I never learned who he was or whether he found what he was looking for.

Several of the privates were told "no soldiers allowed" when they tried to get into a teenage night spot in front of Days Inn.

"That's a fucking," one complained to me. "Here we are fighting for our country and we can't even go in there and get a little trim."

Sean "South Bronx" Petersen told me he and his buddy ran into big trouble Saturday night when they ventured onto Victory Drive. I could not decide then or now whether the episode actually happened or was one of those "can you top this" fanciful stories soldiers tell each other after every leave. But here is what Petersen said happened while he stood outside the motel room off Victory Drive where his buddy was being serviced by a white prostitute with one brown and one blue eye.

"Straight up, this is how it is," a big black man warned as he pressed a revolver against Petersen's chest. "You're going to give me everything you got, or you and your buddy are going to be in a bad way in the morning."

"I knew it was a setup," Petersen said. "Three black guys in two cars drove up." Petersen gave them his money. They drove away. His half-drunk buddy emerged from the motel room not realizing what had happened outside the door while he was trying to get his forty dollars' worth out of the prostitute. He had just enough money left to take a taxi back to Days Inn for the rest of the night.

The first pass of Spank Barker, Chris Cashman and Little Henson typified that of the young marrieds and fathers who could not afford to have their wives fly to Benning for the weekend.

"We bummed around Columbus Mall," Spank told me afterward. "Finally found your book [*Supercarrier*] in a bookstore there and bought it. Went to a movie. *Hamburger Hill*. We walked around a lot, going into the shops. Kept running into drill sergeants. Thought that was kind of neat. They said they were out shopping. But they were watching out for us. They asked us if we had gotten into any trouble. They told us to stay together.

"All three of us had a craving for McDonald's. I ordered the big hamburger, a large milkshake and some fries. I got through only half of it and had to push it away. It didn't taste good. And I guess my stomach shrunk up. I came in the Army as a little fat kid—205 pounds and 5 feet 5. Guess I'm down to 185."

Spank, who marked his 21st birthday just before basic started, and Cashman, 26, were among the few privates on leave who were old enough to drink legally. They and Henson, who did not drink, ended their evening at the Bombay Bicycle Club, a somewhat fancy bar and restaurant a short way from Fort Benning's main gate. Spank ordered a rum Coke, followed by a Miller draft; Henson a nonalcoholic Green Dragon Sea Breeze; Cashman a tall beer. Then it was time to call a cab to take them back to the barracks for another Saturday night of sleeping alone in bunks while their bodies ached for the sweet smell and sexiness of their wives. They told themselves they were doing the right thing for their families and prayed they were right.

"My pass was pretty boring, really," said Fred Cole, 18, of West Plains, Missouri, who had a face and eyebrows reminiscent of Spock in the television show *Star Trek*.

"I went out with mom and dad and a friend from home, Russ Jeremiah. We took dad's '66 Chevy Impala convertible and hit town full force. Went to the Aztec Club. Couldn't get in. They were carding guys. Got our old standard, Miller Lite, and put it in the car. Ate at Ethel's Bar and Grill. Called The Lite Crew back home. My nickname back home was Psycho. Here they call me Spock.

"For breakfast on Sunday, I ate ten Krystal hamburgers. I needed that pass. I was starting to freak out. I was really well-known back home. Not seeing everybody is the worst part. In high school, I was into baseball, football and beer drinking. I played defensive back in football and center field in baseball. My baseball coach told me, 'Hey, you got talent.' I blew it.

"But I wouldn't trade this experience for anything. My parents and my best friend told me on pass, 'You've really changed.' I used to rattle on all the time. They say I'm much quieter; seem to have grown up five years.

"When I was in my motel room at the Ramada, I started folding my clothes nice and neat. I couldn't help myself. Just to spite myself, I threw them down on the floor and stuffed them back in the drawers the old way."

I went to Albanese Barracks to see if all my boys made the 5 P.M. formation marking the end of their pass. Brian Trotter was there.

But he did not know it. His buddies were holding him up. Drill Sergeant Rodriguez looked over his walking wounded and shouted out to the formation: "We drank some beer, didn't we?"

"Yes, Drill Sergeant," the sagging troops answered in unison.

"Beer is bad for the body.

"We ate some junk food, didn't we?"

"Yes, Drill Sergeant."

"Junk food is bad for the body.

"We smoked some cigarettes, didn't we?"

"Yes, Drill Sergeant."

"Smoking's bad for the body.

"Did you have a nice weekend?"

"Yes, Drill Sergeant."

Rodriguez ordered them to open ranks to provide room for calisthenics. I heard the groans and sensed the anguish. Then Rodriguez, after demanding just a couple of push-ups to remind his charges they were back in the Army, dismissed them for evening chow and their controlled life of no beer, no junk food, no cigarettes and—worst of all for these young men at the height of their sexual desires and powers—no sex. There are no women in the American infantry. And the Army women who perform non-combat jobs at Fort Benning were out of reach, and usually out of sight, of the trainees confined to Sand Hill. Even seeing a woman fleetingly in the post exchange at Sand Hill was painful for the men with six weeks of advanced infantry training to go without getting off the base again. They would have to live off the adventures, real or imagined, from the first pass until graduation day, when they would be freed again by the Green Machine for a celebration before reporting to their regular Army units.

# 6. Captain Fleenor

Captain James R. Fleenor II struck me as a worried father waiting for his teenaged sons to return home with the family car as he waited for his soldiers of Delta Company to report back from their first pass. He was relieved when First Sergeant Williams reported to him that nobody had gone AWOL, had been arrested or had broken any bones or noses, neither their own nor anyone else's. His boys instead were safely bedded down for the night. They had survived the Army's seven weeks of basic training. Tomorrow they would start their final six weeks of infantry training by entering Phase III of One Station Unit Training, still called AIT for advanced individual training in the field. The drills had imposed their authority on the trainees. The trainees had adjusted themselves to this new life. AIT would be the downhill side of the training mountain. The commanding officer of Delta Company could risk relaxing a little bit.

"Let's get some lunch," Jim told me with a smile during the first week of AIT. Lunch to Jim Fleenor meant only one place and only one dish: Country's Bar-B-Q down the highway from the base in Columbus for chopped Bar-B-Q pork. In dark moments, he told me, he thought of tossing over his Army career and opening up a Country's Bar-B-Q in his beloved home state of Kentucky.

As soon as we entered Country's, the waitresses buzzed around Jim like moths around a flame. He was easily their favorite customer. I came to learn through more meals at Country's than I

119

care to remember that these pretty women went for Jim because he was fun, decent and, most important of all, safe. Jim was a straight arrow and the waitresses knew it. They could hug him and never worry about a pinch in the behind or a proposition. The strongest drink he ever ordered was iced tea.

I had been watching Fleenor handle all types of crises in the office and out in the field for two months by the time we had what turned out to be a long, philosophical lunch. I had talked to the drills and the troops about him. The drills knew where he stood and respected him. The troops sensed he cared about them. Soldiers' minds are the best threshers I have ever seen. They can tell wheat from chaff in minutes when it comes to their leaders. They had decided Fleenor was wheat. "I want to be like him. . . . He's a good guy . . . I've never spoken to him but I know he cares about us . . . He acts like an officer." Those were among the statements the soldiers made about their leader, Captain Fleenor.

Unlike so many other officers I have known through the years, Fleenor never issued any bulletins describing his philosophy of command. He just practiced it. I decided I would be comfortable sharing a foxhole with Jim Fleenor. More important, I thought if my son, Jim, were to end up in Fleenor's infantry company in a war, Fleenor would do his damnedest to keep Jim and the rest of the soldiers alive.

Yet, despite all that, I doubted Jim Fleenor would make general in America's peacetime Army. I had seen the Army's value system change in the two decades of covering it as a military reporter. The mud soldiers, the ones who were best with troops and worst in the catacombs of the Pentagon or procurement centers, were no longer the prized officers. The all-volunteer Army of the late 1980s was favoring managers, not mud soldiers. It seemed more important to know how to talk in a briefing room than how to lead and fight in the mud. The go-along-to-get-along ethic of the peacetime Army fostered fawning before superiors and backstabbing of competitors. Jim was a take-me-as-I-am kind of guy who put his God, his family, his men and his country ahead of his Army career.

Off duty, Fleenor and his wife, Bobbie, never tried to make the scene at Benning's Officers' Club to enhance Jim's career. Their lives in the few hours the Army left for them to spend together were spent watching television at home with their three children, going to church or visiting First Sergeant Williams. "I love Ted Williams," he told me one day in a way that sounded natural coming from him. On another day, "I love Charlie Butler," the black drill sergeant who had told me: "I like the C.O. Only problem I have with him is that he keeps us out in the field too much."

Fleenor knew Butler felt this way and just laughed when I asked him about it. Fleenor was not hung up on containing his affection for fellow human beings in the interest of projecting a "command presence." This transmitted, I decided after months of pondering the quality, to the waitresses at Country's, to the drills who drank stuff a lot heavier than iced tea and to the troops, most of whom had never met an Army officer before.

"I wish I could be like him one day," Private James E. Proctor II told me in discussing Fleenor. "He's highly motivated, gets everybody else motivated. Yet he walks around cool, calm and collected. Never says much. Doesn't yell at people. I'd feel safe in battle with him. He wouldn't crack under the pressure. The figure of him walking around, standing tall in his uniform—that kind of thing motivates me."

How do we attract the Fleenors into the infantry where even in peacetime they know they will be hot in Georgia, cold and hungry on some lonely prairie in Kansas, itchy in buggy woods in North Carolina? They also know that in wartime young infantry officers are the first to get killed. Unlike the 18-year-olds who are blinded by the prospect of adventure when they sign up for the infantry, the Fleenors know the realities. They also have college degrees that would enable them to obtain higher-paying jobs in civilian life than the Army can offer them. So where do the Fleenors come from? Why do they volunteer for infantry—the hardest and riskiest branch?

I asked Jim Fleenor these and other questions during a long lunch at Country's. I wanted other civilians to get a look inside one of the best and brightest of this new generation of Army officers. I knew he and Johnny Libs would have made a great team in the battle of Xa Cam My in 1966. Fleenor started the story of his life with his hero, James Fleenor, his father.

"My father came out of the mountains around McRoberts, Kentucky. He was the only kid from his family to get a high school diploma. He tried to enlist in the Army for the Korean War but couldn't get in. His father had died from the miner's black lung

121

disease. My father wanted a different fate. He worked his way through Eastern Kentucky University, got a job selling insurance. Hated it. Took a job teaching history in Monroe, Ohio; eventually became principal of Madison High School in Richmond, Kentucky. I'm awfully proud of my father. My father knows everybody. People come to him. I really respect that in my father."

Jim and his sister, Debbie, went to Madison High School while their father was principal. Jim got straight A's; he was class valedictorian, captain of the football team, and absolutely miserable. Fellow students resented his achievements, attributing his successes to his father's position. He became close friends with the class salutatorian, a black girl. She was a great girl, his best friend at a time when he had few others. He was religious and color blind when it came to people. "My world collapsed," Jim told me, when his father objected to the relationship. A black girl was not likely to be accepted in the community. He felt disillusioned with himself, with his hero father. He turned to God for the strength to get through this biggest crisis of his life. He received it.

"I chose God. I no longer required my father to be perfect." He decided he wanted to go to West Point and become an Army officer. "I told God I didn't want to kill, that it was against my nature. I became convinced that God wanted me to go to West Point. Call it a still voice inside. Intuition. Whatever. The Bible, in the Ten Commandments, says thou shalt not kill, but more correct is thou shalt not murder. The Bible in other translations than the King James version, says thou shalt not murder. The difference between killing and murder was the state of the heart."

Fleenor told me his faith sustained him through his unhappy high school years. The kids at Madison got sick of him being called up on the stage of the auditorium to receive award after award. But just before graduating from Madison, a classmate confided to Principal Fleenor: "You know, Mr. Fleenor, Jim deserved all the awards he got." Even more stunning to the shy Jim Fleenor, he recalled, was the moment the cheerleader he had coveted but did not dare ask for a date wrapped her arms around him and said, "I'm going to miss you."

Admitted to West Point, Jim Fleenor soon felt his fears realized. At Madison High, where the senior class numbered fifty students, he had been a big fish in an awfully small pond. He found at West Point he could not excel in either academics or athletics. Again, his faith helped carry him through. So did Steve Parshley, who was also religious and a plodder when it came to mastering the courses at The Point. Jim told me that after hours of studying in one of those forbidding gray buildings at The Point, "Parshley's law" would be invoked with this summons: "Time to close out the books and bring out the Bible." They would laugh, close their textbooks, read a section from the Bible, and pray they would be up to the test on the morrow.

"I was always scared at West Point," Jim told me, "because I thought my education had been inferior. I struggled through the courses, boxed as my sport activity. Still, it was the most rewarding experience of my life. I had this feeling of belonging to a team, of surviving a hostile environment. I wanted to command soldiers but I worried about my looking down on them. I didn't want to do that. I didn't want to be a desk officer. I wanted to be with infantrymen. Your infantryman is still the most important person on the battlefield. I also feel that's where it's happening in the Army."

He said in contrast to West Point where duty, honor, country meant something and "you could leave your wallet out and get it back," the regular Army turned out to be a place with "a lot of lying, cheating and backstabbing." He said he managed to block out these realities most of the time and concentrate on the fulfilling job of turning teenagers into able apprentice infantrymen.

"This is the best job in the Army I've ever had. I get no greater joy in life than teaching. What I enjoy most of all is teaching." He conceded that working from 5 A.M. to 7 P.M. or 9 P.M. six days a week strained his home life. "We don't talk as much as we used to," he said of his wife, "and the kids don't see a lot of me. I hardly ever see them in the best of times. It's usually at the end of the day when the kids are cranky."

Fleenor was 29 years old when we had our long talk. He loved the teaching part of the Army but despised the political, backstabbing part. Whenever he got time to think about something besides Delta Company, which was not often, he asked himself whether the Army was the best place for him to spend his life. He worried about missing it if he left, feeling guilty about deserting his boys. Yet what could he do in civilian life that would compare with the intimacy of the infantry and the sense of hanging it out for your country?

"I guess I'm a cross between an idealist and a realist," Fleenor told me as we rose from the booth in the nearly deserted restaurant.

# 7. Broken and Mended Men

Brad, not his real name, could no longer stand fellow soldiers berating him as "creep, pussy and faggot" for failing to keep up with the infantry training and pulling the platoon down. He waited until the rest of the platoon left its sleeping room in Albanese Barracks, gulped down a whole bottle of pain-killer pills prescribed for his muscle pains and looked around the barracks for a place to die. He chose a far corner of the shower in the rear of the sleeping area. Nobody would find him there until the pills had ended his misery forever, the 18-year-old recruit from Michigan figured.

Just by luck, a drill sergeant walking through the deserted barracks looked in the bathroom and discovered Brad unconscious on the floor of the shower. The teenager was rushed to the hospital where he recovered. I talked to him afterward. He was being processed out of the Army. He told me to go ahead and use his name. It was as if he wanted something to show for his pain at Fort Benning. But I am leaving it out for fear of adding to his pain later in life.

Brad was one of four trainees in Delta Company who found Army training so intolerable that they tried to kill themselves to get out of it. Trying to "be all you can be" the Army way is not for everyone. Captain Fleenor considered Brad's suicide attempt the most serious because the lonely, depressed youth had not told anyone what he had done to himself. The other three had informed their buddies, apparently in hopes of being dragged back from death's door after having taken the most drastic step they could think of to convince the Army to let them go home. I wanted to try to learn from these teenaged volunteers, who had had big dreams, what it was about Army basic training that made escaping it more important than life itself.

Brad looked spooked when we met in the day room of Delta Company. The day room was where the troops hung out when they were given permission to do so. It was the air-conditioned living room for the company's soldiers. It had easy chairs, a television set and a pool table. The chair Brad was sitting in swallowed him up. He looked like a beaten spaniel with glasses. Poor kid, I thought.

When Brad rose to shake my hand, he moved awkwardly, effeminately. I thought to myself that high school must have been hell for him and he soon confirmed this. I sat in the chair facing him and tried to ease into the question of how anything in basic training could be bad enough to impel him to kill himself. His sentences came out in an I-don't-care-anymore monotone.

"I was bored back home. There was nothing there. I was making $3.50 an hour working odd hours at the Ponderosa fast food restaurant. My brother had been in the Army. I wanted the $5,000 bonus for enlisting in the infantry. I just kind of drifted into it."

Brad told me his parents were divorced. His father was a truck driver. Brad felt his father had given up on him. Brad thought joining the Army would please his dad. Brad also needed a steady job. Right after Brad signed up for the infantry, high-paying construction jobs opened up in his home town.

"I told the sergeant at the processing station in Detroit that I didn't want to go in. He told me to make the best of it. At Benning they just kept pushing me. They yell at you all the time. Then the guys in my platoon started picking on me. They called me fag and pussy. They had done that all through high school because I was real friendly with another guy. Some of the guys in the platoon stuck up for me.

"I'm just not capable of being here. It was just a mistake I made. I didn't have the motivation or strength to do forty-two push-ups. I feel defeated but happy. I learned something about myself, about my vulnerabilities and strengths. I can work on them. I'm not angry at the Army. I'm angry at them in Detroit for not letting me out when I told them I didn't want to go. I knew I couldn't do it."

"But why go so far as to kill yourself?" I pressed. "Why did you do it?" I asked Brad.

"I couldn't take it anymore."

He was still talking in that controlled monotone. I could not break through to the volcano that must have been smoldering inside him. I asked the pitiful kid as we parted: "Were you just trying to get out of the Army or life itself?"

He gave me a long look. There was hurt in his large eyes. We stared at each other for several tense seconds. I was still waiting for his answer. Brad's answer finally came. It was just one word: "Both."

The second teenager I talked to who had attempted suicide exhibited none of Brad's timidity which might have made an Army psychologist dubious about his suitability for military service. He was suave, articulate, highly intelligent and graceful in a manly way—everything Brad was not. But this young man whom I will call Dave, at his request, admitted to me that he had an inner compass that could not stay fixed on any one course. He said he was always on the edge of turmoil inside. He told me that he had a hair-trigger temper and could not stand to take orders. A drill sergeant yelling at him set his compass spinning.

In one of our long talks, which Dave seemed to relish, the troubled young man said that during basic training he felt as if the Army had locked him in a cell emotionally and he had to do the equivalent of beat his head on the bars until somebody let him out.

"My father was in the Navy for twenty-four years. I've moved approximately fourteen times. I joined the Army because some friends and I were talking about it, and it seemed like a good idea at the time. I have a temper, and I hate people telling me what to do."

As a teenager in California, he told me he flaunted his rebel qualities by wearing his hair spiked and decorating his body with silver. The Army shaved off his hair at the processing station but he carried his combination radio and tape player off the bus with him when he reported to Delta Company, making him a target for the drills during Shock Treatment.

"What kind of music do you play on this thing?" the drill asked Dave in inspecting his boom box, which was destined to go into the storeroom with civilian suitcases.

"New Wave, Carib."

"You like punk?"

"Yes, Drill Sergeant."

"You're a fat punk!"

"Yes, Drill Sergeant."

"Your name begin with a B or a V?" Dave told him.

"Shit! That means you're going to be in my platoon."

"Hey!" the drill called to his fellow sergeants. "We've got another fat boy over here. All you people who are fat boys aren't going to be fat boys when you leave."

Dave told me that after Shock Treatment he went up to his bunk in the sleeping bay where the drill ordered him to remake his bed ten times. Dave told me he said to himself, "Shit! I don't want this." So when the drill sergeant announced that anyone who wanted to get out of the Army should come see him in his office at the front of the sleeping bay, Dave went to the open doorway. He told me this is what followed:

"Drill Sergeant. I don't want to be here."

"Close the door, son." He did.

"Now goddamn it," Drill Sergeant Williams raged, "why the fuck do you want to get out of the Army?"

"I just don't want to be here, Drill Sergeant."

"Drop! Give me some push-ups!

"Give me some flutter kicks!

"Give me some more push-ups!

"Now get the fuck out of my face."

Dave began to walk out of the drill sergeant's office.

"Too slow! Get back down there and give me some push-ups.

"Get out!

"Too slow!

"Get back in here and drop! You don't want to be here?"

"No, Drill Sergeant."

"Get the fuck out of my face."

Dave said he left the drill sergeant's office sweating, spent, furious, bitter. At that moment he said he hated the Army and everybody in it and vowed to escape. He said he resolved to keep his mouth shut to avoid further punishment until he plotted his escape. He passed out from the heat at rifle practice one August day. He told me the drills accused him of faking the heat injury. I figured they might have been right. Dave told me, and his superiors confirmed it, that right after that episode he gulped down the whole bottle of Motrin tablets he had been given for pain. I knew from talking to other recruits that he told one of them what he had done. The soldier told the drill sergeant who, in turn, took Dave to the hospital where his stomach was pumped out. He was returned to duty. The disciplinary reports indicate the drill sergeants looked upon Dave as a rebel who needed to be broken down rather than as a sick teenager who should be discharged from the Army on medical grounds. One report reads:

> At Fort Benning on or about 24 August 1987, you did, for the purpose of avoiding continued military service attempt to commit suicide by taking approximately 30 Motrin pills in violation of Article 115 of the Uniform Code of Military Justice. . . .
>
> . . . While being counseled about your actions last night that you wanted to commit suicide, your reply was: "I am getting the fuck out of the Army."
>
> At that time formation was called and I told you to get your gear and go down [from Albanese Barracks] for formation.
>
> You instead went in front of your wall locker and sat down and did not want to move. Once again I gave you an order to get your gear and go to formation. You ignored me. So I ordered you once again, and you still did not move. At that time I left and went to see the senior drill sergeant. Private _____, behavior like this will not be tolerated in this U.S. Army. So I am recommending you for a field grade Article 15.

An Article 15 is like a misdemeanor for which the captain in charge of the company determines the punishment rather than go through a legal proceeding like a court martial. Dave's sitdown strike still did not persuade the command that it should let him out of the Army. He tried to scream his protest in other ways, as this other Army report reveals:

> Private _____, you came up to me at Eagle Talon [training ground] and stated: "Take my weapon before I hurt someone." I then asked you who you were going to hurt, and you said: "I can't say."
>
> I later asked you again, and you said it was Drill Sergeant Zuniga you would have hurt. These actions will not be tolerated in Delta Company in the U.S. Army.

A few days later the desperate, rebellious, angry, hurt and probably dangerous private was at last sent to Community Mental Health Services at Benning where I had talked to Major

Deal about the psychological harm yelling and screaming at misfits can cause. After interviewing Dave, the mental health clinic sent this report back to Delta Company:

> Soldier was seen at command request due to suicidal ideations. Soldier stated that if he doesn't get out of the Army, he is going to kill himself. Soldier has thought of ways to harm himself just to show his unit that he is serious about getting out of the Army.
>
> The problems presented by this individual are not amenable to hospitalization, transfer, treatment or any other type of duty within the military. It is unlikely that efforts to rehabilitate or develop this individual into a satisfactory member of the military will be successful. If this individual is made to continue on active duty, he will probably become an extremely disruptive influence to unit morale and mission and be at risk for acting-out behavior. Based upon the conditions and problems presented by this soldier, it is strongly recommended that he be separated by the military.

The command took the psychologist's advice and prepared the paperwork to push Dave out of the Army. He was handed a paper explaining why, by the numbers:

> 1. You have made suicidal gestures by taking a large number of Motrin.
> 2. You have communicated threats toward your superiors.
> 3. Your lack of teamwork is a great strain on the morale and cohesiveness of your entire platoon.

After sixty-two traumatic days of Army training at Benning, Dave finally was sent home. I talked to him several times, including the day he left. He said his drill sergeants had broken the rules by punching him. I could not prove his charge but believed it, knowing how much he had infuriated and frustrated them. Dave was a classic training risk with what the drills called "an attitude." Their philosophy was to punch him mentally, if not physically, until he broke apart so they could put him back together again their way. I felt Dave's pain, understood the drills' frustration and was grateful the Army had sympathetic counselors like Major Deal to provide an out for such teenagers who never would be able to cope with military life. As Dave packed his gear before boarding the bus that would take him out of Fort Benning forever, he told me: "I'm glad to be going home to California. I'm never looking back at this place."

The other two suicide attempts were aborted quickly. Both trainees drank down glass cleaner, told their buddies what they had done and had their stomachs pumped out before the poison had inflicted serious injury. One of these two was discharged and the second was kept in the Army against the advice of psychologists who interviewed him. "If I ever saw a kid I could save, he was it," Fleenor told me in explaining why he had kept Private X in his company in the belief he could turn him into a volunteer-Army success story.

For every Brad or Dave the drills drove to attempting suicide, there were scores of other kids they drove into making something of themselves. The unique chemistry of Army basic training succeeded in many cases after despairing parents, teachers, coaches, ministers, psychiatrists and girlfriends had given up on the rebellious young men. I met many of these kids and parents while following Delta Company through basic and advanced individual training at Benning. Whether they will stay changed for life remains an open question. But the parents of two of them, "Budweiser" and Glen, told me they were astonished by the transformation the Army had wrought in their sons in a matter of weeks after every civilian institution had failed in years of trying to change their behavior. They predicted, and prayed, that their boys would not reverse course and take up their old ways after leaving Benning.

Budweiser had just turned 17 when we met. His honesty about himself—"I fucked up a lot"—and his raw idealism—"I think if you write my story the way it really is, it might help some other kids out there straighten up"—was uplifting after years of covering Washington bureaucrats who never admit to making a mistake and keep angling to make themselves look good.

"I ran away when I was 8 years old," Budweiser told me as we sat at a table in Albanese Barracks with the tape recorder between us. "After that it was all downhill." He recounted years of rebellion against his father, a Baptist preacher, and his mother, who once jumped in the back seat of the car where he was sitting and pounded him from head to foot in her fury over him staying out all night without calling home. "I could never hit my mother back."

Budweiser was a fast, shifty running back and loved football. He made the varsity in his freshman year. But he seldom cracked a book and could not concentrate in class "because I was stoned all the time. I'd go through a dime bag a day. I'd get high right before school, after gym. After football practice we'd get stoned. After the game we'd get stoned. I couldn't play stoned. I tried that once. Me and my friends would party Sunday night with Budweiser and grass and go to school Monday drunk. My nickname in high school was Budweiser."

Budweiser said he flunked eighth grade twice and quit school for the first time when he was 16 and still in the eighth grade. He fought with his parents constantly while living with them in Virginia, left the house to move in with a friend in Lynchburg. His friend's father let him rent an apartment in Lynchburg above his vacuum cleaner store, called Mr. Sweeper. "I lied my ass off to land a cook's job" at an area hospital, Budweiser said in relating the life that led him to the Army and Fort Benning where we got to know each other.

"I told them I had two years of college and knew all about diets for diabetics and all that shit. I looked old. I had a full mustache and a full head of hair. I can be a con man when I want to. I was making good money. We'd finish work at the hospital about 3 in the afternoon, play tennis in the high school courts and then get stoned and drunk at my place or somebody else's and get up at 5 the next morning to get to the hospital by 6. My attitude was fuck everybody. Hey, fuck everything, it's my life. I had a lot of good times. I had a lot of bad and lonely times. A lot of drunk and lonely times. I was in love and everything. Broke up with my girl in Roanoke because of me moving away. I was spending $100 to $150 a week on good dope just to mellow out. I never considered myself addicted. A lot of my friends at the hospital snorted snow [cocaine]."

Budweiser said he miraculously avoided collisions during this life in the fast lane until the night he took his landlord's car for a high-speed dash through Lynchburg "to see if any girls were up." He told me he was so stoned and drunk that he rationalized his landlord would not mind if he borrowed his 1976 Plymouth station wagon for the 2 A.M. spin.

"I get drunk and do dumb things. I got that piece of shit flying. I was having a good old time. Went through downtown Lynchburg at 95 miles an hour. I came off some ramp . . . all of sudden I see red lights in the back. Oh shit, I thought. I was drunker than dogshit."

Budweiser was still 16 and a first offender. The judge sent him home to his parents and put him on probation for six months. Every time he came home drunk, one of his parents would report his misbehavior to his parole officer. He thought he would explode if he did not escape his surroundings. He tried to go back to ninth grade but, "I couldn't stand the silly shit they asked me to do. My parents were pushing me, 'Go in the Army.' I more or less said fuck you; I'm going to make my own decisions."

His life took its first turn toward the high road when he met and fell in love with a college girl who did not know he was only 16. He said he messed up the relationship by going out and getting drunk every so often and then waking her up at 2 in the morning by knocking on her dormitory door. She stopped seeing Budweiser. He quit high school again, along with his part-time job. He said he resorted to stealing to support himself but felt low doing it. He remembered the pamphlet the Army recruiter had left at his house in Roanoke. He went to the recruiting station, learned he would have to get the equivalent of a high school diploma to win admittance to the Army. He studied hard for the first time in years to pass the test for a general equivalency diploma (GED).

"I didn't think I'd pass the test. But I passed it. I ran in to the recruiter shouting, 'I passed it! I passed it.' "

The recruiter sent Budweiser to the processing center in Richmond. "I want the soonest thing I can get," he told the clerk scanning the computerized list of vacancies. The infantry, she told the eager 17-year-old, will take you the soonest.

"What is infantry?" Budweiser asked.

She ran the television tape of what an infantryman does. He saw men swinging from ropes, beating their way through the bush, running and shooting.

"That's what I want to do right there!"

The processing center gave him a bus ticket and told him he would be leaving Roanoke for Fort Benning in four days. He went home and waited until his mother and father were together in the living room. He sprung his surprise without warning: "I joined the Army. I'm leaving in four days."

He said his parents were thrilled, embraced him warmly for the first time in years. His fellow teenagers could not believe Budweiser had joined the United States Army. "They all said: 'Man, Budweiser ain't going to make it. He's nothing but a shithead.' I had a bad reputation all over the place. My best friend drove me to the bus station. He didn't think I'd make it. But he hoped I would. He wanted the best for me. As we sat in the car together he gave me some last words: 'Man, you'll never make it. My brother's in the Navy. It's tough, man. Hang tough, Dude. More power to you.' "

Budweiser took the bus to the airport and flew to Benning from there. "I was scared shitless. I asked myself, 'Why am I doing this?' During that put 'em up, put 'em down part of Shock Treatment I told myself, 'Fuck this shit. I'll sneak out of here. I'll go AWOL.' But I made some friends. They kept me going. I found out I could go three weeks without smoking. I began to mature in a hurry. I told myself, 'Now's your chance to build a good reputation.' Making it through basic training boosted my sense of myself three million percent. I started calling the folks at home. I sat up here thinking one night and wrote them a letter apologizing for all the bullshit I'd given them. I'm a hard-headed, stupid son of a bitch. I still feel bad about what I did. I wish I could change it, but I can't. I love my parents. It was both of our faults. They fucked up a lot. But I didn't help none. I fucked up a lot. They loved my letter. They cried. They wrote me back. Everything was smooth. They're happy for me.

"The best thing about the Army is that it made me grow up. It made me see life, made me see reality. I used to think I was number one, and nobody else mattered other than me. And I still take care of number one first. But right after me, instead of saying fuck everybody else, I'm number one and I take care of number two. I'd stay in the foxhole even if I didn't like the son of a bitch I was sharing it with. I don't like a lot of fuckers in here. But they're my buddies and I've got to take care of them. And I expect them to take care of me."

"O. K.," I interjected. "The Army has changed Budweiser for all time as far as we know. You have got a grip on your life in this, your seventeenth year. Does Budweiser have a new dream for himself?"

"My dream? I've always wanted to play professional ball. I guess it's a little too late for that. I might make a life out of this."

"Why the Army infantry where life is so hard? Why not another service?"

"The Marines are fucked. They're some dumb motherfuckers. Air Force are pansies, and I don't want to go out on the sea for six goddamn months."

"Do you want to be an officer?"

"Hell no. I don't want to go above the rank where I can't go into combat and fight. It's like if we go to war, I don't want to be sitting right behind the line telling everybody what to do. I want to be the one who goes across the line and fights."

"You know you get killed that way," I said with a smile as we sat at the table in the 3d Platoon's lounge in Albanese Barracks.

"Yeah, well. I'd still rather be the one to go."

"Who would you most like to be like in the world—your role model?"

"Drill Sergeant Zuniga. He's got guts and he's got stamina."

It hit me hard. Here was this 17-year-old kid who at one time hated his parents; hated his teachers; hated most of his schoolmates; had been getting blasted on booze and drugs since age 14; had broken into houses to support his wild but depressing life-style as a boy with no place that felt like home; had spent time in a juvenile detention home after being arrested during a 95-mile-an-hour drunken joyride in a stolen car in redneckville; had stood humiliated before a judge; been beat up; had said fuck everybody and everything; craved release from the drills when we talked, especially Zuniga who was always on his ass—probably because he knew Budweiser could take it and liked being noticed; craved a cigarette, a beer, maybe some snow, a woman and long hair. Yet he was saying out loud with raw sincerity and conviction: "Listen, America. I've fucked up a lot. But if you ever get in trouble, I want to be the one who goes out and dies fighting for you. And listen Zuniga, you little fucker, I'm going to be tougher than you—you magnificent son of a bitch."

Put me in a foxhole with the Budweisers, not the Establishment prissies who always seem to get the most out of the sacrifices these Invisible Patriots make every time they take the point for the country. One of my newspaper colleagues in Washington, who never spent an uncomfortable night in his life, asked me with a wrinkled nose why I was running around Georgia with a bunch of privates rather than covering the military establishment in air-conditioned Washington. He will never know because he will never feel the lift these knocked-about kids like Budweiser give you if you build a bridge to them and listen to their hearts.

Glen, 17, of Texas had joined Budweiser and me at the table and listened to the last part of our conversation. I had asked him to join us to broaden my portrait of young men whose broken lives had been mended by the special glue that basic training produces. Like Budweiser, Glen admitted to having been a colossal fuck-up since his early teens and felt the Army had changed him for good. Again, it was too early to say if this was true. He would not have drill sergeants watching his every move once he left Benning and joined his regular unit where he would be able to wiggle around the rules. But Glen's parents told me during their visit to Fort Benning that they dared hoped their son was changed for good. They wondered how the Army had managed to change him after so many doctors, ministers and psychiatrist had failed to do so. I tried to draw the explanation out of this Army volunteer of the 1980s in a long session one quiet night in the barracks.

"I ran away from home when I was 13," Glen began with a devilish smile.

He reminded me of Peck's bad boy when he smiled. It made him look as if he had just gotten away with something. His smile took me back to my own Millburn, New Jersey, high school days when my buddy, Matt Galbraith, lit up classrooms and living rooms with the same kind of mischievous look.

Glen was small, wiry and had a squinty face that prompted his fellow soldiers to nickname him "Rat." He talked easily, sometimes pridefully, about his rebel years. Years of fuck-everybody-and-everything. He said his philosophy was, "This is my life, goddamn it. I'll do what I want with it.

"I was in junior high and had just started on dope and didn't give a fuck about nothing. I was an only child. I'm not saying my parents gave me everything. But if I needed something bad enough, it was there. My dad had a 'Vet [Corvette], my mom a Caprice and they bought me a Monza when I got 16. They were loving parents. They taught me right from wrong." His father, crippled by an accident in which the pickup he was riding in rolled over six times, was a municipal judge in a little Texas town and his mother was district clerk for the county.

"My parents didn't really find out I was doing drugs until I was 16. I'd come home stoned. Smoked dope, did a little coke but never shot up. I got introduced to paper acid. I liked that buzz. It was my favorite. [Paper acid comes on paper one-fourth the size of a postage stamp which users stick on the tip of their tongues. The LSD in the paper is absorbed by the blood, creating hallucinations.] It cost four or five bucks for one little piece. They come in sheets of 100 with names like The World, Saturn, Polka Dot.

"Acid was getting scarce in town. So I started smoking more dope. My best friend was a dealer. No problem getting a bag here and there. I'd pay him back when I could. I'd stay stoned at school. I never took a book home the whole time I was in high school. Flunked tenth grade. Never did pass again. Come home. My best friend would come over. Smoke a joint or two out in my car which had tinted glass. Parents couldn't see what we were doing. My dad came out one day and found a roller. He was pissed off. Went and told my mom . . .

"Got to the point where we got kind of burnt-out on weed. Stopped going to school. Didn't give a fuck. My motto was, 'You only live once, so do it.' Got into coke pretty good. Started stealing stuff from my parents to get money to buy coke. Had a job working at the Chamber of Commerce putting up signs for a lady for $3.25 an hour. I'd only work a couple of times a month for $10 or $15 a day. I started forging checks [by signing the lady's name on Chamber of Commerce checks made out to himself]. Totaled out to $800 to $900 worth of checks. Got caught when they came back. Chamber had a meeting on it. One lady out of the twelve voted to press charges. But they let me keep the job. I had a reputation for being a bad kid. My mom and dad had to pay for it.

"Got into skateboarding. Could only do it when I was high. I was wearing my hair down to my shoulders but cut real short on top and spiked. Was still living home. My parents grounded me. I'd sneak out the window at nights. My mother locked the window after I'd sneaked out one night. Came home and slept in the garage.

"Started tenth grade for the second time. Went to school stoned every day. If I wasn't stoned, I'd be flying on acid. I was spending twenty-five bucks a day on pot. I'd get about five bucks a day from my parents for lunch, and I was working. Making about eighty bucks a week. Got a lot of dope free from my friend, the dealer. He was 14 but was big and had a beard and everything. I'd have supper at my house and then go over to his grandmother's house where he lived and smoke six or seven joints. Leave his house about 9:30; go home; take a shower, go to bed; out my window, and come home any time from 4:30 to 6:30 in the morning.

"I'd sleep through school. My highest average in biology after going through tenth grade twice was 17 out of 100. I hated biology. I'd never do the work. I was good in auto mechanics. Been taking carburetors apart with my dad since I was 13. That's why right now I'm a mechanic, 11 Mike [the Army designation].

"Sometimes I'd cuss out the teachers, get in fights over shitty stuff. Vice principal called the cops on me a couple times. They never did find nothing" in searching for dope.

I asked Glen if his parents, pillars in their town, did not try to intervene, to change the course of his life before he destroyed himself.

"Yeah. They'd always tell me to stay home. 'You're gone too much. You're always over at your friend's house every night.' I'd tell 'em, 'I don't like it here. There's nothing to do.' They bought me an Atari. I'd take it to his [the dope dealer's] house to play. I felt better watching TV at his house than watching TV at my house. What it was, I think—I'm not sure—was that because my dad was a judge and I was such a fuck-up in town, it didn't go together. Was like magnets not attracting each other. That's the way we were going.

"It was October 1986 that I went to school for four weeks straight flying acid. You ain't supposed to do that because that will fuck you up. If you get some good stuff, the buzz can last you twelve hours. Most I ever took was two-and-a-half hits at one time. That gave me a bad trip. I took them because somebody had smashed up the front end of my car and I didn't know what to tell my dad. I didn't go home until the next morning. That night we were sitting at this chick's house. We were all flying, and I was looking at the cat. The cat did a back flip. My whole mind went crazy. Her mom walked in the door—her mom didn't care, bought us beer and stuff. I went crazy, starting yelling and stuff. In my hallucinating I saw her Mom's face cave in. I went out to the pool and went crazy on the dog there, starting kicking it and stuff to get it out of there. I went crazy. I jumped in my car and drove off. My best friend, the one who was giving me the dope, was with me that night. I left everybody at the house and came back four hours later calmed down. They said I went crazy inside the house, tearing stuff up. Her mom was trying to stop me. They told my parents about it.

"My parents put me in _____ Hospital . . . the first of November. It's a thirty-five-day program where you work your way up one level after another. Took me close to three months to get out. All the people in there are related to it [drug abuse].

"I started thinking how much I had hurt my parents through all these drugs. I went to Alcoholics Anonymous meetings at the same time because I was drinking a lot, too. I went to Palmer Drug Abuse Program. Once I started thinking about it, I signed papers to stay in the hospital. They were giving me some kind of drug to slow me down because I was coming down off the drugs and was hyper. Then I'd get in moods where I was so drowsy—I could sleep twenty-four-hour periods. They'd drag me up. Sometimes coming off all those drugs I'd go crazy because I had been doing acid, coke, freon, paint—anything I could catch a buzz off of.

"At the hospital they have a 12-by-12 room called seclusion. I stayed in there for five weeks in level one. One day they took us out to play baseball. I had the chance, hopped the fence and I was gone. Six of us took off. I had a baseball bat. E_____ who jumped the fence with me called his girlfriend to pick us up. Slept in an abandoned house that night. The girl and E_____'s friend brought some joints over laced with heroin. We got stoned quick.

"Next morning we went to the mall where everybody knows me. We were all fucked up, didn't know what we were doing. Wanted to play games and stuff. A security guard stopped us and told us not to leave the mall," evidently because he believed the youths had escaped from somewhere.

"I called my best friend to come pick me up so I could go home for a while. My parents didn't know where I was. They knew I had broke out. I stayed with my friend, D_____, for two or three days. My parents still didn't know where I was. Called A _____ [who had escaped the hospital with him] and his friends said he had gotten busted and been taken back to the hospital. They told me, 'The cops are looking for you hard.' I had my friend drive me to Corpus and drop me off. This was about December 10, 1986.

"I called home. My dad asked where I was. I told him Corpus. They told me there was an all-points bulletin looking for me all over the state. I didn't know if that was true or not. I started getting scared. I didn't have nowhere to run no more. I was leeching off my friends. I was sneaking in D_____'s [the 14-year-old dope dealer] every night. His grandmother didn't even know I was staying there. I'd sneak out of his house at 6 in the morning while he went to school. I didn't have nowhere to sleep in the daytime. I went from 130 pounds to 110, 105 in a six-month period. Started thinking; went back into the hospital. From that time on, I only fucked up once. That was when I went home for Christmas. I came back to the hospital with a bag. They fucked me up for that. I had to go back to level one.

"Then I started thinking about my mom and dad and what would be better than this kind of life, because it wasn't worth a shit. I never thought of suicide. There's nothing I'd take my life for. Ever since then I was making levels week after week. I was doing great, going home on weekends. My parents and I were getting along great. They had already paid $2,000 to $3,000 for hot checks that I had written off their bank account. The hospital was $400 a day. Insurance paid for 80 percent of it. It totaled out to like $25,000 for three months. They had to pay like $3,000 or $4,000 because they had good insurance.

"I got out at the end of February. My seventeenth birthday was March 14. My parents were proud of me and everything. I stayed out of drugs for a while. But I had met friends in the hospital and didn't stay straight. I started getting into drugs. My parents thought I was going to Palmer Drug Abuse Program and Alcoholics Anonymous meetings. But all I was doing was going to Corpus and getting stoned and frying out. I had my car back. I started all over again. Back to my same old self. This is when I finally said, 'Fuck school; fuck my parents. I don't want no more of it.'

"My parents had found some of my joints I had hidden in my room. My dad turned them in to the cops. I was dead shocked but kind of understood because he's in law enforcement and stuff. And he's gotten me out of so much trouble, it's pathetic.

"I took off from the house in my car. Came back later. We started talking about it. My parents said we thought you were off of it. I said I couldn't hack it without it. It's kind of like, if you don't get accepted somewhere, you're going to do something. I started thinking again. But I just couldn't pull away [from drugs and friends]. I was having too much of a good time. Started frying again on acid. Fronting it [buying it now but paying later]. Getting behind in payments. Was stealing beer from where I worked . . . Lost my job. Starting talking to my dad about quitting school. He didn't want that.

"I got busted for shoplifting in Corpus. Had ripped off a couple pair of shades, tapes. They took me to jail and I had two joints in my pocket. The handcuffs were loose enough for me to get the joints out of my pocket and stick them down by my nuts. When they strip-searched me I grabbed my underwear off so the joints wouldn't fall out. They never found them.

"My mom and dad came and picked me up the next morning. Got in a bitching session. My dad said, 'You want me to just leave you in there?' I said, 'I think it would be better than staying at home.' He put me in the car. We went home. Talked about it. Didn't put me on restriction or nothing. He said, 'I think you've had punishment enough.' I didn't quit smoking or nothing. I was hard-headed. Didn't listen to nobody.

"I was still in tenth grade when I should have been a senior. Just before my class graduated I quit school and starting thinking, What am I going to do with my life? My parents were totally broken up about me. I felt bad. I got more into drugs. I was stealing from my parents—jewelry. I'd sell necklaces that were worth $200 for a $20 bag. My dad had a .38 special. He knew I was stealing stuff from my mom. The .38 special came up missing. It was chrome-plated. His step-daddy had given it to him before he died. I really didn't steal it. But I had so many friends in the house, and I was so fucked up all the time. Some of the people were real dicks. To this day he still thinks I took it.

"I would never listen to my parents. But my friend who I was getting all the dope from started talking to me. He said I was getting too fucked up, that I was doing too much drugs. I don't know what it was, but it snapped on me when he started talking to me.

"My dad started talking to me about the Army. From the start it sounded good to me. Thirty days' vacation and all that good stuff. My dad had tried to raise me right but was about to give up on me. They tell me I had stuck a knife to a guy's throat and beat him up. They were going to try me on June 30th. I went to my recruiter and started talking to him close to the end of June. The recruiter was telling my dad behind my back that he didn't think I was going to be able to pass the test. He told him a good score is a 50 and he expected me to make about a 38. I could memorize stuff easy. I started studying that book [for the GED test], a big old thick mother. And I did great on the test. I made a 64 on the ASVAB [Armed Service Vocational Aptitude Battery] and my GT [general test] scores were high enough where I could qualify for anything I wanted in the Army.

"I was getting back and forth to San Antonio to the MEPS [Military Entrance Processing Station] station by bus. I was getting stoned on the bus in the bathroom in the back because they've got those vents. I lied my ass off to get in this Army. Told them I had no record, no tickets, no nothing. I was still on probation at the time. My court date was still set. My dad went to the judge and asked him to close out my records. The judge said he would sit on the case about me holding the knife to the guy's neck and if I didn't get in the Army, he would reopen it. The judge told my dad that I was looking at five to ten years in the penitentiary for assault and battery with a deadly weapon.

"The charge was pending on me. I started talking with my parents, started communicating. I could never get off the drugs. I was still stealing from them, and they knew it. But this time my feelings were so down; I was so low in the gutter. On June 28 the Army sent me to the MEPS station. I told them I wanted to leave as soon as possible. I got my job [a slot in the infantry]. My dad had told me: 'The only way you're going to earn our trust back is to do something positive.' I called him from the MEPS station that night and said, 'I'm in, Dad.' Talked to my mom on the phone. She started crying she was so happy. Made me feel bad. I started crying on the phone talking to her. She said, 'I love you,' and all this."

The Army gave Glen a plane ticket to Atlanta. He got stoned in the airport men's room by smoking two joints and then boarded the bus for Fort Benning. He sat next to another volunteer on the bus who had traded drugs heavily. He was beginning to feel at home with this and other bad boys he met at the Reception Station at Benning on July 2. The Army kept them in the barracks there for a week, waiting for the other future members of Delta Company to arrive. Glen flaunted authority for the last time before entering basic training by smoking the cigarettes he found on the street while assigned to cleanup details at Benning. By Monday of July 4th weekend, he had received his uniform, had had his hair shorn off and had looked in the mirror at himself: "Goddamn, what a change!"

Glen told me that he found Shock Treatment a shock, basic training a strain mentally and physically. "The only thing keeping me going was my parents, how proud they'd be. I'd be on a run, and I'd think, 'My parents. Left foot, Dad. Right foot, Mom.' It helped me go through basic.

"I started feeling good about myself. I've been gaining weight. I was 112 back at the MEPS station. Right now I weigh about 130, 135. I'm feeling real good about joining the Army. It's the best thing that ever happened in my life; the best thing that's happened to me. All I've been trying to do is make it up to my parents. I bought my mom a gold necklace with a diamond in the middle. I bought my grandmother a cross. I talked to her on the phone. She told me she was so proud of me and everything. I cried my ass off. I apologized to her for all the stuff because she had gone through it, too. I've been getting letters from friends—I can't call them friends because I didn't hang around with them or nothing. One guy named Bubba lives around the corner from me. In seventh and eighth grade we were pretty good friends, but I wandered off from the jock life because I was going into skating. All them jocks turned against me. He started writing me. He goes, 'A lot of people here in school can't even believe you went. They didn't think you'd make it.' My mom and dad were sending me cards and stuff about how a family should be. It was motivating me more and everything.

"I know I've improved since I got here. The way I grew up I didn't take shit from nobody. I haven't changed that much because it's so hard to change my attitude, the way I was. But since I've been in the Army, it's helped me so much that I've improved 100 percent from the way I was. For anybody who wants to get in the Army right now, it's great. Because my mom and dad are so proud of me, it makes me feel so good inside. I've never felt this way in my life before."

Glen had finished the story of his life. Glen, Budweiser and Barry—another reformed drug abuser who joined the Army to get straight—and I had all listened with intense attention as the four of us sat around the little card table in the lounge in 3d Platoon's sleeping bay. Nobody said anything for a long moment. I felt like a lay priest who had just heard two confessions, Budweiser's and Glen's. I could tell they felt good about somebody hearing them out, taking down their story, passing it on. "Writing them in a book might help some other kids from getting so fucked up,"

Budweiser had told me at the onset. I did not know about that. But I did know the Army worked some kind of magic on hard-heads like Budweiser and Glen—at least during their first months in uniform. Would these converts stay converted?

While the feeling of intimacy at the table was still warm, I tried to pull out of these 17-year-olds why the drill instructors and others in this military society had succeeded in turning them around while the experts in civilian society had failed.

"It's discipline," Glen replied. "They've got the best discipline I've ever been through. They put fear in us. I know they've put fear in me from head to toe. I've been scared of them ever since Shock Treatment. I'd keep Shock Treatment. It does a whole lot of good. It separates the people who want to be here and ones that don't.

"Discipline and the learning, like shooting the M-16. I've been hunting but never shot nothing like the M-16. And the hand grenades. It's a wonderful feeling.

"Here, like cleaning up the barracks, you got to work like a team. If one person fucks up, the whole platoon is going to get punished for it. It's the team thing that works with it. When I was back home, most of the friends I hung around with weren't my friends. But once you get here and make a friend, I'm not going to say all of them, but most of them, are your friends for life. You've got to work as a team, or you're not going to make it. You've got to learn. Because if you ever have to go to war, you got to have a strong enough friendship and know enough to cover your ass first and them second."

"But when you were in the hospital," I pressed Glen, "you were under tight control—somebody could order you to make your bed. So what's different here?"

"I wouldn't have to do it."

"So the difference here is that there's no escape from the discipline, right?"

"Right. You have to do it, or you're going home. And most of the people who come here come on a voluntary basis and they don't want to go home."

"But a lot of guys here said, 'Fuck it!' and wouldn't do what they were told."

"Yeah," Glen said. "But they're not here right now. They've gone home."

I turned to Budweiser sitting there listening to Glen and asked what made him put up with all the aggravation of drill sergeants yelling at him and being cut off from everything he pursued back home at such great pain and risk.

"Like Glen said about going home and having respect," Budweiser replied. "Your parents have respect for you. A soldier, you know, is a man."

"Your friends, too," Glen interjected. "If I went home right now, they wouldn't respect me as much. They'd say I was a quitter and stuff. I knew if I went home they'd reject me even worse."

"But you quit the hospital, so why not quit the Army?" I asked. "What's the difference?"

"Who gives a fuck about the hospital?" Budweiser answered. "It's temporary, man."

"That was just games back then," Glen agreed.

"Yeah," I continued, "but two days after you get home from the Army no one is going to make a big deal of your quitting. It would be just one more failure. You flunked out of school, you flunked out of the hospital, you flunked out of the Army. So what's the big difference about flunking out of the Army?"

"This is where you make your money," Budweiser replied. "This is where you grow up."

"As a teenager you got time," Glen added. He explained in jumbled sentences that he had learned as a boy that his misbehavior while growing up would be tolerated by adults and cheered by his peers but that in the Army everyone expected him to act like a man at last.

"Yeah, but see," he struggled in trying to say that, "now that I'm in the Army, if I was to go home, I'd be marked for life."

"It's manhood," Budweiser added. "Like me, I like challenges. The other things—they were temporary. Fuck. This is it. If you can't do this, you're fucked."

A soldier came into the lounge to tell Budweiser and Glen they had to report to a work detail. I left them in Albanese Barracks and walked out in to the twilight. I reflected on our conversation as I looked at the little dots of light in the valley below me. I marveled at the turnaround in attitude since Vietnam. In the 1960s many teenagers went to Canada to stay out of the Army, or to college if they had the money. They did not consider this dishonorable. Some of those who had been drafted would do almost anything to get out of the Army. And here these two one-time bad boys, Budweiser and Glen, were trying to change their lives to conform to the resurrected ethic that serving in the military was the honorable thing to do. Failing to live up to that solemn obligation would be dishonoring yourself. Would the Army seize this golden moment by keeping the dreams of these volunteers alive and building on them? Or would they treat these new soldiers like serfs once they got away from Benning and into their regular units, kicking away the opportunity? The next months would tell.

# 8. Homestretch

"Like my new Revlon fucking compact?" Timothy N. Tasse, 18, of Worcester, Massachusetts, asked me as I watched him and others in Drill Sergeant Zuniga's 3d Platoon put on war paint by streaking each other's faces with light- and dark-green lipsticks. "I'm going out on a date. Sometime."

It had been six weeks since Tasse and others in Delta Company had seen or smelled, far less touched, a young woman. It had been that long since their one and only pass that allowed them to leave the Army reservation. But somehow almost everyone in Delta Company had hung in and made it to September. The trainees were finally in the homestretch. Graduation was only a few days away. But they had to pass the infantry's final exams to march before their parents sitting in the grandstand off the parade ground on graduation day. I could feel their anxiety as I talked to the young troopers during these last days in Benning. The new soldiers were anxious to graduate, to wear the blue cord signifying infantryman, but once again were nervous about what lay ahead of them outside their now-familiar world of Sand Hill. They were like prisoners about to be released from jail and wondering if they could adjust to the supposedly normal life outside the walls.

Two parts of the infantry's final exams were called STX, for situational training exercise, and FTX, for field training exercise. Tasse and other trainees were putting on war paint for STX. Their 3d Platoon under the leadership of Drill Sergeant Zuniga was supposed to sneak through the woods without getting killed by snipers hidden in the brush and to knock out a machine-gun nest. I thought how the Vietnam Charlie Company could have benefitted from this training. Both attackers and defenders in this exercise would know who killed whom because their weapons would fire laser beams that followed the path of real bullets when the trigger was pulled, exploding the blank bullets in the chamber for added realism. Button-like sensors on the helmets and web gear of the troopers would ring whenever a trooper was hit by a laser beam. This laser training equipment is called MILES, for multiple integrated laser engagement system.

I was going to walk behind Zuniga and his troopers when they attacked the "enemy" M-60 machine gun. Probably like Sergeant Charlie Urconis before him, Zuniga called his men around him to remind them what might happen and how they were to respond. He warned them that they might be shelled by simulated artillery (called indirect fire) and gassed as they tried to weave their way through the snipers.

"The first guy who spots the 60," Zuniga told his soldiers in reference to the enemy machine gun, "tell me where it is. If indirect fire lands on us, move away from it. When the 60 pops, move away from it. I'll empty that smoke, and then we'll start peeling away from the 60. We'll retrograde until we're out of danger.

"If a sniper hits on the left, get down. Alpha Fire Team faces left," Zuniga continued. "What do we do if the sniper hits us at 6 o'clock [from the rear of the advancing 3d Platoon]?"

"About-face and get down," his troops answered.

"We're going to get the 60," Zuniga said in his final pep talk just before pushing across the road and entering the wooded combat zone. "That's our mission. If I call your number, I want you to respond. After each attack, we must consolidate and reorganize. Nobody has got to the bunker yet. We'll get the bunker. If you make a mistake, don't get out of shape and believe you're the biggest fuck-up in the world.

"Once we cross there," Zuniga continued, pointing to the road marking the line of departure [LD], "treat everything as dangerous. If you've got to go pee-pee, go to the pee-pee room fast. Lock and load [the M-16 rifles]. Make sure your MILES is in."

I joined Lieutenant Raines walking behind Zuniga's platoon. Raines carried a notebook to record what the attackers did right and wrong. He would hold a critique right after the attack. We watched the forward part of Zuniga's platoon enter the woods where the enemy was hidden. Zuniga sent out two squads, one to the right and one to the left, to look for enemy soldiers who might be trying to ambush the platoon.

"Putting out left and right security, that's good," Raines commented, scribbling a note in his book. "Squad leader is the last one across the LD. Brings in that security. Good. Good. By the book."

"Gas!" a trooper screamed, pulling his mask on. It was a false alarm. He felt ashamed for panicking. The platoon stopped to regroup. Zuniga walked over to the trooper who had sounded the false alarm and said consolingly: "Don't worry about it. Just keep going. Blow it off! Blow it off! Understand?"

"Yes, Drill Sergeant."

The platoon pushed on. The flat *snap* of a sniper's M-16 broke the quiet of the woods.

"Alpha Team," Zuniga shouted. "Pull back to the left! What's your ammo?"

The squad leader gave his report. I could tell from the hand signals and high-pitched voices of Zuniga and his men that their hearts were pumping fast, just as they would be in combat. Everyone was trying so hard to win. I marvelled at the dedication of this new generation of infantrymen as I walked along behind them with Raines. Johnny Libs would have been proud to lead this new breed.

"Turn around, you!" Zuniga shouted to a trooper who was facing away from the sound of the sniper's fire.

"I'm dead, Drill Sergeant."

The deeper *boom-boom* of the M-60 shattered the woods, drowning out the flatter snaps of the M-16s being fired by the attackers and snipers.

"I see the 60!" Private Jimmy L. Russell Jr., 18, of Gray, Georgia, shouted to Zuniga. The drill sergeant set off the smoke grenade to hide his troops as he directed them into the formation he wanted for knocking out the machine gun.

Raines suspended the fight. He figured, with the M-60 located, Zuniga's platoon had won the fight, thanks to Russell spotting the machine gun.

"House Mouse!" Zuniga shouted across the clearing to Russell, who got his nickname from being platoon clerk. "House Mouse!" Zuniga repeated, smiling with a joy that lit up the dark woods.

"We would have wiped you out if Jimmy Russell hadn't discovered the 60," remarked a disconsolate enemy gunner.

Russell had told me he had joined the Army "to become a man the hard way." This day he indeed felt like a man.

Raines called Zuniga and his platoon around him. He delivered his criticisms, which were few, and sketched the just-completed movements and countermovements in the dirt.

"The best thing was, you were aggressive," Raines said. "But never attack a sniper in force for fear of running into an ambush." I could not help wondering if that was what Charlie Company had done in 1966.

"If bullets are flying at you, you fire back in the direction of fire," Raines stressed.

"Come here, House Mouse," Zuniga called to Russell after Raines had finished. Zuniga patted the private's head and said, "If I had had a LAW [light antitank weapon], I would have blown that bunker away."

Raines interrupted the brief celebration by announcing Lieutenant Colonel Gordon Lam, battalion commander, was going to walk behind Zuniga and his boys in a repeat attack on the snipers and machine-gun position, which would be hidden in a new place.

"The Colonel's coming through on this one," Raines said and went into a mock faint.

"We won't let you down," one of the troopers told Zuniga. "We'll fuck 'em up."

During this second assault through the woods, I walked behind the platoon with Command Sergeant Major Sidney L. Raspberry, 47, of Birmingham, Alabama, a husky black man who towered above my 6-foot height. We chatted while Zuniga and his men paused to snoop and went into low and high crawls to evade sniper fire. It was slow going, with frequent stops, just as in real combat. I asked Raspberry during these pauses why he had joined the Army, whether he thought he had done better in it than out of it.

As a black boy growing up in the South, he told me, he found himself at a dead end, like so many of the young soldiers in the woods in front of us. He joined the Army in 1958 in hopes it would be a way up; had served in Vietnam with the Kit Carson scouts, former Vietcong who joined the American side and fought their former comrades. After thirty years in uniform, Raspberry had moved to the top of the Army's enlisted ranks and was grateful and proud.

"I don't believe I could have advanced as well in civilian life. I was one of eight kids. There was no way for me to go to school. If you don't have the education, you don't get the money. Companies don't care what you majored in as long as you get the piece of paper. Then they give you the money.

"I really love being an infantryman. I get a sensation out of helping people. I like talking to young sergeants, giving them a map and showing them how to get ahead. The Army is really looking up. But the top people have to keep pushing their knowledge down because the experience in middle management is not there. I consider myself a senior trainer."

This is exactly what the post-Vietnam, untested volunteers need, I thought. Trainers like Raspberry to tell them what is real and what is not; what is important; what is not important; how to fight and live.

I told Raspberry as we walked along how astonished I was during my months at Benning to hear blacks calling each other "nigger" with no racial implications. When I first heard the term, I braced for an explosion. But none ever came. Both blacks and whites in razzing each other called each other nigger. It had lost its fire as a racial epithet with this new generation and become just another knocking term, like knucklehead. I felt glad about it. Race relations were healthy. There was some black-white tension, but not much. Raspberry told me he had a tough time dealing with the young blacks who knew nothing about even the most recent struggle of their race, the one led by the late black preacher, Martin Luther King Jr.

"Nigger means a different thing to them than it does to me," Raspberry said there in the middle of the Georgia woods. "They don't even know who Martin Luther King is unless they read it in a history book." This decorated sergeant walking with me knew he owed a lot to King. And although he despaired that the young black troops in the woods with us did not know how hard it had been to win their rights, we two men of the older generation—a white reporter and a black sergeant—could walk together through the woods talking about the term "nigger" with neither of us getting emotional. I felt even that little difference was progress. It made me feel better about the world as I looked back to my searing days as a young police reporter when I saw white cops beat up defenseless blacks in New Jersey.

Our conversation was interrupted by Colonel Lam dispensing advice to the privates maneuvering through the woods. One private decided to get in the act, shouting this advice to his buddy trying to survive the snipers who kept firing as the platoon advanced through the woods: "It helps when you spread out."

"No shit, Sherlock," his buddy answered.

I laughed. I was back in the real world of the American mud soldier.

Zuniga's platoon did well despite all the high-level supervision. But West Pointer Raines conceded to me that real battles seldom are won by the book. "If you do everything right, nobody gets the Medal of Honor." I thought of Sergeant Robbie Robinson charging the Vietcong's .50-caliber machine gun singlehanded. Not by the Army book. But he might well have turned that battle because he followed his own book.

I followed the 2d Platoon through the woods during its attack. I discovered Chris Cashman sitting on the ground, obviously disgusted with himself. He had failed to stay low. He was the squad leader. His "death" had jeopardized the men in his squad following him. He felt right after his sensors started ringing that he actually had been killed. He shared with me the immediate thoughts of the "dead" infantryman: "My first thought was, 'Aw shit! Who's going to take care of my family?' Then I thought, 'I let down the people behind me.' When Drill Sergeant Rodriguez came up and I was lying there on the ground, he looked down at me as if to say, 'You dumb shit.'

"Getting killed made me wake up. I realized if something did come up and we went to war, I should tell myself: 'Don't try to be a Rambo by exposing yourself.' It's the first time I've ever taken anything that seriously. I realized I had gotten myself killed before I ever saw my baby son, Christopher Junior."

I left the STX assaults in the woods for the foxholes Delta Company was digging in another part of the woods. The idea of this part of advanced individual training was to teach the infantryman how to burrow into Mother Earth to improve his chances of surviving an attack by a big force. The Army book, which the trainees had to follow, called for digging foxholes almost shoulder-deep with firing ports on the left and right sides and a thick roof of timbers and dirt on top to protect them from grenades, mortars and artillery fragments. Two men shared one foxhole.

"It's not a foxhole anymore," Drill Sergeant Stover told me, shaking his head with obvious disgust at the Army's changed terminology as he supervised the digging. "It's a fighting position."

Drill Sergeant Rodriguez was using his usual warm sarcasm to urge his troops in 2d Platoon to keep digging their "fighting positions" so they would pass the upcoming inspection during this FTX.

"What are you doing?" he asked a sweaty trooper leaning on his pick.

"Resting, Drill Sergeant."

"Think the enemy is going to let you rest?" Trying to get his platoon dug in before dark, Rodriguez added, "Do you know how to mount a flashlight on that pick?"

Moving on to Spank Barker's fighting position, Rodriguez looked down into the cavity he and his foxhole mate had dug. "Little wide in there."

"I'm a little wide," Spank replied, but narrowed the trench at the bottom of the foxhole so it would pass inspection the next day.

Stover walked out into the clearing in front of the foxholes. He praised the construction of one of them in the platoon's interlocking lines of defensive fire. "That's good. From 35 meters you can't see it. A man with a grenade can't see it."

I walked along the W-shaped line of foxholes and encountered a distressed Tweety Selvester. He broke down and cried when he saw me, sobbing out his story: "This is the worst day of my life. I've already called my mom to come to my graduation. She's flying all the way from California, but I'm not going to graduate. I couldn't do the forty-two push-ups. I did them. But they screwed me. They didn't count some of them I did."

I checked with Captain Fleenor. He confirmed that Tweety would not graduate if he did not do his forty-two push-ups in another test Fleenor had arranged. The other physical requirements for an 18-year-old like Selvester to graduate were to perform sixty-eight sit-ups and run 2 miles in fifteen minutes and fifty-four seconds. I wondered why the Army insisted on doing each of those requirements rather than develop a combined score that would test the overall physical fitness of the soldier. Fleenor told me battalion would probably just hold Selvester at Benning a

153

couple of weeks to strengthen his upper body. Then Selvester would join his company at Fort Riley, Kansas. "It's not the end of the world," Fleenor said with a smile. But it was for Tweety—at least for the moment.

I thought the trainees learned more about fighting and winning battles in those few days of assaults through the woods than in all the weeks of sitting in grandstands and lying in ranges. I wished the Army would conduct those patrols with laser weapons every two weeks during the thirteen weeks of training even if some of the courses, like the one on setting out claymore mines, had to be scrapped or taught later at the units, which is what actually happens anyway. The realistic attacks were not only instructive but fun. It was what most of the troops had hoped to do when they signed up for the infantry.

The bad news of advanced individual training, I discovered in my final weeks with Delta Company, was an antitank weapon called the Dragon made by the McDonnell Douglas Corporation. I carried it at night, sat under it to aim it, heard the lectures on what it could and could not do, talked to the gunners who had fired it. I concluded that the fact that we were still expecting the individual foot soldier in the late 1980s to use the Dragon to try to stop a Soviet tank was nothing short of a national disgrace.

The Dragon is shaped like a cylindrical vacuum cleaner. A missile is fired out of the short cylinder. The infantryman has to carry the Dragon on his back with a single strap. I found that carrying the Dragon through the woods is indeed like carrying a vacuum cleaner. The damn thing does not sit balanced on your back but keeps sliding around. I also discovered that it is likely to slip under your stomach or chest when you fall on the ground to fire, knocking your wind out or cracking your ribs. I saw my worst fears confirmed when a trooper of the new Charlie Company had to be evacuated for medical treatment after he fell chest-first on the Dragon he was carrying in the dark.

Aiming the Dragon requires assuming a sitting position and holding the fat tube above your lap. Once fired, the Dragon's antitank missile trails wire behind it as it flies along. You keep the cross-hairs of the Dragon sight on the tank, with your moves transmitted out over the trailing wire as electrical signals that correct the missile's flight path. The Dragon cannot be fired through brush or over water because this would cut or short-circuit the wire umbilical cord. Worst of all, the Dragon gunner is supposed to sit stock-still out on the open ground while guiding the missile through the air and into the enemy tank. The Dragon instructors told the privates to be sure to hold the cross-hairs on the target for fifteen seconds without moving. They added grimly that the Soviet T-72 tank requires only five seconds to swivel its big gun and blast the Dragon gunner. As if to make it easier for the Soviet tank crew searching the battlefield for antitank gunners, the Dragon sends up a distinctive plume of smoke the instant it is fired, like waving a red flag at a bull. Finally, the Soviet armor is so tough that the Dragon would bounce off most parts of the tank hull.

I asked one of the trainees who had been selected to be a Dragon gunner how he felt about this weapon. This is what he said angrily into my tape recorder: "It pees me off that somebody got millions of dollars to build this weapon that's no dern good. In a war I'd never use the thing. Maybe I'd get court-martialed, but at least I wouldn't get killed."

A retired infantry colonel who commanded a brigade on the NATO front line in Europe told me: "If we sent troops to fight modern Soviet tanks with the Dragon, we'd find 'lost' Dragons all over the place. American soldiers know when something is no good and just throw it away in battle rather than carry it." His theory has not been tested because the Dragon has not gone to war.

I could not fathom how the American foot soldier had received such short shrift when it came to combating Soviet tanks. I had flown mock aerial combat in the back seat of a Navy F-14 fighter plane and worked the firing systems that enable either the backseater or the pilot up front to fire a missile at an enemy plane and then break off the attack to avoid being hit by return fire. I could not believe the Army had not given its foot soldier such a "fire-and-forget" weapon to stop what the generals have said is the Soviet's biggest single edge over the United States in conventional weaponry, tanks.

Armed with first-hand experience with the Dragon and testimony from Army troopers who recoiled from the idea of using it in wartime, I broke off from the troopers to ask the Army why it had left the lone infantryman so under-armed. I expected to get the you-don't-know-what-you're-talking-about defense. But instead the Army's chief executive for overseeing the development and production of weapons, Under Secretary of the Army James R.

155

Ambrose, admitted the bureaucracy had failed the mud soldier when it came to giving him an effective antitank weapon. This is what Ambrose said in an interview in his Pentagon office:

"You're looking at something that should have gotten changed out a long time ago. It was part of the general failure—whether by the Army, Department of Defense, the Congress or everybody together—to perceive that there has to be a shorter cycle" in developing new weapons to keep up with the threat.

"An institutional reason" for not improving existing weapons like the Dragon, Ambrose continued, "is the fear that if you say we can fix this one up somewhat, then you won't get more. My view is that you ought to have one weapon pretty fully fielded, you ought to have one that's just going into service, and you ought to have something on the drawing board. That isn't any different than automobiles, computers, airplanes or whatever in the private sector.

"But there are all kinds of institutional inhibitions against working that way. You see those operating in the Dragon, which the Army has known for a long time was not a particularly good weapon: short range, not particularly lethal, knock your ear off if you're not careful. We want to get rid of it as fast as we can. It should have been done long ago."

I asked why the Army had not put a higher priority on arming the individual mud soldier who takes the greatest risks in wartime. Ambrose agreed there had been a wrong order of priority among uniformed Army leaders, declaring that when it came to dividing up the money pie in secret budget meetings they favored "tanks, Bradley fighting vehicles, Apache helicopters and stuff like that. Even the Infantry favored getting the Bradley, not the infantryman stuff. I thought the infantryman was getting short-sheeted big time and told the Army over and over that you're focused on the machinery, not the people. You've got to keep the people alive."

In refreshing contrast to the Dragon, I saw during the last part of the troops' training that the Army had improved such old reliables as the hand grenade since Vietnam and introduced a fast-firing, lethal and light gun called the SAW (squad automatic weapon).

"Forget about the way John Wayne throws grenades in the

156

movies," the sergeants told the trainees nearing graduation as infantrymen. "Throw it like a baseball." And to help break the John Wayne arm motion, the new grenade is shaped like a baseball, not a pineapple.

I fired the SAW with no practice and mowed down the targets with ease. I thought, what a difference SAWs could have made to the old Charlie Company trying to blast the Vietcong snipers out of the trees.

The physical highlight of the final part of the thirteen weeks of infantry training was running through the Confidence Course at Benning. It included diving onto rolling logs, jumping over walls, climbing up and down ropes, going hand over hand along elevated ladders and "the slide for life." The slide for life required the recruit to climb a tower made of cross logs with a platform at the top. Each succeeding cross log was higher and thus harder to reach and hoist up to than the previous one. Drill sergeants told me that some trainees always froze with fright high on the tower, especially if they looked down. I went through most of the confidence course obstacles but not all of them. I reached the base of the slide-for-life tower. A trainee was stuck two-thirds of the way to the top. Drill Sergeant Stover, standing on the platform atop the tower, yelled at him to keep climbing. The trainee stayed put like an impaled fly with extra-big eyes.

"What the hell," I said to myself, "give it a try." I started climbing up the tower. If you went slowly and kept looking up rather than down, the climb was less unnerving. When I got to the top, Stover fashioned the safety belt around my waist and pointed down the rope slanting back toward the ground. The "slide" required going down that rope with your ankles crossed above the rope and your hands walking down it while your arched back hung down from the rope high above the ground.

"Head first or feet first?" Stover asked me with that smile that made the trainees believe they could do anything as long as he led them.

"Head first," I replied. This was easier on the arms but scarier.

"You're history," Stover said as I started down the rope.

Again, it looked harder to do than it was. Also, I could not hesitate once the trainees on the ground had spotted me. They were laughing and clapping as this crazy guy in their midst, who they knew had to be more than 50 years old although I did not admit it, took his slide for life. One of them grabbed the camera I had left on the ground to record the event. He could not work the shutter. So I have no photographic proof, just a lot of high-spirited witnesses.

"Hey, Mr. Wilson's doing it," Private Joseph E. Booth Jr., 25, of Houston, Texas, yelled up to his buddy still frozen on the cross-logs of the platform. His buddy became unfrozen and resumed his climb. He completed his slide for life.

"George Patton sat right here," Colonel Richard S. Siegfried said as he motioned me to a chair beside the revered place where World War II's hardest charging general, George S. Patton, had sat forty-five years earlier. The office was on the second floor of a dilapidated, white frame building on a rise in the Sand Hill training complex. Patton had used the office while developing armor tactics from 1940 to 1942. The current occupant of Patton's old office had the responsibility for turning 30,000 civilians a year into infantrymen. Siegfried's formal title was Commander, U.S. Army Infantry Training Center. I had come to Siegfried's office to learn what he thought of this new generation of volunteer infantryman, whether he thought suspending the draft was a mistake. I never can resist asking why a man joins the high-risk infantry in the first place, and opened with that question.

"Call me Steve," Siegfried began. As he talked, I mused at the vivid contrasts between Siegfried and Patton. Siegfried was warm, squat, old-shoe. Patton had been cold, tall, patrician. Siegfried came from a family of modest income and married a woman, Margaret "Maggie" Ann Everhart, from the same economic level. Siegfried thought he would make his living by playing blues on the piano. Patton believed he was destined to lead great armies in great battles; Siegfried joined the Army as an enlisted man in 1961, four years after graduating from high school in Columbus, Ohio. Patton had gone to West Point and become an officer.

Siegfried and Patton were alike, however, in their reverence for military men who hung it out for their country. Siegfried said he was uplifted as a boy by the retired Navy chiefs who came to his house to play pinochle with his father, also a former chief.

"They didn't talk about money or themselves," Siegfried recalled. "They talked about what had to be done to save the Navy. They related to something bigger than themselves. I loved to listen to them talk as I brought drinks and pretzels to the table. I was proud of my father, Robert Siegfried, and wanted to find something to hook into bigger than myself, as he had done." It turned out to be the infantry for this one-time blues piano player.

"In the infantry I found something that was bigger than me. There is something very special about being an infantryman. I tell my soldiers, 'Hey, they're very few of us, and we're very special to this nation. That's a real thing. There are just not many men who will go off and do what an infantryman does. That flag is not going to fall as long as you've got an infantry corps that is proud and well trained.'"

Like Johnny Libs, Siegfried's Vietnam experience left pain in his heart. With considerable reluctance Siegfried had jumped over the firebreak between enlisted man and officer, taking his officer infantry training at Benning. He commanded Bravo Company, Fifth Battalion (Mechanized), Sixtieth Infantry in Vietnam in 1967.

"I liked leading. I think I can do that well. But I hated talking to those young chargers in my company in Vietnam. Here I was privileged to command, and yet I couldn't answer their questions very well about why we weren't respected in the villages we went to . Where's the feeling for us? Out in the little villages we saw the good we were doing and we didn't see anything good coming out of it. The trauma for me as a young commander was convincing my men that they would get their recognition.

"You see yourself doing good. You see your soldiers die. But you never see headlines saying Old Bravo Company did very good for the old U.S. No one came out of my units feeling that we had lost anything on the ground. We out-guerrillaed the guerrilla on his own turf over and over again. Yet my men never got any credit for it, either over there or over here. That hurts me."

Our conversation jumped from the Army of draftees who fought the Vietnam War to the Army of volunteers who had no war to fight in 1987 when I joined the infantry as a chronicler. I asked Siegfried whether it bothered him that in ending the draft the U.S. government had abandoned the principle that every man must share the burden of defending his country.

"I always believed the volunteer Army was the best kind of an

Army," Siegfried replied. "Maybe I'm an idealist, but the perfect world is a world where young Americans want to volunteer to serve their country in some manner. The perfect world is an America which creates this pride in its homes, in its churches—an America which creates this fervor for national service for some period of time. If these young Americans come see the Army before deciding where to serve, we'll get our share. My vision of America would be a national feeling, a pride, an ethos that compel young men and women to volunteer."

I pressed him on the danger of the all-volunteer Army becoming so separated from the mainstream of America and its government that we will find ourselves with a high-paid version of the French Foreign Legion. Siegfried rejected this notion outright, declaring the draft would have to be reactivated if the United States went to war, if for no other reason than that the 1987 Army of 781,000 men and women, about half the number on active duty in 1968 at the height of the Vietnam War, was too small to fight a war by itself.

"Armies don't fight wars. Countries fight wars. I hope to hell we learned that in Vietnam. We've got a very small standing Army. So the argument that this small standing Army is going off to fight the war is fallacious. A country fights a war. If it doesn't, then we shouldn't send an army."

I brought the discussion down to the task at hand: turning the Selvesters, Proctors, Hensons, Adkinses, Murrays, Barkers, Cashmans, Austermans into infantrymen who would fight, hold and die—like the men of the old Charlie Company had done in 1966. Siegfried had no doubt this new breed would fight, partly because they themselves had decided they wanted to be soldiers.

"These volunteers I'm training today are not here because some judge sent them here, saying, 'You can't make it in society. I'm going to let the Army square you away.' They're not here trying to get away from mom and dad, not because they can't find a job. A lot of them signed up because of the educational opportunities, whether their families could afford it or not. A lot of them came for adventure; a lot came to grow up. Some of them love the Army.

"It's a different environment today than the one we had during the Vietnam War. They volunteered to be here. They want to succeed. Our power should be based on this desire—the soldier's desire to succeed on a team bigger than himself. If they are not trying hard to succeed, they will be punished by being sent home. These guys want to do well, want to become part of the team. That all by itself creates an atmosphere that you see all around you.

"I'm under-black," Siegfried had told me, explaining that by 1987 many blacks had figured out that getting trained as a rifleman did not lead to a high-paying job in civilian life after leaving the military. So blacks were favoring what Siegfried called "the soft skills," like those of computer operators, nurses, mechanics, administrators—all training that was more likely to impress a civilian employer than a sharpshooting rifleman or antitank gunner. In 1984, 15.4 percent of the 25,888 infantry trainees who had gone through Benning were black. The proportion of blacks had declined to 12.1 percent in 1987 when 24,970 men were in training, according to Benning's figures.

"This new atmosphere, this desire to succeed in the Army is part of the renewal of national pride," Siegfried continued. "A lot of it came out of Washington, D.C., from Ronald Reagan. There's a new renaissance that we can feel down here and see in the new soldiers. There's a new 'Let's come to grips with Vietnam' feeling. Finally we're saying, 'Hey, it's an honorable thing to be a service-man or woman.' It's an upsurge that we in the training command can build on if we're smart about the way we train these new soldiers.

"I want to make very, very sure that we teach the skills that a Skill Level One infantryman needs to know to keep himself alive and to function as an individual member of an infantry unit. I want him to know those skills so well that he can call them back instantly.

"The first time a bullet whizzed by my ear in Vietnam, I was scared to death. And I was the company commander! The first ten to fifteen minutes of that engagement I was looking after Steve. I hate to admit that to you, but I've got to tell you the truth. I didn't call back what I had learned here in Officers' Candidate School and all those other places. I called back what old Carl Burton, my drill sergeant, had taught me: 'Do a low crawl; a high crawl; put a rifle to your shoulder; make a target fall.' I want my guys to be able to call that back instantly."

I felt as I left Siegfried's office that the young men I had seen transformed in thirteen weeks would do well in a firefight if they had sergeants as good as Stover and officers as good as Fleenor. These apprentice infantrymen were looking forward to gradua-tion, which was the Army's formal way of marking their passage from raw volunteer to blue-corded infantryman. One of what

Siegfried had called the "very few, very special." Trainees were telephoning and writing parents and girlfriends to fly to Fort Benning to see them graduate. I was looking forward to the graduation of my boys as well. I listened to a group of them shouting out their new-found pride as a cadence as they marched along a road weaving through the barracks of Sand Hill:

> *We're standing tall;*
> *We're looking good.*
> *We ought to be in Hollywood.*
> *One-two; three-four.*

# 9. Graduation

The big day of graduation—October 9, 1987—broke chilly but clear. Parents from all over the United States had flown to Fort Benning to watch this event marking the metamorphosis of their sons from boy to soldier. I talked with many of them as they gathered in clots around the cement plaza under Albanese Barracks to catch a glance of their sons before the formal ceremony on the parade ground a short distance away. Black parents were dressed up the most, with several fathers wearing dark suits and ties. I wondered as I studied them whether this was because seeing their sons formally certified as United States infantrymen was a more solemn moment for them than for the more casually dressed white relatives. I knew that several of the black graduates, including James E. Proctor II and Steven Henson, had been bounced from one ghetto apartment to another while growing up. So for their relatives, the graduation signified that they were indeed getting higher in their hard climb up the mountain.

Of the 209 young men who had gotten off the bus in July to report to Delta Company and undergo Shock Treatment, 183 would graduate this day. Of the original starters, four had attempted suicide to end the pain of Army training. One would graduate today and the other three had been sent home. The rest of the missing had been discharged for physical reasons, such as vulnerability to heat; been held over for more training, as in the case of Selvester; been adjudged unfit for military service. One trainee had been yanked from the graduation list at the last minute when the FBI notified Delta Company that he was wanted for a long list of drug crimes.

I talked with parents about the transformation of their sons. The most common comment I heard was: "He's so much quieter. More mature."

I was braced to meet a distraught Karen Selvester who had flown all the way from California only to learn her son would not graduate because he never did push out that forty-second push-up to pass his final physicals. But instead of encountering a tearful mother and son, I found the happiest couple I had ever seen holding each other, laughing, crying, talking. Karen Selvester and her remade son were joyous to be reunited after thirteen weeks of mutual trauma. Graduation could wait. They had each other.

"Isn't she great?" Tweety asked me, holding out his mother to me on the plaza under Albanese Barracks where the then-overweight boy had suffered through Shock Treatment thirteen weeks earlier.

I asked Karen Selvester: "Has your boy changed?"

"Oh yes!" she said, giving him another hug and smile.

Steve Henson's mother, Betty, was there to salute her son for having made it through. So were Mr. and Mrs. Norman L. Adkins. They had flown from West Virginia to witness their son graduate and receive two awards. Doctors had warned Mr. Adkins that he was too sick to make the trip. He told me he was not going to miss Norman's graduation, even if it killed him. Relatives of the former bad boys, Budweiser and Glen, also had flown to Georgia to be uplifted by the sight of these teenagers achieving the biggest success of their young lives.

We all left the plaza for the parade ground. We filed into the grandstand while cold still held the morning. I sat in a front bleacher seat with Jim Fleenor. The troops stood off in the distance, at the far end of the parade ground, dressed in jungle fatigues and carrying their M-16 rifles. The relatives struggled to identify their soldier, whose face was obscured by his helmet. There were squeals of, "There he is!" and much camera-clicking before the loudspeaker boomed out the sobering poem, "I Am the Infantry." The poem opened with these lines:

"I am the Infantry—Queen of Battle. For two centuries I have kept our nation safe, purchasing freedom with my blood. To tyrants, I am the day of reckoning; to the suppressed, the hope of the future. Where the fighting is thick, there am I. I am the Infantry! Follow Me!"

First Sergeant Ted Williams, facing the reviewing stand, boomed out from the heart of the formation that the men standing on the parade ground were now infantrymen ready to take their posts for America anywhere in the world. The band played; men marched; parents cried. I felt engulfed in their sea of emotion. I wrote down what I thought many of them must be feeling:

"OK, Brother. I got no stocks; I got no bonds. I ain't rich. But that's my boy out there defending America. He's a United States infantryman. He's doing something great. He made it. He's a somebody for the rest of his life. Nobody's going to take this day away from him. Nobody's going to take this day away from me. That's my boy out there, America. See him? He's standing tall. So am I. And I don't care who knows it."

The time in the ceremony came to present the distinguished honor graduate of Delta Company, the most outstanding soldier of the 209 who started infantry training in July. Out of the ranks stepped James E. Proctor II, the young man who had grown up in the ghettos of New Jersey; had fallen in with hoodlums in West Germany; had changed course in high school and resolved to live up to the Army's recruiting slogan, "Be all you can be." He had done just that in the crucible of Sand Hill.

Other trainees were called forward to be honored. Norman Adkins made his parents prouder than ever when the West Virginia soldier marched to the podium twice—once to receive the "excellence in infantry skills" award and a second time to be presented the medal for "excellence in physical readiness."

Also singled out for distinction were many members of the new Charlie Company. Michael A. "Chief" Austerman—the former Navy man who found civilian life so boring he joined the infantry—received the award for excellence with the TOW anti-tank weapon; Chris Cashman, the 26-year-old soldier who discovered he had stayed in Australia too long playing rugby, was promoted to the rank of E-2, halfway between a raw private and private first class.

Drill Sergeant Mario A. Zuniga, "Z Monster," won the coveted "Drill Sergeant of the Cycle Award." His 3d Platoon was named "Honor Platoon."

While sitting there feeling proud of the young men I had come to know and admire over the past thirteen weeks, I heard Lieutenant Colonel Gordon R. Lam, commander of the Second Battalion, call out my name, requesting that I come forward. He graciously presented me with a picture of Albanese Barracks with a metal plaque within the frame reading: "Thanks for seeing the other side of the tent."

The band struck up "Follow Me" and then the graduates of Delta Company, with flags flying, passed in review, looking "eyes right" toward the grandstand where their loved ones started crying all over again. The new infantrymen were soon a thin line moving up the hill toward Albanese Barracks where they would change into their Army greens and then be reunited with their families. For all the soldiers, whether their families came to graduation or not, the rest of Friday was free. The next day they would start yet another new life at their assigned duty station or go home for their first leave.

The men in 2d and 4th platoons, as soon as they were formed at Benning, had been designated to go to Fort Riley in the heart of Kansas right after graduation to become the new embodiment of the Charlie Company that fought in the jungle outside Courtenay rubber plantation twenty-one years earlier. They would remain welded together—no transfers to other units to pursue such original dreams as becoming a paratrooper—for three years. They would do their first year at Benning and Fort Riley and the following two years in West Germany. Only after this three-year period would the company break up. The Army called this experiment in togetherness COHORT, an acronym for cohesion, operational readiness and training. When the Army launched COHORT in 1980, it said the idea was to "determine the Army's capability of supporting a unit replacement system designed to reduce turbulence, improve stability and enhance the cohesion and readiness of units."

Rather than repeat the system of past wars where a lone, green soldier would report to a company to take the place of someone who had been wounded or killed, the Army wondered if an entire company could replace one in the line. In theory, the replacement company would be an experienced team skilled at fighting side by side. Too many confused, lone replacements got killed in their first hours of battle action for not knowing what to do, how to survive. COHORT advocates often cited the chilling quote from Major General Clarence R. Huebner, a World War II commander of the First Infantry Division, who in railing against sending green, confused, lone replacements to the front said: "We haven't time to dig graves. These boys don't last long enough to reach foxholes."

But would three years of togetherness within Charlie Company unify or divide? Would the men meld into a winning team through COHORT's bonding or a losing team as the men got sick of each other from constant rubbing together in the pressure cooker that is the infantry? I would follow Charlie Company long enough to find out. I had already heard from sergeants and officers at Benning that COHORT had turned out to be a bad idea. But the happy graduates did not know this. They were looking forward to flying to Riley and joining The Big Red One, First Infantry Division (Mechanized).

Captain Fleenor drove me to the airfield at Benning to fly with the new Charlie Company to Fort Riley. I thought it was classy of Drill Sergeants Rodriguez and Stover to take time out from their Saturday to come to the field to bid their former charges goodbye and wish them good luck. I felt enriched from coming to know Rodriguez, Stover and the other dedicated drills of Delta Company who had transformed the young men whose passage I had been chronicling. The drills had surprised and touched me a few hours earlier by presenting me with a statue of an infantryman with an inscription underneath that read: "Many thanks." Fleenor told me it had surprised him, too, that the drills had done that, commenting: "I guess we all like somebody who will listen to us."

Once airborne, the graduates took a last look down at Fort Benning with no sign of regret over leaving the base. They plugged earphones from their Walkmans into their ears, settled back to sleep or just stared silently into space. Their new captain and first sergeant, Michael McMahon and Russell Snyder, sat in front of the plane dividing on paper their unknown riflemen into the four platoons of the new Charlie Company.

"If you could get out of the Army right now with no penalty, would you do it?" I asked each of the sixty-six graduates on the plane. Just five of the sixty-six said they would get out. Most of the troopers said: "I'm glad I joined." They were less sure they could stand going through basic training for a second time. But knowing that basic and advanced individual training were behind them, they were looking ahead to a new kind of Army life at Fort Riley. There would be such a thing as off-duty, they had been told, when they could sleep with women, drink beer, watch television, read magazines, drive cars, buy junk food. This freedom alone was enough to make these freshly frocked infantrymen feel positive about going to a base called Fort Riley out on the Kansas plains.

When the airliner reached Kansas, everyone looked down at the brown prairie and wondered what the Army would have them doing there. Ty Barker and Chris Cashman had told their wives to travel to Fort Riley and look for places to live. Cashman studied the boxy buildings spread out below us and wondered which one held his wife, Kerry, and their newly born son he had not yet seen. Elation was rising inside him. He could not wait to hold his wife, their daughter and new son. Get this plane on the ground!

# 10. Fort Riley

Driving from the airport at Manhattan, "The Little Apple," toward the old cavalry outpost of Fort Riley disabused me of the notion that the Kansas prairie is flat. I felt instead as if I were driving through a rolling sea of brown grass with big waves peaking up above the horizon. I envisioned Lieutenant Colonel George A. Custer galloping around this rolling prairie with his Seventh Cavalry when it was stationed at Fort Riley in 1866 with the mission of keeping the trails and expeditions into the nation's new heartland safe from the Indians. Custer became famous on the morning of June 25, 1876, by disobeying orders to await a second column of cavalry and pushing ahead alone into a huge Indian encampment on the banks of the Little Bighorn River in the Montana Territory. His outnumbered force was wiped out by Indian braves. The cavalry's only known survivor of the Battle of the Little Bighorn was a severely wounded horse named Comanche. But once inside the old cavalry redoubt of Fort Riley, I discovered the Army has chosen to celebrate Custer as a hero, not shun him because he was an officer who disobeyed orders and got himself and the 266 men with him killed by the Sioux and Cheyenne Indians.

The high knob of prairie grass and limestone where the new soldiers of Charlie Company were checking into three-story, brick barracks turned out to be Custer Hill. A venerable home on the fort is called Custer House, and one of Riley's main roads is Custer Avenue. Walking around Custer Hill joshing with the young men

169

of Charlie Company, I felt the force of the prairie wind. Old hands told me that that wind would turn icy come winter and cut through everything in its path, including the infantryman's best cold-weather gear. The prairie wind already had the feel of winter in it. I knew we would be going out on the prairie soon to practice for the mock war against the Russians in California's Mojave Desert. How would these motivated but inexperienced teenaged infantrymen hold up staying out on the freezing prairie day after day and night after night?

The first days and nights at Riley, the new troops were too happy about regaining their freedom to worry about what was ahead of them on the prairie beyond Custer Hill. I ran into smiling troopers as I explored Riley. "I love this feeling of freedom," Steve Henson told me as we walked into the bowling alley together on Custer Hill to bowl a few games. He won. No drill sergeants kept the new men of Charlie Company from bowling, drinking beer at the noncommissioned officers' club or trying to find women and entertainment in Junction City, the town at the edge of the base.

I had heard Junction City was one of the junkiest cities in the United States, inspiring the nickname Junk City. I decided after exploring the crossroads on the prairie that the nickname was deserved. Driving across the Republican River Bridge into the town revealed one long, fine mesh net for soldiers' dollars. In just the first mile beyond the bridge I saw this parade of dollar catchers: U.S. Grant, A Drinking Establishment; Alibi; Hunan Chinese Restaurant; Oriental Foods; Pizza Palace; Popingo Movie Rentals; Devon Home Center "where you can get easy credit"; Riverbend trailer court; Rib House Bar-B-Q; Domino's Pizza; liquor store; A-1 Taxi Co.; Avenue Coin Laundry; Hollywood Supper Club—Wet T-Shirt Contest; Korean Martial Arts Academy; Rendezvous Lounge; Two Hour Cleaner and Laundry; Coin-a-Matic Laundry; Kim's Used Furniture; liquor store; Jim Clark used cars; Mercury Finance Loans; Cottonwood Trailer Park. The rest of the miles of Junction City's downtown went like that as well. It looked like blatant "gimme, gimme, gimme" with no inviting classy bar or restaurant in sight.

Taking to the sidewalk, I met Precious on Eleventh Street just off the main thoroughfare, named Washington Street. She was a black prostitute who said she had already met some of the boys freshly arrived from Fort Benning. They were starving for her love, she said, but she had not raised her price above the standard

"$40 for one time." She added that her services were available right now for the same price and pointed to a small wooden building down an alley. I laughed and wished her well, continuing on down the sidewalk while she clicked off toward the parked Buick Regal where she sat hour after hour beckoning to GIs strolling along Washington Street in a usually vain search for girls their own age. Most of the bars of Junction City refused to serve the teenaged soldiers, driving them into the noncommissioned officers' clubs on base where beer was easier to come by, 21 or not. Junction City got no better during the rest of my walking tour. It seemed to be a string of used-car lots, dreary bars, tacky shops and fast-food eateries. It was obvious that the year the men of Charlie Company would have to serve at Riley would seem like five years to the privates lusting for young girls and bright lights.

Driving Ty Barker, Chris Cashman and their wives around Junction City in my rental car to look for places to live, I learned how young married soldiers with little rank had to live at Fort Riley. Riley's housing office had told the wives that the fort had no housing for families of such low rank. The only housing in Junction City within their price range turned out to be mobile homes in grim trailer parks featuring sagging trailers, disassembled cars and weedy patches of grass. The going price for the exhausted-looking, two-bedroom trailers was from $200 to $300 a month, not counting the cost of electricity and other utilities, which would be high in the severe winter ahead. I saw the trailers had no walls under them and wondered how the young wives would cope when cold wind shot up through the trailer floors. The Barkers and Cashmans rented trailers across the highway from each other. It was obvious to them that they would have to buy cars for shopping and escape.

Back inside the fort, I explored the winding, tree-lined streets of the main post, where high-ranking officers lived. The contrast with the privates' trailer homes was dramatic. I saw stately homes built of blocks of yellow limestone with broad porches inviting leisurely Sunday brunches or summer evening cocktails. Most of the porches turned around the front corner of the houses, softening the hard appearance of the limestone walls. I envisioned the good times that must have taken place inside those houses during the early 1900s when cavalrymen were the kings of the laid-back Army. The homes obviously had living and dining rooms big enough for dancing. How many parties had this block known in those gentler times when the horse helped glamorize Army life and the Bomb that changed everything had not yet been invented?

Fort Riley sponsored a formal welcoming ceremony for new arrivals the second Monday we were there. I filed into the movie theater on the main base with my boys from Benning to hear the lectures. The first speaker was a sergeant who sounded disconnected from the post-Vietnam Army, from the volunteers sitting in the audience in front of him. Standing on the movie theater stage, the sergeant spoke as if he assumed these still-forming teenagers were like the hardened bums of the *From Here to Eternity* army and needed to hear his version of soldier-to-soldier talk:

"Now, when you were going with your wife, you took her to some good restaurants. Where do you take her now? Burger King and McDonalds. I'm telling you true, right?

"With all due respect to everyone," the sergeant standing on the stage continued, "your drawers have poop stains in them, and your wife has to wash that. Think about it, married male soldier.

"You been in a restaurant, and the kid is in a high chair and he throws up all over you and your food. What did you do? You gave it to your wife.

"Your wife has got to put up with all that stuff. Your wife is the most important person in your life. Take care of your wife and children.

"Don't go out and get a disease and give it to her and blame it on her for giving it to you. Your wife is supposed to be the beautifulest person in your life. Abuse is a crime. Your wife was not made to be beaten on.

"If you have an urge for sex, don't take it out on the child. To rape a child is totally insane."

The sergeant's speech was interrupted by the bang of doors being opened in the back of the theater and the clatter of many boots.

"Attention!"

We all stood for the entrance of Brigadier General Jerry R. Rutherford, assistant division commander. He welcomed the new arrivals to Riley, declaring that in joining the First Infantry Division (Mechanized), The Big Red One, "You've joined an elite division." He told the young infantrymen that their mission was "to train to go to war if deterrence fails." A few more welcome-

172

aboard words and he was gone, walking out quickly the same way he came in, entourage in tow.

Division Sergeant Major Julio Diaz took over the welcoming ceremony. He projected warmth and wit and caring, offsetting the message of low expectations issued by the sergeant who preceded him.

"They say Kansas is in the middle of nowhere," Diaz told the young soldiers who had just been dumped on an isolated prairie. "It's in the middle of the United States.

"They say if you wanted trees, you had to bring them with you. That's lies. Since 1917 we've been planting them.

"They say we have no hills in Kansas. They're full of shit."

"Some say there's no big town around Fort Riley. You've got Salina and Kansas City and seven different gymnasiums to keep you skinny."

Diaz turned fatherly, warning the young troopers about the used cars Junction City dealers would try to sell them.

"Your warranty expires two hours after you leave the lot. They're put together with Krazy Glue."

On payday, Diaz continued, some woman will ask: " 'Hey, you want to come to my house for a drink?' You'll never make it to the house."

He told the new infantrymen that they were not allowed to wear Army fatigues in a restaurant or liquor store. He ordered them to act and dress like squared-away soldiers in town as well as on the base. "You are a soldier twenty-four hours a day. If you see a guy with a ragged shirt, he's one of those National Guard or Reserve guys."

The speakers went on too long. Soldiers began nodding off. One of their new sergeants ran around waking them up. He ordered the ones completely asleep to stand in the back of the theater while the lectures droned on.

I thought these leaders of The Big Red One had missed an opportunity to link this newly arrived COHORT company to the division with words that would inspire them to grab the First Infantry Flag and hold it high. Here were teenagers longing to belong to something bigger than themselves. Many of them came to Riley with a grudge against The Big Red One because the Army at the Benning reception station had forced them into the COHORT Company destined for Riley. They had hoped to go into the paratroopers or Rangers. They needed words to offset their resentment at being ordered into the mechanized infantry. I knew from my seven months aboard the aircraft carrier USS *John F. Kennedy* that teenagers can be made to feel pride in their ship or outfit. The *Kennedy* is far from the Navy's newest aircraft carrier. But her officers managed to communicate to every new man who reported aboard the *Kennedy* that he had just joined a special ship, a special group of men entrusted to sail her. This spirit, generated time after time, has kept the *Kennedy* a winner in the fleet year after year. I felt as I sat in the dank movie theater at Riley that the show-me new soldiers joining The Big Red One from Benning could have used an uplifting, inspirational welcome—like the one Major Mark P. Hertling heard and then wrote about in *Military Review:*

The colonel, whom Hertling did not identify, addressed his new troops

in an uncharacteristically soft voice, one which could almost not be heard in the back of the auditorium. He was telling a story about one of his tours in Vietnam when he was a lieutenant. His unit had been ambushed by a North Vietnamese army unit. Most of the soldiers in the company were killed in the first few minutes of battle. The Colonel found himself the ranking man.

While performing the critical leadership tasks of redistributing ammunition and repositioning those who were still alive, the Colonel found Specialist Fourth Class David K. Stoddard. Stoddard was bleeding profusely from a stomach wound, the result of a mortar round that landed nearby. Stoddard was pushing his intestines back into his body with leaves and twigs intermixed between his fingers and stomach. The Colonel realized two things as he approached this soldier: Stoddard was going to die, and Stoddard knew it . . .

On one of his checks of the perimeter, he tried comforting Stoddard by telling him he would be all right, and that the unit would stop the enemy. He then asked Stoddard if he could hold on just a little longer. On 26 February 1968, on Hill 614, Specialist Four David K. Stoddard spoke his last words in answering that question: "No sweat, sir. You can count on me. We'll stop 'em."

Several years later, the Colonel visited David's mother, Mrs. Mary Stoddard. As he was leaving, she posed one question: "They won't remember him, will they? No one will remember my David or care about any of the things he was fighting for." He replied, "Miss Mary, as long as I'm alive they'll always remember your son."

The Colonel began walking off the stage, but turned back to his new soldiers in case they had not received the message: "You're all heroes. It's too bad some of you don't let everyone know it every day. The way I look at it, any soldier in this Army who goes AWOL or who doesn't do his job so someone else has to, or who doesn't wear his uniform with pride—well, it's almost like they're pissing on the grave of David K. Stoddard."

I knew the freshly graduated infantrymen of Charlie Company would have flamed up inside if they had heard such a speech. Instead they heard about poop in their underwear. I knew the new troops were better than that. I knew the First Infantry Division was better than that. And I knew that the Army of 1987 was better than that. But the new arrivals did not know that. We walked out of the movie theater. The troops formed up. Their new sergeants ordered the men to do push-ups in the parking lot for falling asleep during the welcoming remarks. Some welcome, I thought to myself, for men who had been forced into a COHORT company bound for Germany; had trained intensively for thirteen weeks at Benning; had not taken the customary leave after graduating from basic and advanced training, meaning they could not go home and see their families and friends and show off their Class A greens; had been flown instead directly to Riley in the middle of nowhere with the warning that they would be out in the field for weeks to get ready for National Training Center maneuvers. I saw trouble ahead and wondered who was making these decisions already dispiriting the new Charlie Company.

Leaving the theater area and the new troopers "on your face," I wandered through the new cavalry museum nearby in hopes of getting some perspective on mechanized infantry before going out in the field to see it in action. Many of the cavalrymen, I learned, dismounted from their horses after reaching the edge of the battle area. They proceeded on foot with their rifles to fight like regular infantrymen, not to swing sabers down on enemy soldiers from atop their horses. The horses for these dismounted cavalrymen were taxicabs to get them near the action in a hurry. General Douglas MacArthur in 1933 made the case for a better taxi than the horse in a statement displayed in the U.S. Cavalry Museum at

Riley: "The horse has no higher mobility today than he had a thousand years ago." How that statement must have infuriated the never-say-die cavalrymen of the day. The cavalrymen would not give up on the horse even during World War II, as evidenced in the museum by the model of a horse wearing a goofy-looking gas mask during chemical warfare training at Riley in 1942. But MacArthur and his allies ultimately won out. Armored taxis replaced the horse for getting riflemen to the edge of the battle, to the dismay of the cavalrymen who knew glory at Riley before war became so complicated and dangerous for the mud soldier. The men of the new Charlie Company were to learn how to drive and ride in these mechanical horses in the coming months. The Army still says soldiers "dismount" from these armored vehicles.

"This is what I joined the Army for—excitement!" James E. Proctor II yelled over to me from the vehicle that had replaced the horse for taking men to the battle area. It is a metal box with treads called an M-113 armored personnel carrier. Its nicknames were "APC" and "track." Proctor and I were among the new arrivals from Benning learning to drive the M-113. Proctor was anxious to take his track up and down the hills and valleys of the rolling trail he was driving. "Let's go! Let's go!"

I was in the driver's seat of the track next to Proctor's, enjoying driving it every bit as much as he was. A big gas pedal is on the floor. A simple gear shift is near your right knee. Two upright rods, called laterals, come up from the floor. The left lateral controls the left track and the right lateral the right one. Pull back on the left lateral, and the left tread slows or stops to enable you to swing left. Pull back on the right lateral, and you turn right. I found driving the track was like sailing a sailboat. The less you fidgeted with the controls, the smoother the ride.

The old M-113 had plenty of guts left, pulling itself out of stream beds and clanking up the steep bank. But I found riding in the back of the track no fun at all, especially if the roof hatch was closed and a hot-rod was driving up front. Everything was worse at night. You bounced against the hard walls and fittings, got your feet caught in the litter of boxes and other gear on the floor of the track, stepped on someone else or felt him stepping on you. I smashed two watches against the steel insides of the track before I wised up and stopped wearing one. I also learned how to brace my body so it did not bang into steel as we jolted along inside the track. For all the discomfort, I heard little bitching from these new GIs who got bounced a lot more than I did inside the tracks. They just went with the flow, even breaking into song once in a while. I marveled anew at the resilience and dedication of the American soldier as we jolted day and night along the prairie trying to be mechanized infantry good enough to defeat a simulated Soviet motorized rifle regiment in the make-believe war in the Mojave Desert five weeks hence.

In Vietnam the United States deployed the M-113 we were practicing with to a limited extent. Israel used the M-113 with great success in the Sinai Desert. But modern guns are far ahead of the M-113. The sides of the vehicle would not stop Soviet fire. Everyone inside an M-113 would almost certainly die if the vehicle was hit with one of these new weapons that would send shrapnel ricocheting all around the inside of the hull that carried up to nine soldiers. I decided I would prefer to walk rather than ride in a combat zone. Walking would at least give the illusion of controlling your fate. It would also avoid the bruising bumps, smells generated by sweaty and flatulent troopers and the claustrophobia of being buttoned up inside a steel box. The Army has high hopes for its new taxicab, the Bradley Fighting Vehicle, which is replacing the M-113. Thank you, Army. But I would still rather walk when the shooting starts.

We started to walk down the tank trail as darkness pushed the last shards of October daylight out of the sky. Captain Michael J. McMahon, Charlie Company commander, wanted to get the troops Benning had just sent him accustomed to soldiering in the dark. He knew that much of the fighting they would do at the National Training Center in the Mojave Desert at Fort Irwin, California, would be conducted at night. Charlie Company, despite its lack of experience, would be part of the Second Battalion of the Sixteenth Infantry Regiment which the Army had chosen to fight a Soviet motorized rifle regiment at the National Training Center (NTC) for two weeks, starting right after Thanksgiving. Companies that go to the NTC usually have more experience than this new edition of Charlie Company. The battles would be highly realistic. The simulated Soviet regiment would use actual Soviet armor or look-alikes; employ actual Soviet tactics while enjoying the 3-to-1 edge in manpower confronting the North Atlantic Treaty Organization along the European front. As in the mock battles in the last days of training at Benning, MILES equipment would be used so the referees could tell who killed whom in the two weeks of day and night battles in the Mojave Desert. McMahon wanted his new company to do well even though he had green officers and green troops and had never been in combat himself. He intended to press everyone in the company hard.

I was carrying a light pack and sleeping bag and stumbling like everyone else over the trail's black clumps of dirt, which had been kicked up by the steel treads of M-1 tanks and M-113 armored personnel carriers. Feeling the ice in the October air, I mused how quickly winter comes to Kansas. Suddenly the soldier struggling along in front of me with that damned Dragon antitank missile on his back pitched forward. He belly flopped toward the rough ground. The Dragon swung under him. His rib cage smashed onto the bulbous ring at the end of the Dragon tube.

I rushed up to the fallen soldier and saw it was Edward W. Giroux, 17, of Weymouth, Massachusetts. He had rolled over on his back and was writhing with pain. I feared he had cracked or broken some ribs on the Dragon. Son of a carpenter, Giroux had told me he had joined the Army with high hopes for adventure as a paratrooper while putting money away for college. The company evacuated Giroux to the rear. His injuries turned out to be only bruises. I carried Giroux's Dragon on out to the bivouac area in the dark. Its unwieldiness refueled my contempt for this obsolete antitank weapon which we have inflicted on the American foot soldier.

"Mr. Wilson," Norman Adkins asked when we reached the campsite. "Sleep in our tent. Murray and me are short. There's plenty of room."

Another trooper heard the invitation, glanced at the two fireplugs named Adkins and Murray and quipped: "Mr. Wilson, I see two stumps in front of me." Adkins was 5 feet 4 inches tall and David Sean "Smurf" Murray, 20, of New Cumberland, West Virginia, an even 5 feet. I had developed deep affection for these two Smurfs from West Virginia. Adkins talked endlessly to Murray about settling on a farm together in West Virginia after they finished their Army careers. Murray, also a former high school wrestling champion, listened to Adkins but did not commit himself. Murray had already married his high school sweetheart, Ruth, and they had a baby girl, Heather.

"I had lots of scholarship offers" as a result of being named the outstanding wrestler of the Ohio Valley Conference, Murray told me while the three of us stood in the tall grass outside the tent, schmoozing. "I didn't want to go to college. And you had to know somebody to get a job at the brick factory near me. Things were closing down. Worked at the racetrack as a busboy for $3.35 an hour. Then my fiancée got pregnant. Figured the Army would pay for the baby. I plan to make the Army my career. I want to be able to retire young and spend the rest of my life doing what I want to do."

I declined the offer of the tent and lay out instead on the open prairie under a sweet-smelling hemlock. I studied the stars and listened to the barking of coyotes foraging somewhere close by. I rejoiced that coyotes had survived in spite of Army tanks and troop carriers tearing up their territory.

During the coldest part of the night, I heard the sergeant wake up Adkins and Murray and order them to put on their BDUs (battle dress uniforms) and helmets to stand guard over the camp. The young soldiers did not bitch about drawing the detail. I heard Adkins say, "OK, Sergeant." I admired the uncomplaining way these soldiers left their warm sleeping bags to stand out on the frosty prairie practicing for a war that might never come.

It was still dark and cold when the troopers were roused for stand-to, the procedure of getting ready to repel a surprise, pre-dawn attack. After stand-to, we went to the truck that had brought out breakfast from the chow hall at Custer Hill. I rejoined Adkins and Murray outside their tent. There was slack time. Time to talk. Even to get philosophical.

Adkins and I compared notes on the coyotes we had heard during the night. He said he not only had heard the coyotes but had smelled them. "My daddy taught me how to smell out animals during our hunting trips back home." Then the dedicated mud soldier looked at me uncertainly and said: "Mr. Wilson, may I ask you a question? Why is there this feeling against us in some places when we're doing the job nobody else wants to do?"

I had not heard a soldier ask that question since my combat reporting days in Vietnam in 1968 and 1972. I did not think the new generation of soldiers sensed such resentment among civilians, especially if they came from a pro-military state like West Virginia. I fumbled for the answer. I told Adkins that most of the country appreciated what he was doing. "Hey," I said, "you'll be a hero back home in West Virginia."

179

"That's true," Adkins agreed with a smile. "My mom said to be sure to wear my Class As," the Army's dress green uniform.

The daylight training consisted mainly of the new soldiers of Charlie Company sitting on an open patch of ground and listening to their platoon sergeants lecture them on old subjects, such as how to use the Dragon and LAW antitank missiles, how to string communications wire. The Army's idea for training soldiers seems to be repeat, repeat, repeat no matter how boring it gets. Doggerel helped relieve the monotony of sergeants standing in the grass reading out of training manuals or saying the obvious one more time. The Dragon gunner, for example, is supposed to determine if his Dragon missile has gone bad in storage by reading a humidity meter on it before firing the weapon. If the color was blue, the Dragon was ready to fire. If the color was white, the missile had a 50-50 chance of firing and leaving the tube when the trigger was pulled. If the color was pink, the Dragon was unsafe to fire even if a Soviet tank was charging into the company. The memory crutch was: "blue is true; white's all right; pink stinks." The sergeants' instruction made me more convinced than ever that Dragon gunners in a real war would simply "lose" those risky weapons on the battlefield.

I talked at length during training breaks to one of Charlie Company's veteran sergeants. He was in despair at receiving only sixty-six troopers from Benning instead of the expected eighty-six. Adding Riley's thirty commissioned and noncommissioned officers, the new Charlie Company would total only ninety-six men, fewer than the 134 in the old Charlie Company that fought near the Courtenay rubber plantation in 1966, unless the togetherness restraints of COHORT were broken and Charlie received more men from other units. Additional full-time riflemen were lost to the need to make them drivers of the M-113 tracks.

"When you really look at it," said the sergeant, "one sergeant gets three soldiers to train out here because the drivers are back at the base learning how to drive tracks. The CO [commanding officer] can say we're going to kill 'em at the National Training Center next month. But I've been there before. Be realistic. We're going to get waxed.

"I have to give the basics to them out here because they're all green soldiers, and I'm supposed to get them ready for NTC. They're going to hate the Army because it's basic training all over again. And then they're going to have to train again when they get back here from NTC.

"COHORT units are terrible. People get sick of each other, having to stick together for three years. The COHORT units have more suicides, more AWOLS."

He and other members of the Army's middle management, including some officers, told me that the generals did not seem to realize the polarization that can take place in a company that is frozen in size and personnel for three years. They said illness and other unforeseen development always results in troopers leaving a COHORT unit. Army personnel chiefs do not fill these vacancies in the interest of preserving cohesiveness, I was told, resulting in shifting more of the load on the relatively few men in an infantry unit who already do most of the work. I was told that the previous COHORT Charlie Company that came from Benning to Riley became dangerously polarized. I confirmed through legal authorities that two soldiers in the previous Charlie Company had been convicted of murdering a third private on April 20, 1985. The murderers—Private Wayne R. Partridge and Private Timothy Scott Kennan—shot Private Francis R. Badame with a crossbow and then beat him to death with a trench shovel, according to court records. His body was found in a shallow grave on the banks of the Republican River in Junction City.

Even applying my usual discount for healthy soldier bitching and allowing that the crossbow murder was a freak event that could happen anywhere, I concluded out there on the cold Kansas prairie that these sergeants who actually have to take green soldiers to war had made an impressive case against Army personnel chiefs who kept privates and sergeants glued together in the same COHORT outfit for three years.

The drizzly Sunday of October 25, 1987, on the prairie almost killed Steve Henson and his dream of completing his Army tour and returning to Baltimore to become a policeman "to do good." I had slept out with the company in the woods off abandoned farm fields the previous rainy night. In the morning I joined Johnny Libs's old 2d Platoon for the day's training. We started off the day with a church service and after breakfast spent most of the morning walking through the wet woods searching for a part that the brush had pulled off the M-60 machine gun Kevin Brewton, 18, of Beatrice, Alabama, was carrying. Lieutenant John Kiser, who planned to become a chaplain after serving as an infantry platoon leader and staff officer, led the patrols in search of the lost part. We found it.

The drizzle turned to rain. The temperature dropped. It was absolutely miserable weather for the troops. Yet they were expected to give rapt attention to the platoon sergeant reading from a field manual the do's and don'ts for dismounting from an M-113 APC. We stood under trees to reduce the amount of ice-water rain going down our necks. The platoon wore rubber boots, rubber jackets, rubber pants. But the pre-winter cold and wet still penetrated. I suppose the Army has reasons for keeping troops out in the rain on a Sunday in peacetime to listen to a sergeant read haltingly from a manual rather than give such instruction in a warm classroom on the base, but I could not fathom those reasons at the time or since. It just seemed to be practicing misery for no apparent gain in knowledge—certainly not in enthusiasm for the infantry. Why not study how much so-called "collective" training is necessary to keep a company ready to fight? Would teenaged math students learn more math if they were kept in class from 8 A.M. to 6 P.M.? Would standing them out in the rain to listen to the teacher read out of the math book teach them anything? I doubted it. Why this Army fear of letting soldiers study college courses, rest or play basketball when there is no meaningful work to do or the weather is miserable? Why all this make-work and motion to no end in peacetime? Is there no Army leader who dares to break the mold and give these new, brighter troops interesting work to do rather than just keep everybody moving under the old "asses and elbows" syndrome? I realized out there on the prairie that it was easier for the Army just to keep doing the same old, unimaginative training in regular units rather than change. But I felt Army leaders were prematurely ending their golden age of recruiting by making training so damn boring and unnecessarily uncomfortable. The kids, I figured, would never sign up for seconds once their enlistments expired if this was all there was to being all you can be.

While I was standing under a tree in the rain with one platoon, Steve Henson was marching in the wet with another. Platoon Leader Lieutenant Eric Hungerford had misjudged what the weather would do once they set out from the base camp. He figured the morning drizzle would not turn into rain. Unlike the troops I was with, Henson and his fellow soldiers had no rain

# GRADUATION

At last.   (*Washington Post* photograph by Dudley M. Brooks)

Kristian "Tweety" Selvester and his mother, Karen, are reunited.

# CAPTAIN JAMES R. FLEENOR II

# HAIL AND FAREWELL

vard Green greets family at graduation.

"I made it!" Marcus Foreman tells folks.

Have to say goodbye.

Author flies with Benning graduates to Fort Riley.

# OUR NEW SOLDIERS

Christopher Cashman.
(*Washington Post* photograph by Dudley M. Brooks)

Marcus Foreman.

Nathaniel Brown.

Mark Grant.

Glen Norton.

Glenn Dowe.

Ty "Spank" Barker.

Kevin Brewton.

Aaron Henson.

Eric Harbour.

Patrick Dickerson.

# FORT RILEY

James E. Proctor II in M-113 track.

Norman Adkins sights in cursed Dragon antitank weapon.

First Sergeant Russell Snyder.

Sergeant Ronald Reichle.

# FIGHTING THE "RUSSIANS"

Captain Michael J. McMahon plots Charlie Company attack in Mojave Desert at the National Training Center.

Tired troops have heard it all before.

Observer-Controller (on stool) tells Charlie Company officers why they lost the battle.

Sean and Ruth Murray with daughter Heather.

Ty and Rhonda Barker (*left*) with Kerry and Christopher Cashman and their two chil
in Junction City trailer park.

jackets, no rain pants and no rubber galoshes over their black boots. Henson had told the medic before his platoon started out for the patrol in the rain that he felt sick. The medic found congestion in Henson's lungs. Hungerford decided against leaving Henson in the rear and brought him along on what he thought would be an unstrenuous patrol. Henson afterward reconstructed for me what had happened to him.

"After breakfast the whole platoon rounded up. Had me carrying the Viper [antitank weapon] and M-16. It was drizzling a little bit. We didn't have our raincoats at all. Walked a mile out there, and rain starts coming down hard. None of the guys had their raincoats, so Lieutenant Hungerford says, 'Let's find cover.' But before he said go for cover, we stood in the rain.

"We started walking along again. Then we found cover under some trees. Lieutenant Hungerford assigned three guys to go back and get our raincoats for us. These guys took one and a half hours to get back. By the time they got back, everybody was drenched to the bone.

"Before the boys got back, Lieutenant Hungerford taught a class out there in the rain under the trees. We're standing there, and he's trying to teach us about reconn patrol, using little sticks in the ground and everything. He saw the guys weren't into it because of the rain. The mud was 2 to 3 inches thick. Our boots were drenched through. We had no galoshes. Just these black boots. We went out unprepared.

"I was feeling drowsy and dizzy and coughing and wheezing and shivering. I've learned whenever you tell a sergeant or an officer you're sick, they totally blank you out. They always think you're trying to get out of training.

"A command sergeant major saw us and said to Hungerford, 'It's cold; it's raining. You can put your guys in the back of the truck so they can eat their MRE's [cold Meals Ready to Eat, which come in a plastic case]. He had to tell a lieutenant this. He should have known this.

"I was feeling really bad. The command sergeant major told us he would give us some hot water. I was really feeling scared. I felt myself drooling. I had trouble breathing. I made some hot chocolate with the hot water. It tore my body up.

"Sergeant [Bobby] Miller called us out of the truck, 'Let's go, let's go.' He looked at me and said, 'You all right, Henson?' I said

183

'I'm not.' He said, 'Well, don't worry, you'll make it.' I just looked at him.

"We walked. I was staggering. I just couldn't walk straight. We got about seven minutes away from the truck, and I just fell flat on my face. I was shivering and shaking and everything.

"First person I saw was Sergeant [Willie] Glover. Sergeant Glover was at the end of the line, but he was the first one there. That told me something right away. He told me, 'You'll be OK. You'll be OK.'

"He was fussing at Miller because Miller didn't want to cut off my MILES equipment and my shirt and everything. I heard Glover say, 'I don't give a fuck. Cut this so the man don't die.' I couldn't breathe."

I checked with Miller afterward. He said Henson was confused about Miller's role. Miller said he worked as quickly as he could to cut off Henson's MILES gear. He added that he had recommended to Hungerford that Henson be excused from the patrol.

"I took hold of Glover. They kept saying, 'Let him go, let him go.' Even though I tried, I couldn't do it. I was really scared. I couldn't breathe or anything.

"I saw Cashman looking down on me. I heard him say, 'Hang in there, Henson. Hang in there, man. You got a girl back there just waiting for you. Donna. And I can't live without you. Come on. You're a strong man.'

"I was dozing off. My eyes were closing. I was dying out. So the guys were saying, 'Keep your eyes open. Keep your eyes open.' Glover said, 'Come on man, react. Keep your eyes open.'

"I heard him, but I couldn't react. I heard them say, 'He's out! He's out!' "

At this crucial moment, Henson and I learned later, a medic from another unit maneuvering in the area shoved an antisuffocation tube in the shape of an L down Henson's throat to keep air going from his mouth into his lower throat. Another medic in the area, who luckily came to the field fully equipped, rushed up to Henson and clamped an oxygen mask over his face. The medic kept squeezing oxygen into Henson until he resumed normal breathing.

"I finally opened my eyes up. Every two or three minutes I was having small convulsions, throwing up and everything. At the same time I was hyperventilating. I was having hypothermia. I was scared. I was crying and everything. It was like death flashing in my mind, saying this is the time.

"I heard Glover say, 'You're going to live.' I said, 'No I'm not.' I saw Hungerford and Miller standing back. What kind of people are they?

"They carried me into a helicopter."

A doctor from the medical unit, which luckily was out training on the same Sunday, climbed into the helicopter with Henson.

"I was so scared. I really felt myself dying. The doctor in the helicopter told me: 'Your buddies down there did a good job. You almost died. They saved your life.'

"That Sergeant Glover showed me something. He stayed with me the whole time and said, 'You're going to make it.' "

I asked Hungerford afterward if he considered Henson's collapse serious. "He stopped breathing twice and passed out once," the lieutenant replied in characterizing the training accident as indeed serious.

Captain McMahon heard about my inquiries into Henson's collapse while we were still in the woods together and Henson was in the base hospital. He said he understood that I had to ferret out the facts but warned me that I might shake the confidence of the troops in the command in doing so. He was sincere in saying that, not threatening or nasty. But I did not see it his way at all. The troops, in my view, appreciated visible signs of interest and concern about one of their number. Their confidence in the command had already been shaken. My inquiries were not unlike their own in trying to find out what had really happened to their buddy that rainy Sunday in the wooded part of the prairie.

I accompanied McMahon to the hospital to visit Henson. The scared teenager had recovered by then. Doctors said Henson had an asthmatic condition. Henson told me he had never experienced such trouble in playing a variety of sports during high school. McMahon told the troops afterward that Henson had suffered a "minor" setback. The captain no doubt believed it was minor because this is what the hospital officials, who saw Henson only after the worst of his ordeal was over, told him. But the troops knew it was more than that. Inadvertently downplaying Henson's collapse that fellow soldiers considered serious opened up a credibility gap between the new soldiers of Charlie Company and their commanders that was to widen in the coming months. I thought back to how successful Second Lieutenant Raines's confession of command error had been in narrowing the credibility gap that had opened up when drill sergeants at Benning had overexercised many of their troops into heat injuries. "The command made mistakes today," Raines had told the troops the day of the heat injuries. The Benning battalion launched an investigation. Two drill sergeants received letters of reprimand. By contrast, it was business as usual at Charlie Company after Henson's collapse as far as the troops could tell. Troops complained to me that their officers and sergeants at Riley were not as interested in taking care of the troops as they were in advancing their careers. They noted that Hungerford was on his way to becoming a captain. They contended that their sergeants should know what they were teaching rather than read information out of a book. Perhaps these new arrivals from Benning were rushing to wrong judgments in their first month at Riley. But rightly or wrongly, this is the crucial time for the command to project interest in the troops' welfare.

Henson himself told me that what happened to him had killed his enthusiasm for the infantry but not for the whole Army. He said he was considering suing Hungerford and/or the Army. His mother, Betty, who had fought her way out of the ghetto, talked him out of it. Mrs. Henson told me later that she had told her son that "God decided it was not your time." She said she had urged her son to put the accident behind him and resume the pursuit of his dream. I realize from humping around with troops in Vietnam that infantrymen have to learn to put up with harsh conditions, including being cold and wet. I also realize that in peacetime a commander's priorities are supposed to be his men first, his mission second and himself third. I pondered the Henson incident from the leadership standpoint and wondered how the West German Army would have handled it. Contrary to the popular myth, the German army is a brotherly army. Leaders are supposed to be ceaseless in caring for their troops. Junior officers are expected to argue with senior officers before a decision is made. Commanders have wide latitude in deciding how to accomplish their missions. The German army outfought its opponents unit for unit during World War II, military histories document, but were overwhelmed ultimately by the mass of the allies arrayed against it. One of the German army's bedrock documents on leadership is "Truppenfuhrung" of 1936. It states officers must exhibit "cold-bloodedness, determination and courage" in combat to inspire his troops."He must, however, also find his way to his subordinates' hearts and gain their confidence by understanding their feelings and their thoughts. His care for them must never cease. Mutual confidence is the secure basis for discipline in times of need and danger. . . . The troops' forces must be conserved so that the highest demands can be made on them at the decisive moment. . . ."

Captain McMahon had a sign hanging in his office that read AN ORGANIZATION DOES WELL ONLY THOSE THINGS THE BOSS CHECKS. He was relentless in practicing his philosophy of micromanagement. His lieutenants felt his pressure continuously. Sergeants complained to me that his micromanagement resulted in the lieutenants trying to do the same thing with the sergeants, undercutting the sergeants' authority over their troops and often resulting in everybody working longer than necessary doing the same things twice. McMahon's leave-no-stone-unturned approach prompted several of his lieutenants to tell me, "He's sure to make general."

Maybe the lieutenants are right. They probably are, given the Army's obsession with "managers." But there was such a difference in the human engineering practiced by Captain Fleenor of Delta Company at Benning and Captain McMahon of Charlie Company at Riley. Fleenor loved soldiers as individuals and projected this. McMahon must have loved them, too, because he worked as hard as they in preparing them for war. He was as wet and cold as they. He did not stay in his office but went with them to the field. Yet, probably unfairly, this projected to the troops as "hard core" rather than caring. He got the nickname "Ranger Mac" from pushing his men so hard. He had earned his Ranger tab. First Sergeant Russell Snyder, a Vietnam veteran with a more laid-back style, projected caring to the men of Charlie Company. They returned his affection.

Yet despite McMahon's hard-charging style and difficulty in making small talk with his men, most of the critical troopers named him when I asked which officer they would feel safest with in battle. The point here is that training and leading soldiers and still having them feel you care more for them than yourself is one of the most complex and challenging jobs in the world. The hours are long, the pay is low and the appreciation may never be expressed. The country is lucky to have the Fleenors and McMahons in uniform to take on this challenge. I had no doubt that they would lay down their lives unquestioningly for their country, for their men. But it struck me at Riley that it is even more important and difficult for officers and sergeants to project caring to their men in peacetime than in wartime. The need for sacrifice is obvious during wartime.

I asked McMahon—who like Fleenor is a West Pointer, husband and father—why he had chosen the infantry for his Army career, where life is so hard in peacetime and so short in wartime.

"The chance to work with people," he replied, "to make them do things. The challenge. You're betting your own life and everyone else's on your ability, on your leadership."

I thought of the old Charlie Company that had run into a Vietcong base camp and ended up surrounded. I continued the colloquy: "Sure, it's a challenge. But if you're just 100 meters off in leading your men in combat, you get people killed. Isn't that excruciating to contemplate?"

"It's hard to explain when you think about it. That's why you have to take peacetime training seriously."

My time at Riley hardened my conviction that many of today's officers do not really know today's soldiers, although they think they do. Today's private is different in many important ways from the private in Johnny Libs's platoon a generation ago. Today's private has a dream for himself, which he expects the Army to help him fulfill. Today's officer needs to know this difference from personal exposure to the new soldier in an environment where the officer is a peer, not the authority figure.

I left Riley in late October after spending three weeks with the fresh infantry graduates from Benning in the field, in the barracks and in Junction City. I felt depressed as I departed. Their enthusiasm was evaporating. I feared Charlie Company would unravel as the men concluded the Army was not living up to the slogan that attracted them in the first place: "Be all you can be." I hoped fighting the mock Russians at the National Training Center in December would rekindle the fire in these mud soldiers I had come to know and admire. I would rejoin them in the Mojave Desert to watch the new Charlie Company fight its first "war."

# 11. Fighting the Russians

"Our job," said Captain McMahon, Charlie Company commander, "is to make them shoot at us so the tanks can shoot at them. That's the breaks. But their weapons," he said of the Russians, "aren't as good as ours, so we should be all right."

It was early December 1987, in the Mojave Desert outside Barstow, California. We were on a flat spot in that brownish red desert rimmed with mountains forming part of the world's biggest outdoor classroom for mechanized warfare, the Army's National Training Center.

Charlie Company had been flown to the edge of the battle area and then been driven to the base camp at Fort Irwin, California, on Thanksgiving weekend. Now it was camped out near the "enemy" in the Mojave Desert. The enemy was a simulated Soviet motorized rifle regiment armed with Russian armor and weapons. The regiment of specially trained Americans dressed as Russian troops would use the Soviet tactics of ganging up on a perceived weak spot in the American defenses and punching through it. The Russians would enjoy 3-to-1 odds or better at the spot they picked to penetrate, as would be the case along the North Atlantic Treaty Organization front line in Europe.

To win against such odds, the American battalion task force, which included Charlie Company, would have to employ its superior weaponry, principally the M-1 Abrams tank, at the right place and right time. Key to success in these battles would be knowing where the enemy was and driving him into a kill sack where tanks and artillery could kill him. Artillery, ditches and land mines all were supposed to be employed to drive the enemy into the killing zone chosen by the American forces.

"It's really not much different between what we're trying to do here and the Battle of Waterloo" in Belgium where the English defeated Napoleon in 1815, Colonel William West, commander of the observer-controllers, told me. The English drove Napoleon's cavalry into the squares of infantry where the English troops knocked the French off their horses and killed them, he noted. But here at the National Training Center, the desert was home to the Russians troops known as the OpFor, for Opposing Force. They would use stealth, the terrain and smoke to cover their movements in the desert.

Both sides would use rifles, antitank missiles, tank cannon, artillery, mortars, bombs and mines. Soldiers would know when they had been hit but would not die. They would be attacked with beams of light, laser beams, not lead or shrapnel. When you pulled the trigger on your M-16 rifle, Dragon antitank weapon or M-1 tank cannon, a laser beam would shoot out across the desert. If the simulated bullet hit a Russian soldier or the simulated Dragon missile his tank, sensors on the Russian's body would ring or his tank's rooftop light would flash yellow. The American soldiers dressed and armed like Russians would fire laser beams from their weapons back at the Americans the same way. The laser fire was part of the MILES (Multiple Integrated Laser Engagement System) the troops of Charlie Company had first used at Fort Benning. The MILES system would be one way to prove who won and who lost. The computerized printout of who did what would be another. The Army had wired the desert and focused camera eyes on it to show the combatants after the battle why they had lived or died.

This particular night Charlie Company was supposed to participate in a "deliberate attack." Its M-113 armored personnel carriers were to rumble across the desert floor to draw fire from the Russians hidden somewhere in the valley or on the mountain behind it known as The Whale because it looked like one.

The American M-1 tanks would shoot at the Russians and their vehicles once Charlie Company and other units located them. The M-113s, while drawing Russian fire, would try to get through it and taxi their infantry within a short hike of the enemy forces. Charlie Company troops might charge out of the tracks at some point and attack the Russians hidden in The Whale's crevices. It might get down to rifleman against rifleman in the dark desert.

It was 4 P.M. when I jumped in the M-113 commanded by Lieutenant Brian Strong, 1st Platoon leader. He was a tall, easy-going West Pointer who worked his troops hard but had their affection and respect. "If he tells you to jump off something, he will do it first," said one soldier. "But if you piss him off, he'll slam dunk you in a heartbeat." Strong told me he had chosen the infantry because "I wanted to be down to work with the men where it sucks the most. I like to work with people."

We pulled up the rear door of the track and started its powerful diesel engine. Brian and I stood with two other troopers on the floor of the vehicle so the upper third of our bodies stuck out the open hatch in the track's roof. The M-113 driver sat on a seat up front with his head sticking out of a hatch shaped like a manhole cover. The five of us could study the landscape all around us. Three riflemen were lying in twisted positions on benches running along the right and left sides of the track. Nobody could sit or lie down comfortably because all kinds of boxes and lumpy gear littered the insides of our metal cocoon.

We started bouncing across the desert floor. Our immediate task in this fading daylight was to practice driving through the antitank barrier we had built against Russian vehicles. We did not want to get stuck in our barbed wire come nightfall. We also were supposed to familiarize ourselves with the course to the LD, line of departure, so each armored vehicle in Charlie Company would push off for the battle zone from the same spot at its assigned time, not wander around the desert in the dark by itself.

All this emphasis on rehearsal in the American Army of the 1980s, I mused, is such a contrast with what I saw in Vietnam almost two decades earlier. Back then, many brash American commanders had scoffed at the elaborate rehearsals "the gooks" conducted before launching a night attack. I thought about the North Vietnamese night attack in 1968 that almost wiped out an American fire base on a hill in the Highlands of South Vietnam near Dakto.

I had walked into the fire base the morning after the night attack. An Army helicopter pilot had dropped me on an open spot a half mile outside the fire-base perimeter. He did not want to go any closer for fear North Vietnamese might still be hiding in the woods nearby and shoot him down.

191

"What the hell are you doing out here?" a GI forward observer outside the fire-base perimeter yelled to me as I walked toward the concertina-wire donut surrounding his unit's position on the sides of a rounded hill. "We're expecting another attack."

"That's OK," I smiled. "I'm a reporter from *The Washington Post*. I want to go in and talk to you guys about your fire fight last night. Hear it was a little hairy."

Inside the wire, groggy troopers told me how elaborately the North Vietnamese had rehearsed their night attack without being detected. They had picked out the weak point in the fire base's defenses, a tongue of ground forming an easy avenue of approach to the higher ground of the hill. Sometime during the day, or perhaps at night, the troopers said, the North Vietnamese had quietly strung a long wire from their launching point in the woods all the way up to the bottom part of that tongue of ground. In the darkest part of the night, the North Vietnamese infantrymen lined up under the far end of that wire in the woods. Their sappers and wire-cutting troops stood at the front of the column. On command, the North Vietnamese infantrymen grabbed the wire overhead with one hand and moved quietly through the dark woods toward the perimeter of the fire base. When they reached the open ground just outside the wire, the North Vietnamese made a screaming attack through the hole their sappers made in the wire.

The defenders from the night before told me the North Vietnamese kept running up the tongue of ground leading to the interior of the fire base. They encountered a long trench just vacated by surprised and confused American troops trying to organize a counterattack farther up the hill. The North Vietnamese troops, who probably had been marching toward their jump-off point day and night, spotted jugs of Kool-Aid in the abandoned trench. The North Vietnamese stopped their charge up the hill long enough to drink deeply from the jugs of Kool-Aid. This pause gave the American defenders the extra seconds needed to regroup. They charged back down the hill and wiped out the first wave of North Vietnamese standing in the trench. The North Vietnamese attack lost its momentum and was called off. Suddenly the North Vietnamese were gone, the American troopers told me, probably to rehearse an attack somewhere else in the hotly contested Highlands.

Lieutenant Strong, rehearsing his own attack with the care of those North Vietnamese officers of two decades earlier, ordered the driver of his M-113 to stop at the obstacle our Blue Force engineers were constructing. The Army engineer at the obstacle yelled from the ground up to Strong, who was leaning down from the left forward corner of the hatch: "I don't know what the fuck is going on, sir! We've changed this plan six or seven times already. We're not moving until you implement us in your plan."

Strong did his best to explain the plan. The back door of the track opened. We jumped out of the cramped M-113 vehicle and stood together on the desert floor while the driver of the armored personnel carrier practiced driving through the opening at the edge of the barrier. A light rain began to fall. Everyone's rain gear was in the vehicle driving back and forth past the obstacle. The spectacular orange sun fell behind the tall mountains rimming the Mojave, suddenly causing the low creosote bushes to throw long shadows on the desert floor. A chilly wind pushed the rain through our clothes and onto our skin. We suddenly felt cold and wet.

"It just doesn't get any better than this!" quipped Specialist Fourth Kenneth Chiles, 23, of St. Petersburg, Florida.

God bless you, Chiles, I said to myself. The black soldier's humor warmed me. We got to talking there on the desert floor as the twilight blackened into night. Every soldier has a story to tell if you reach out to him and listen. Chiles told me he was a championship wide receiver on his high school football team; had received several college scholarship offers; had gotten his girl pregnant just before high school graduation; felt obliged to get a job in a hurry to support her and their son, Jamol, now two. Chiles joined the Army. "The first morning I woke up and asked myself, 'What am I doing in the Army?' "

He talked with no bitterness about his lost opportunities. That was just life as non-Establishment kids lived it. They took things as they came with resignation, grace and humor. I always felt humbled by this inner grace that I so often encountered in these soldiers asking for just a sliver of America's rock in return for defending it with their lives. I heard quips from other soldiers as we stood or sat in clumps on the scruffy sand and grass of the Mojave Desert, waiting for our part of the night battle to begin.

"I foresee an early death," somebody said.

I caught the eye of Alphabet Florczyk, who wanted to be a Ranger but was tolerating the less glamorous life of mechanized infantryman. "I love this," the indomitable trooper told me with feeling.

After Strong had briefed his squad leaders by gathering them in his track, each sergeant went to his own vehicle to wait for the platoon leader to push off toward the mountain in the shape of a whale. We fired up the company tracks and lumbered off in spread-out formation. Strong kept scanning the terrain all around him with field glasses that could see in the dark. The radio was a constant jabber of talk, most of it unintelligible to me. Every once in a while I would hear the calm voice of McMahon, Charlie Company's commander, issuing from the radio box. We could not see his track. Strong kept telling his driver to change course as he searched for enemy positions on the distant mountain. We were soon swerving in and out of dry river beds on the desert floor called *wadis*, zigging left and zagging right. The observer-controller who was following our every move by tailing us in the oversize jeep nicknamed the "Hum-Vee" waved Strong to a stop. He walked over to the tense lieutenant trying to get into the fight he could not find on the dark desert and asked: "Brian, what are you doing?"

"Proceeding to the battle area."

"How far away do you think you are?"

I could not hear Strong's answer, but the observer-controller shook his head and corrected the lieutenant trying to find the fight: "I'll give you a hint, Brian. You're a hell of a lot farther away than that."

We got going again. I could see we were drawing closer to The Whale. But the crystal-clear desert night air makes everything look closer than it really is. We were still far from the battle. We bounced around. Stopped. Started. Stopped. Zigged and zagged. We were LID—lost in the desert. We never did get into the battle. We saw flashes off in the distance and the blinking lights of destroyed vehicles. The troops were long past caring where they were or what was going on outside their metal coffin. They had twisted their bodies around every which way looking for comfort among the litter of hard objects inside the track. They looked like strands of spaghetti. To them, the night had just been another bumpy ride in the dark—an update from the "another walk in the sun" complaint I had heard in Vietnam. The days of eating MRE's on the desert had turned their insides into gas chambers that erupted more often than Old Faithful. Every time I bent down from the open hatch and stuck my head into the hull of the vehicle to retrieve something, I felt like I was hanging upside down in an outhouse.

The word finally came over the radio that the night attack was over. We cranked up the M-113, turned around and headed back toward the base camp as the sun reappeared above the mountains in a burst of glorious light. Lieutenant Strong was embarrassed that we had never found our war. "Oh George. Oh George," he kept saying as we bounced back toward Charlie Company's base camp. I tried to reassure him that anybody could get lost at night in the desert or anywhere else. And I meant it. Fighting at night is blind man's bluff without something as simple as the North Vietnamese's overhead wire or a position indicator on the armored vehicle to tell you where you are. I felt the Army should have put position indicators on all its armored vehicles years ago and wondered why it was always the inexpensive but vital items—like clear, rugged radios—that never got bought as billions got spent.

"Hey, Brian! That's fortunes of war," I told Strong in trying to get him to shake off the bad night in the Mojave. I felt he and other armor officers out there on the black desert had learned something without anybody dying from the mistakes green commanders always make. I felt sorriest for the troops who had spent the whole night inside their bouncing metal box without seeing, doing or learning anything then or afterward from this deliberate attack in the dark. Soldiering is like that much of the time. Too much of the time.

"We didn't have enough intelligence for a deliberate attack," acknowledged Lieutenant Colonel Joseph G. Terry Jr., battalion task force commander—the head of the Blue Force, which had taken on the Russians in the night battle around The Whale.

Terry was sitting inside a big van on the desert that had been turned into a classroom for all the officers participating in the exercise. Standing in front of this class as teacher and critic was an officer who had endeared himself to me by saying at the outset: "I'm still Lieutenant Colonel Daniel Butler."

Butler, with the help of marvelous displays on the screen beside him, was telling Terry, McMahon and other leaders what had gone wrong and right in the night battle I had participated in twenty-four hours earlier.

"We lost our eyes for an important time," Butler said of the Blue Force, which had lost to the Opposing Force. "All those positions were dug in during broad daylight. There was a big hole in reconnaissance."

While Charlie Company and other units were planning and rehearsing in daylight for an attack on the Russians hidden on The Whale, Butler explained, the Russians had moved infantry with antiarmor weapons down on the valley floor in front of the mountain where they dug foxholes. The foxholes could not be seen at night. The Russian infantry in the foxholes on the valley floor had picked off American armor charging toward the mountain.

Butler ran down the list of losses. The Americans' M-1 tanks had destroyed many Russian vehicles, but that alone was not enough to enable the infantry to seize and hold the high ground of The Whale. Few Blue Force infantry platoons had climbed The Whale, largely because the fire of the American M-1 tanks and the close-in punch of the infantry had not been coordinated.

"Our tanks were the big killers," Butler said. "Use of tanks and infantry together is a fine art."

There was no yelling. No haranguing in the van. It was a calm, diplomatic dissection of how, when, where and why the Americans had lost this night battle to the Russians. The attackers and defenders got to explain themselves. I was watching this after-action review, called an AAR, not from inside the tent but from the Star Wars building on Fort Irwin, which received it live by a television hookup. I learned more by watching and listening to this AAR on the mock battle than I had learned from some of the real battles I had been in two decades earlier in Vietnam. Often in Vietnam there would be a quick burst of fire between the front of the company and an unseen enemy force to the side of our line of march. Such battles were often over in five minutes, with nobody knowing what had happened or why it had happened. The National Training Center battles were different in that they were recorded on tape and film and then shown like a football game film to some, but unfortunately not all, of the players.

I watched the after-action reviews after every battle and then rejoined Charlie Company. I was always dismayed, often infuriated, by how little the soldiers had been told about the battles they fought. The observer-controllers would conduct critiques with the officers and sometimes the sergeants about the battles just fought. But by the time these analyses were related to the troops, if they were related at all, they were virtually meaningless.

The after-action review process during my two weeks at the National Training Center in December 1987 was like only letting the backs, not the linemen, see the films of the football game they had played on Sunday.

"We're just training aids for the officers," was the complaint I heard over and over again from troops on the desert. "Nothing I've learned here I couldn't have learned at Fort Riley."

"It pees me off, Mr. Wilson," said one outstanding soldier in Charlie Company, "that they tell us how great we done after every battle when we know durn well we lost. It's as if they think we can't take the truth or that they think they can fool us."

It was as if Army officers had a mindset against taking soldiers into their confidence. I saw no reason why a video cassette of the officers' after-action report could not have been shown to the troops in the field. It would have done wonders to keep up their interest and enthusiasm in what they were supposed to be doing: learning how to fight and win. I wondered why Army commanders did not throw a sheet over an M-113 and show the televised after-action review to the troops. Why not make soldiering meaningful and fun whenever you can?

"This has been just riding around," said Private James Gordon, 18, of Orange Park, Florida, of his National Training Center experience. He joined the Army thinking he would be practicing to play Rambo. "A real cluster fuck. It's a joke. I haven't learned anything. You'd think they could pass the word down the chain quicker about what they wanted done so we could do something during the day instead of digging at night. They won't let us wear warm boots out here. Can't mail letters. No mail coming in."

"I learned a little bit about the desert," said a trooper after several days in the Mojave. "But this is boring, boring, boring. We've got twenty rounds of ammunition for three weeks. You'd think they could liven it up a bit."

"We filled enough sandbags to stretch from here to Fort Riley," Tweety Selvester told me. "I felt like a slave—digging, digging, digging."

"Think they could put us in a deuce [two-ton truck] and give us a shower," said a sweat-encrusted Sergeant Leslie Whitmore after being in the Mojave for more than two weeks.

"I saw the lights of the Dust Bowl!" interjected Sergeant

Ronald Reichle in referring to the troop encampment inside Fort Irwin where there were crude showers.

"Gave me a hard on," joked Private Nathaniel Brown, 18, of Medford, Oregon.

"Well," I consoled that December afternoon, "only fifteen shopping days till Christmas."

"My sister has five dates set up for when I get home at Christmas," Brown said. "I'm going to bag every one of them."

"That's the American soldier!" laughed Mark Grant.

"Yeah, and you know when I'm home watching TV and some good-looking chick comes on, I'm going to say, 'Look at that bitch with the big fucking tits' and my mom will go crazy."

I fell into talking with Grant as we waited for word of what command wanted Charlie Company to do next. The sun was high up in the clouds. We felt warm. He felt unhassled for a change. He said he joined the Army so he could support the woman he wanted to marry, Mary, and her three kids and the one of his own. Grant said she was back in Madras, Oregon, living in public housing and struggling. He said he did not mind soldiering. He felt he had finally found a place where he fit after years of drifting around Oregon.

"My feet hurt," he said with a smile. "My back's sore. I'm constipated. I got hemorrhoids. But this is better than sitting around all day—sometimes!

"When I get back to the Dust Bowl, they're going to think I went AWOL because I'm going to stay in that shower for so long."

Brown, Grant and others in the squad were ordered to climb into the M-113 for another ride to nowhere across the desert. I climbed in with them. They were dirty, exhausted, itchy. Yet as soon as we started rolling across the desert, Brown and Grant broke into this Christmas song:

> *Deck the halls with marijuana,*
> *Tra la la, la la la la.*

I laughed, which encouraged them to launch into this doggerel loud enough to best the roar of the diesel engine powering us across the Mojave:

> *Jumping off snow-capped mountains;*
> *Slide down slippery lane.*

*Poke my pole in the glory hole,*
*Make those dumb bells ring. Hey!*

Brown and Grant clapped their hands together and laughed.

I glanced up the front of the darkened interior of the track where another one of my favorite soldiers was tolerating the bouncing ride. He was Private Kevin D. Brewton, a tall, rangy black who could have gone to college on a basketball scholarship but wanted to try something adventuresome first.

"My mom, a school teacher, didn't agree with me," Brewton had told me in one of our chats. "She wanted me to go to college. But I saw home boys making it well in the Army, so I decided to do the same thing. It's going to be all right once we get out of Fort Riley. Nothing to do around there for a soldier. Got to go fifty miles to find a girl. Thing to do is get some rank. I like the Army. Just wish I hadn't joined the infantry."

I caught Brewton's eye at the end of one of the routines by Brown and Grant in back of the M-113. He shook his head, smiled and tried to go back to sleep despite the noise, smell and bumps.

"The CO has a gung-ho hair," Grant said by way of explaining why we were bouncing along for no apparent reason.

"I'll give anybody sixty MREs for one cigarette," Grant said. Nobody moved his hand toward his pocket. Brown finally relented and gave Grant a cigarette. "Your theme song should be, 'Wasting away again in Margaritaville,'" Grant told his buddy Brown, who dreamt of getting one of those tall margaritas come Christmas leave. The other six soldiers in the crowded track could not match Brown and Grant for high spiritedness and dismissed them as "Cluster Fucks I and II."

I had been in the track with the eight soldiers less than an hour this particular evening. They had to ride jammed together in the track for almost three weeks. I marveled at how they put up with the thousands of minor irritations, like people stepping in your face as you tried to sleep in the track, and the major ones like little sleep, no showers, lousy food, bruising rides and overwork. But these mud soldiers put up with it all—day after day, night after night. They never thought of themselves as anything special. I sure as hell did. They had done great, even though the company lost battle after battle. They did not make the mistakes. Their leaders did.

"I came out here just to protect my country," Private Marcus D. Foreman told me when the M-113 finally stopped and we dismounted to wait for the next maneuver. "Maybe that's an old thing now. Don't hear it much anymore." His buddies called Foreman "Wizard" because he had an answer for every question they asked him.

"The Army has pretty much lived up to my expectations. It's a job. My friends back home haven't done anything. They've just hung around while I've been to California and shot all these weapons. Too much bullshit here at NTC. Leaders can't get their shit together. We sit around all day. I learned some from that first attack. Showed me it is scary." Foreman, like so many of the mud soldiers, had a dream that many of the people he was protecting by going in the Army would find too modest: "I always wanted to be a police officer in Texas, settle down and have a family."

I walked over to Brown sitting on the ground near the track we had just left. We talked about his life as dark rushed toward the desert.

"I joined because I couldn't get a decent job. I had no high school diploma. Army was the only place that would take me. It's not so bad, I guess. My dad's proud of it.

"My dad is a millwright. He could of been my hero. But I couldn't do anything right or else my dad wasn't willing to tell me. He'd go fishing with friends, and I'd stay with the truck. I said to myself, 'Take it while you can get it. You're with him.' Took a divorce to get us where we were father and son.

"I got into crack in high school. Was selling it when I was supposed to be going to high school. Then I met Tammy. She got me out of it. Took me in, put me to bed and got me through the withdrawal. I don't want anything more to do with drugs."

In the pre-dawn dark of an especially cold morning at Fort Irwin, I slid onto the cold front-passenger seat of Captain Mark Dutton's Hum-Vee to motor through the dark to reach the desert hill Charlie Company would be defending at dawn against the same simulated Soviet motorized rifle regiment that had won all the previous battles against the Americans. Dutton had no compass or other navigational aids. Our headlights were off. There was a little moon and starlight but not much. I could have been on the surface of that moon for all I knew. Dutton knew where he was from years of watching battles as an observer-controller on this Mojave

Desert training ground. It is like he grew up here, I mused, as Dutton threaded his way through the boulder-strewn desert in the dark. The Hum-Vee had no windshield. Our foreheads ached—at least mine did—from the freezing desert air hitting them as we drove along. We finally stopped. It was now gray in the desert. The sun was still behind the mountains. I spotted Charlie Company troopers dug in on the smooth, navigable face of the mountain as well as in impassable crevices and on knobs to the side of it.

"I bet the OpFor comes right up here," Dutton told me. He was pointing down the face of the mountain, which looked to him like a highway for the Soviet regiment. Many of the troopers of Johnny Libs's old 2d Platoon were sitting in foxholes just a few feet from what Dutton saw as the natural avenue of approach. They would get run over by the Russians if Dutton was right—unless they could stop the first wave of armor with the Dragon antitank weapons held by the troopers or with the TOW antitank missiles mounted in jeeps behind this forward line of soldiers. I could not see the TOW vehicles and doubted if they could see Soviet armor once it started climbing the mountain. The TOWs' only chance was to hit the Soviet motorized column as it moved across the desert floor. But the Soviets usually laid down a smokescreen to foil the antitank gunners.

I climbed into an empty foxhole behind the big one occupied by Private Fred D. Cole. He had joined the Army in hopes of proving to everybody back home that he had gone from boy to man. He had hoped to be a paratrooper. But the Army at Benning pushed him into a COHORT platoon destined for Fort Riley. This December morning Cole was carrying a Dragon antitank weapon.

"Here they come!" somebody shouted.

I looked down on the valley floor. The Soviets had generated a big cloud of white-gray smoke. I caught glimpses of vehicles racing through the smoke cloud. Suddenly they were at the foot of our sharp hill. Cole aimed his Dragon at the lead vehicle of the charging column. He pulled the trigger. Nothing. The damn Dragon, which never seemed to work, had failed again.

"Shit!" Cole exclaimed as he examined his worthless weapon.

The Soviet column roared right past Cole and me. The Soviet vehicles spread out after they had penetrated Charlie Company's front line, rolling up the defender's flanks. Cole, Selvester, Sergeant Ronald Reichle and the other Charlie Company defenders on the hill were all "dead"—again. They had been losing battle

201

after battle since taking on the Soviet motorized rifle company on the desert. It was not the GIs' fault. It almost never is. It was their leaders' fault. They failed to prepare and execute in ways that would enable their soldiers to win.

I worried about the battle smarts of this post-Vietnam Army as I watched a representative slice of it lose because of such fund-amental mistakes as failing to send reconnaissance teams out during the day to locate enemy positions before attacking them at night. This particular morning the American commanders had deployed troops smack across the Soviet route of approach rather than concentrate antitank soldiers to the side where the gunners could get flank shots into the thinner side of the armor.

"We in the Army have been kidding ourselves about how long it takes to get good at this stuff," an observer-controller who refereed the U.S. vs. Soviet mock battles told me. "I thought I was a real hotshot platoon leader. Now that I've watched over 300 battles out here, and seen what is really takes to win, I realize I didn't know anything. We've got to keep our platoon leaders and company commanders in the field with their men longer or we're going to lose our ass."

The problem was not that the officers, sergeants and privates failed to work hard. Captain McMahon as Charlie Company commander worked day and night. His voice was hoarse from fatigue, his lips cracked from the dry desert air, and yet he kept going relentlessly. But he had just taken over the company in October and would leave it in March for a nonfield job. His successor would start afresh. The lessons of the National Training Center would have to be relearned because of this revolving-door approach to commanding combat outfits. I came to believe that the Army would have more chance of winning battles against superior odds if it identified exceptional troop leaders in its officer corps and kept them in field jobs rather than rotating them to other specialties after commanding platoons, companies or bat-talions for eighteen to twenty-four months or less. So what if they miss going to the various charm schools called war colleges or taking foreign languages? Promote them for getting good at winning battles in the mud.

Lieutenant Colonel Douglas E. MacFarlane, who as commander of the Sixth Battalion of the Thirty-first Infantry Regiment di-rected the mock Soviet motorized rifle regiment to victory after victory over the American reinforced battalion during my two weeks on the desert, reinforced my view that modern warfare has become too high speed and too sophisticated to allow Army commanders to hopscotch from field commands to staff jobs to colleges to procurement and back to the field. MacFarlane described the typical dilemmas of the new battalion commander fighting the "Soviets" on the benign ground of the National Training Center.

"The battalion commander is out there right now driving along in an armored vehicle at night trying to find out where he is personally. He gets lost like everybody else. He has six company commanders on the radio, all giving him spot reports. He is receiving spot reports from his S-2 [intelligence officer] and demands information from higher headquarters. All this is going on while he is trying to control artillery and tactical air and while he is trying to find the [enemy] scouts. He is trying to get his maneuver forces where they are supposed to get, on ground they don't really understand. All those things can add up to be a very difficult and challenging task for these guys.

"The battalion commander's situation becomes even more chaotic," MacFarlane continued, "once the enemy knocks out his lead columns. What does he do then? Keep maneuvering, bypass the place where he believes the enemy is located or stop? Usually," MacFarlane continued, "the battalion commander stops to try to assess his situation.

"'Gosh, all my scouts are dead. Oh my gosh, the lead team is dead. That's not the way I had it planned. That's not what my overlay [the map of the tactical movements he intended to carry out] says.' Then he gets pounded by artillery" because the enemy sees the American battalion commander has stopped, making his surviving forces easy targets.

"Then he loses another few vehicles," MacFarlane noted. "All of a sudden he just can't make decisions fast enough because too much has gone wrong.

"Once you cross the line of departure, chaos begins at a very low level. Things don't work. People aren't where they are supposed to be. Someone hasn't fueled [his vehicles]. Someone didn't get his ammo. All these things. You can't beat that. That's always going to be there. What you need to do is become accustomed to that. That's what our doctrine says. 'Hey, it's going to be goofed up, so be ready for it. Make sure you spend the time you need to spend to do as much detailed planning as you need to do.' The reason they're not winning out here is that they're learning [from their mistakes]."

After watching the United States battle the simulated Soviet regiment for two weeks in the desert, I told MacFarlane, it struck me that both sides use basically the same tactics.

"Everybody comes to that conclusion after they have been here for a while," he replied. "At our level it's the same. Combat techniques are the same for any army. How the soldier and how his squad and how his platoon function out there are the same for the United States as the Soviet Union."

Then what determines which side wins?

The one "who becomes accustomed to dealing with the realities of maneuver warfare," MacFarlane replied.

MacFarlane, as he had intended, had made his case for spending millions to train battalions at the National Training Center. But I think his comments also helped strengthen the case for establishing a separate career path in the Army for troop commanders so that they and their units would keep getting better. Charlie Company and the rest of the Second Battalion of the Sixteenth Infantry regiment would soon go home for Christmas leave. Most of the officers would leave for other jobs, including Battalion Commander Terry and Charlie Company Commander McMahon. I doubted if the lessons learned at the National Training Center by the battalion officers would be passed on to their successors in full measure because you cannot pass on experience. Yet the Army had spent $5.3 million to send the battalion to this outdoor classroom in the desert. Army statistics on how a succession of battalions did against the Opposing Force show little improvement through the years. The lessons evidently are not being passed on, if indeed they can be. The lesson I drew from the National Training Center was not that the Opposing Force wins because it knows the terrain but that there is no substitute for keeping commanders in the field long enough to make them experts in fighting battles rather than try to make them renaissance men by sending them hopscotching from one job to another.

Soldiers detect almost instantly whether their officers know what they are doing. I wondered how many would become disillusioned with the Army they had joined six months ago because of the way they were treated and led at the National Training Center. Brigadier General Horace G. "Pete" Taylor, commander of the National Training Center, said of this new breed of mud soldier: "They're smart. They have an abundance of common sense. They're educated, but most of all they believe in what they're doing. These young people are the key to what is going to keep our country strong."

Would the leaders of this post-Vietnam, all-volunteer Army lean far enough toward these new soldiers to keep up their enthusiasm? I doubted it from what I had seen at Riley and at the National Training Center but resolved to make new soundings after my mud soldiers had completed their first year in this new Army.

# 12. After One Year

Late summer rains had broken the drought and transformed the Kansas prairie from brown to green when I returned to Fort Riley in September 1988 to see how the young volunteers of Charlie Company had fared in their first year of soldiering with a regular Army unit, The Big Red One. I could tell even before the soldiers told me that something had gone wrong.

For, as I looked over Charlie Company standing within the battalion on the stubble of the Custer Hill parade ground, I saw that a lot of the men from Benning were missing. I also noticed that at least half the sergeants were new and that only one officer was still in the same job he held a year ago. The company's commanding officer, executive officer, first sergeant and two of the three platoon leaders had all been replaced since the COHORT soldiers had reported to Riley in October 1987. Yet the whole idea of COHORT was to prevent this kind of wholesale turnover, which Army leaders believed hurt fighting power and morale. What happened to this COHORT company that started off so well just one year ago?

"Hey! Mr. Wilson!" Private Second Class Lester J. "Sticks" Remington, 19, of Burton, Michigan, called out as I approached the shrunken company standing at ease on the parade ground waiting to start the battalion morning run. "What do you think of the company now? We're a lot smaller, ain't we?"

"And fatter," chimed in Specialist Four James E. Proctor II in launching an attack on Riley's soft physical training program.

206

"Did you hear about A _____?" asked another soldier who seemed happy to see me and anxious to fill me in on what I had missed while away in Washington. "He jumped out a second-story window to get out of here."

"Yeah," said another trooper I knew well from Benning. "And a lot of guys have come up hot on their piss tests. V_____ is in jail. Lots of guys have gone AWOL and are getting kicked out. We're getting all kinds of Article 15s [disciplinary actions that are the military equivalent of civilian traffic tickets, which do not require going to court]."

I felt like the lost member from a walled village who had just found his way back inside where the villagers could not wait to catch him up on all the hot news and gossip he had missed. The new sergeants who had not seen me before eyed me suspiciously. To them I was an outsider who somehow had gotten into their domain.

"Attention!" came the command from the edge of the parade ground. I walked away from Charlie Company, promising to reconnect with my old friends after they had finished the battalion run around The Loop, the road running around the top of Custer Hill.

While the troops were doing the early morning jog, I went into the chow hall, drew a cup of coffee from the big silver urn and sat across the table from Sergeant Angel Rivera, who had helped lead Charlie Company when it first arrived from Benning but had since been transferred to its successor company. The soldiers admired Rivera. I asked him why so many men in Charlie Company had failed to survive this first year at Riley.

"They got dogged too much," Rivera replied. This was soldier talk for overworking and harassing the troops.

I left Rivera to find out how bad the losses really were. I learned that of the sixty-six fully certified infantrymen who had graduated from Benning on October 9, 1987, and reported to Riley immediately afterward, only fifty-one were still in this COHORT company, a 23 percent loss rate. Attrition would soon wipe out the original company if it kept up at this rate. More worrisome, of the fifteen who had left the company, eleven of them, or 73 percent, had been judged so bad that they had to be kicked out of the Army. Their offenses in this first year of soldiering included attempting suicide, going AWOL, deserting, stealing, drunkenness and drug abuse. All this happens in almost every Army unit over time. But the extent of the misbehavior, reflected in the eleven ejections, sounded high to me for a COHORT unit completing its very first year in a regular outfit.

I queried the Army on this point. After researching the question, an Army spokesman said the latest measures of behavior in COHORT units were taken in 1984. Those measures showed that Charlie Company's eighteen Article 15s for its sixty-nine soldiers (sixty-six of whom came from Benning) in their first year at Riley was much higher than the Army-wide average of eighteen Article 15s per 1,000 COHORT soldiers in 1984. Also, the Army said, Charlie Company's five AWOLs among its sixty-nine soldiers in one year was "significantly higher than the COHORT average of 4.2 AWOLs per 1,000." However, to my surprise, the Army said the loss rate in Charlie Company was not unusually high for these supposedly unified COHORT companies. The eleven COHORT soldiers who were kicked out of Charlie Company in its first year at Riley represented an attrition rate of just under 17 percent for disciplinary reasons, not health or other problems, or 1.4 percent loss per month in the company's total of sixty-six Benning graduates. The attrition rate Army-wide for COHORT units in 1984 averaged 12 percent a year, or 1 percent a month, the Army said.

My own observations and those Army statistics confirmed that the Army was not living up to the expectations of many of the post-Vietnam volunteers. A disturbing percentage of these volunteers all across the Army, not just in Charlie Company, obviously lost the motivation that got them through the first stages of their training at centers like Fort Benning. The reverse could be true as well: the volunteers were not living up to the expectations of their sergeants and officers. Either way, high attrition rates in an already small Army are something for the nation to worry about. I decided to ask leaders and soldiers at every level at Riley what had gone wrong with the once high-spirited Charlie Company of 1987–88 in the conviction that the problems in this typical combat outfit would be found in the others forming the forward wall of American and NATO defenses in the post-Vietnam era.

To obtain some historic perspective on the problem, I went to a troop leader who had seen almost everything in his two decades of soldiering: Sergeant Major Noah J. Wright of the 2d Battalion of the Sixteenth Infantry Regiment, Charlie Company's parent battalion.

Wright was sitting behind his desk in battalion headquarters when I asked him the ticklish question of what he personally thought had gone wrong with this 1987–88 edition of Charlie Company at Riley. At first, the decorated sergeant major bobbed and weaved. He could tell I thought he was filibustering. He finally looked me straight in the eye and said, "What the hell! With all my years in, what are they going to do to me?"

"Send you to Fort Riley!" I quipped with a smile.

"It's too high," he said of Charlie Company's attrition rate.

"The basic problem has been leadership. You'll notice out there that I've changed about half the sergeants. You know, the way the system works, a Spec Four [Specialist Four] may be happy driving a truck for the rest of his life. But to keep him in the Army, he has to be promoted to sergeant. And when he gets promoted to sergeant, he becomes responsible for troops whether he wants to lead them or not."

Not every sergeant has the skills needed to lead and teach troops, Wright said. If you miscast sergeants into leadership roles they cannot fulfill, some of their troops will give up on the Army and become so impossible that the Army will also give up on them and discharge them, Wright said.

When the nation switched from the draft to the All-Volunteer Force in 1973, the best and brightest noncommissioned officers did not stay in the Army, Wright contended. But the ones who stayed were the only ones available to promote to key leadership positions, like master sergeant. This resulted in a dip in quality at the senior levels of the NCO Corps, Wright said. The NCO leadership was not as good as it should have been when Charlie reported to Riley and other companies went to other duty stations in 1987 and 1988.

"I don't think the cadre was ready" to train the Benning soldiers who arrived in 1987 to become the new Charlie Company, Wright said. "It was asking for trouble, from a morale standpoint." Not only did the sergeants have to train the soldiers in the infantry tactics they would be expected to know when they reported to the National Training Center, but also in the intricacies of driving and maintaining the M-113 armored personnel carriers the Benning soldiers would use for the first time at Riley.

"The only guy who had experience was [First Sergeant Russell] Snyder," Wright said. Snyder not only was a Vietnam combat veteran but was experienced in mechanized operations like Charlie Company had to execute at the National Training Center after little more than a month of training.

I asked Wright whether the leadership gap would be closed once these bright volunteers who joined the service in the 1980s advanced to middle management level—the NCO Corps. To my surprise, Wright doubted this would happen.

"We went to the all-volunteer Army," Wright acknowledged, "but we're still getting soldiers from the lower middle class. The kids who come to us from high school with a 4.0 average come in for the college money and then leave us. So we're still left with Joe Snuffy with the 2 to 2.5 average from the lower half of his class. We don't have that real high-level guy.

"We're getting the offspring of the hippie generation. We're getting a more educated soldier. But he doesn't have half the discipline of the kids we used to get."

Another sociological change that makes it harder for the Army to keep troops disciplined through constant supervision is the reversal in the single-to-married ratio among young noncommissioned officers, Wright said.

"Twenty years ago," the sergeant major continued in our conversation in his office at battalion headquarters, "70 percent of the young NCOs were single and lived in the barracks. Today 80 to 85 percent of them live in civilian communities and are married. When they get off, they go home" rather than stick with the soldiers.

Wright's conclusion that the whole all-volunteer Army, not just Charlie Company, has a leadership problem encouraged me to dissect it by questioning everyone from privates I knew at Riley to General Carl E. Vuono, Army chief of staff, and General Maxwell R. Thurman, commander of the United States Army Training and Doctrine Command. To continue the inquiry I had started with Wright, I walked toward Charlie Company's van standing on Custer Hill to get amidst the privates from Benning I knew so well. They would tell me straight out what they thought had gone wrong within their Charlie Company, a microcosm of many other combat units in the all-volunteer Army of the 1980s.

"You are going to ride in this thing with us, Mr. Wilson?" asked one of the grunts as I squeezed into their wooden, silver-painted cattle car, a long moving van with benches and handrails inside.

"Sure," I smiled and climbed into the darkened cavern crowded with the young soldiers of Charlie Company.

Private Second Class Anthony L. Suddoth, marking his twenty-first birthday on this September 2, 1988, sang out a few bars of a barracks ditty from the front of the van. "Suddy" was a tall, handsome black from Zion, Illinois, who had told me at Benning that he had joined the Army to take himself off the streets where he was getting into trouble. He had slipped once at Riley, getting caught for drug abuse, but was otherwise doing well in the soldiering he intended to make a career. He had found the social life at Junction City and Manhattan below zero. "They ought to close the fort," he told me. "There's nothing for a soldier to do." His spirits never stayed low for long, however.

"Come on, Suddy!" someone in the crowded troop van yelled out. "Get into it."

"Will you go along?"

"Yeah! Yeah!"

With that, Suddy sang out the first line of one of his hundreds of ditties in his lovely, penetrating voice. The troops repeated the first line after him in kind of a hoarse holler. We all laughed. My old friend Norman Adkins standing beside me in the cattle car shouted in my ear, "I don't know what we'd do without each other."

Suddy started over again. The troops got caught up in his rhythm this time, repeating each line as we jounced down the steep face of Custer Hill in the cattle car:

"Hey! Hey! Captain Jack!" Suddy began.

"Hey! Hey! Captain Jack!" the troops boomed back, and then went through the rest of the ditty that way:

> Meet me down by the railroad track
> With your weapon in your hand.
> I'm going to be a fighting man.
>
> Ho! Ho! Diddly bop!
> I wish I was back on the block
> With some reefer in my hand;
> I'm going to be a smoking man.

The van stopped on the flatland of the old cavalry base near the

Republican River. I joined the pack pushing out the side door of the cattle car and looked around with wonderment at the scene all around me. There were World War II–type barracks stretched across acres of green lawn. I felt as if I were back in the barracks I lived in as a Naval aviation cadet between World War II and Korea. I tapped the side of one of the barracks. It had been coated with aluminum. Moving inside, I saw more fundamental changes. The open bays on the first and second floors of the old barracks had been divided up into private rooms for two or three soldiers, an unheard-of luxury in my ancient past. Washing machines and dryers had been installed in the bathrooms. I laughed to myself as I remembered the shock I had felt as a teenaged cadet when someone stole my skivvies off the clothesline running between barracks ten minutes after I had hung them out to dry.

Moving from room to room in one of the old barracks Charlie Company would occupy until flying to West Germany to start two years of duty holding down part of the North Atlantic Treaty Organization front line, I sat down with the Distinguished Honor Graduate from Fort Benning, James E. Proctor II. I had left him a year earlier as a high-spirited young black man who had helped his mother fight her way out of a New Jersey ghetto, won himself an appointment to the Air Force Academy, let it drop so he could earn money to pay off debts, joined the Army in hopes he would find fun and adventure in the infantry. At Benning, he had looked like the model soldier. At Riley one year later, he looked dispirited and talked that way when I put a tape recorder between us and asked him what had gone wrong in so short a time.

"Nobody has any positive motivation here," Proctor began. He was sitting on one bed in the room and I sat on the other. "Basic training was intense. You had something on the schedule to do, you did it, you were done. You knew what you were going to do the next day. Everybody wants to go back to basic training.

"For E-4 [fourth rung up the enlisted ladder, Specialist Four] and below, everything here sucks. Even the PT Sergeants here get tired after ten push-ups.

"Out in the field, nothing is where it's supposed to be. We're told there's water just up ahead. We get there, no water. If we want water, we have to get it ourselves. The supply system is null and void. It doesn't happen every time, but more times than it should.

"I'm an E-4 now. I go to a meeting on what we're supposed to do. I come back and tell the guys what we're supposed to do. Then we don't do it. So much of our time is wasted. We get dicked around. Maybe it's the schedule. We get one, but we never can follow it.

"We got overworked June and July supporting the ROTC. Some of us worked eighteen hours a day and were still supposed to get up at 3 A.M. to do it all over again. We did this for weeks with no days off. It wasn't necessary to put all that time in. Nobody appreciated it anyway.

"All and all, it's not what I expected. I was full of Rambo. That's why I joined the infantry. This is not Rambo. We're either working all the time or not at all. If we're not training, we're sleeping. And I think the officers and NCOs should know their stuff rather than stand there in the field reading it out of a book."

I asked this black, unmarried soldier, a star performer at both Benning and Riley, whether he would join the Army again in light of his first year's experience. "I'd sign up for the Army, but not COHORT. Everybody gets tired of seeing everybody."

To make sure Proctor was not exaggerating, I sought out several other star soldiers, including Norman L. Adkins and David Sean Murray, the two Smurf wrestlers from West Virginia. I had watched Adkins and Murray soldier in the heat of Georgia, on the cold Kansas prairie and in the Mojave Desert. No demand put upon them by sergeants or officers was too arduous in all those days and nights I had seen them in the field. Their superiors at Riley had recognized their worth and promoted Adkins to private first class and Murray to specialist four. I knew they would not overstate when I asked them independently what had happened to Charlie Company.

"The soldiers ain't bad," Adkins told me. "They tell us, and we do it." He agreed with Proctor that the schedule was one of all go or all stop, that nothing went as scheduled, that he knew the leadership was messed up but did not know whose fault it was. He also agreed that supporting the ROTC cadets burned out the soldiers of Charlie Company.

"We worked thirty-nine days straight, and most of those days were eighteen hours long," Adkins said of the ROTC detail. Afterward, he said with amazement, the Charlie Company commander said the troops had not really done anything all that time. "I couldn't believe it when he said that," Adkins told me.

Murray, in a separate interview, told me the most infuriating part of the ROTC support mission was that most of the overtime that kept him away from his wife, Ruth, and baby, Heather, was unnecessary. Ruth and Heather were alone for most of the day and night for twenty-nine days straight with no days off in between in July 1988, as he put in this kind of day. Murray, the kind of soldier the Army cannot afford to dispirit, told me those days went like this:

Get up at 3 A.M.; drive his pickup truck from his trailer home to Charlie Company's area on Custer Hill; hitch a ride on the company truck to the edge of the woodsy site used by the ROTC cadets in their simulated attacks; report to the formation at 5 A.M.; walk to his position in the woods and stand around until 7 A.M. doing nothing; climb the tree to play sniper for each wave of cadets coming through the woods from 8 A.M. to 5 P.M.; take his rifle to the base camp a half mile away; clean that and other weapons until 10 P.M.; retrieve his pickup truck and return to the trailer at 11 P.M. or midnight when his wife and baby were asleep; get up again at 3 A.M. when his family was still sleeping to start the sniper routine all over again.

"It just wasn't necessary to put in all that time," he told me. "I could have worked from 7 A.M. to 9 P.M. and gotten everything done. I've stopped telling my wife when I'm going to be off because we never get off when they say we're getting off."

In contrast to the ROTC mission, Murray and other soldiers told me, was the second time Charlie Company went to the National Training Center to supplement the "enemy" force, the OpFor.

"First of all it was a thirty-hour bus ride to get there," Murray said. "Then I was only out in the field eight times for no more than two hours during the three weeks we were there. They didn't teach us anything. The rest of the time was just lying around. I never saw so many movies. You'd think they could plan our time better."

Murray does not mind working hard when there is a point to it. The Army wanted to recruit smart and willing soldiers like Murray. But Army leaders do not seem to realize these bright new soldiers believe they have something better to do than stand around like dray horses when there is no load to pull.

Another typical complaint about the roller-coaster pace of the training came from Private First Class Sean "South Bronx" Petersen who said, "They burned me out here. The calendar they had for us here was ridiculous. A lot of people who would have been damn good soldiers went AWOL because of it. You know something has to be wrong when sergeants go AWOL." I confirmed one Charlie Company sergeant had indeed gone AWOL, reportedly to avoid being returned to Germany for more field exercises with the company. He was in the process of being prosecuted when I was at Riley.

"The stuff we were doing was stupid. No reason for it. Get ready for an attack, but nobody comes. Sit there for six hours, pack up your stuff and leave. Then they say we won when we know we hadn't done anything.

"The thing that really got me was ROTC. That was so damn stupid. It was like setting a dinner table for a President. We mowed grass. We had to make little walkways with sandbags. They can't just walk where they want to go. We put up tents. We put up pretty little signs. We made sand boxes for them. Sure, sand boxes are important [for tracing tactical movements]. But these were ridiculous. We put paint in the sand; green trees, green land, blue water, gray roads, black roads.

"At 5 A.M. those of us in the OpFor set the camouflage net over the bleachers. What are we camouflaging them for? Birds? Give me a break. A lot of guys in the OpFor started at 4 A.M. and didn't get home until 9, 10 or 11 at night. If they used a little common sense, they could have made shifts or something."

"ROTC was a complete show for the brass," agreed Corporal John P. Korkue, 23, a four-year veteran of the Air Force who showed himself to be an outstanding infantryman at Benning and was one of the most promising young leaders at Riley. "Sometimes we weren't allowed to take water out to the guys when they needed it because trucking it out might offend the brass."

Private First Class Ty Barker, driver of an M-113, in an interview in his trailer home sounded the same theme I had heard in moving from room to room in the barracks: "They burned everybody out and always kept breaking their promises.

"We'd come back from the field and one second they're saying all we're going to do tonight is wipe the weapons down real good and then we're going to turn them in. Next day when we come in we'll take two, three, four hours—whatever it takes—break the weapons down and bring them to extra clean sparkle. Half the time we would do that till 10 or 11 o'clock at night. Then at 11:20 someone would say, "All right, I want 'em down to POM 4 [squeaky clean]. Then we'd be up on Custer Hill until 4 or 5 in the morning; go home; get an hour's sleep and come back for formation. I slept in the barracks a couple of nights because there was no use in me coming home here.

"When guys have been busting their ass for two or three weeks out in the field and they're dead-ass tired, don't bring them and get their hopes up—which they do all the time. Tell us one thing and do another."

Private Second Class Kristian "Tweety" Selvester, who never worried about anything growing up, told me he was worried about soldiers getting hurt in the field because everybody got so tired. "It's amazing someone wasn't killed. So many nights guys driving the tracks couldn't stay awake. It's a wonder they didn't topple over or run over somebody. You don't need to be running around with weapons when you can't hardly keep your eyes open. Crazy. Crazy this working around the fucking clock. We're all strung out. And there were so many days we went from working like crazy to doing nothing. Nothing at all. Sit around and do nothing. I know we could have had more days off. It was like they were afraid to give us a day off. I don't where this comes from. The lieutenant colonel must get it from the colonel when it comes down from a one-star general. I don't know.

"The leadership has been really wishy-washy. The company is wondering why we're suddenly getting all these Article 15s. Just doesn't make sense to be getting all these Article 15s all of a sudden. Every soldier in our company can't be that messed up. Got to be something wrong somewhere. The sergeants aren't the problem. They're the ones who stick up for us. Goes higher up than that."

Private First Class Travis Linville, 19, of Grand Junction, Colorado, said ROTC "just about killed everybody" and that he and most of the other soldiers in the company were not looking forward to Germany for fear it would be the same kind of endless, exhausting but empty duty in the field.

"The way it works," he said, "is that the company commander takes his training schedule up to battalion and says, 'Look at this training schedule, man. It's just packed with training.' He'll get his pat on the back for the schedule and keep pushing, pushing, pushing it. This is just cheesing. But what about his guys? How about some time off for them?

"One thing I've learned here is that you're not an individual. You're just someone to do something. I think it's the Army. I think it's just the way they've been for so long that they can't change. But I think people respond more by being asked to do something. How do they expect you to reenlist when they give you shit for a year?"

Linville had written on the questionnaire I asked all the members of Charlie Company to fill out at Benning a year earlier: "I was told when I joined that I would go be an accountant. However, someone lied! Now that I'm in The Big Red One I love it! It's great! As long as God guides the way, there's nothing for us to fear."

I was not naïve as I talked with Linville, who won an achievement award for his outstanding performance at Riley, about the need for soldiers to gripe and the need for me to apply a discount. So I asked him if his one year of soldiering had turned him off the military completely.

"No. I'll do my four honorably," he replied, "then go to college and come back into the service as an officer." Linville's next words underscored the losses the Army will suffer in high-quality soldiers if they conclude that the service is wasting their time rather than challenging them with interesting work under a reasonable, reliable work schedule: "I'm not coming back to the infantry. Its organization is all messed up. Maybe I'll go into the Air Force. It looks more organized. Many times a lot of us have said we'd rather be in basic training again because it's more organized. You knew what you were doing all the time. Here the organization is all messed up. Soldiering shouldn't have to be like that."

Ty Barker raised the question in my mind whether the Army had determined scientifically how many training hours are required to teach this new volunteer soldier a skill or was just going by what somebody put down in a book decades ago.

"I went to the EIB [expert infantry badge] course here and learned more in two-and-a-half weeks about my job than I did all the rest of the time here at Riley. And I had a ball. And we always got done by 1700. There's no sense sitting around for sixteen, seventeen, twenty-four hours to do one job. Half the time we sit around half a day waiting. I realize that in the field it's a twenty-four-hour-a-day job. But in garrison it shouldn't be a twenty-hour day.

"We could learn a lot if they'd even the days out and teach infantry jobs. But they don't. Half the time we drive around all day long or all night long. You could knock off from the field problem at 5. If you're staying out all night, have some fun. Arrange to do something to build up self-esteem."

Specialist Four Christopher Cashman made many of the same points when I went to his trailer off the Junction City highway to ask him what he thought had gone right and wrong. This winner of two Army Achievement medals underscored that view by relating what a difference imaginative leadership can make to privates.

"The second time we were at the NTC as part of the OpFor, Lieutenant [Timothy] Fath sent a few of the guys around a hill to hide as the bad guys. Then he asked a few of us left behind how we would go about getting those guys. What a difference! You could just see the guys' eyes shine. One said, 'Sir, if we sent one guy around this way and two others behind the hill, we could catch them off guard and trap them.' And that's what we did. It was just great.

"Lieutenant Fath is the only officer who talks to us that way. I told him afterward what a big difference he had made just by letting us do that little patrol our own way. He told me he would like to do more of that but his hands are tied."

I left Cashman and his wife, Kerry, to return to the old barracks to do more one-on-one interviews with the single soldiers who lived there. I sat down with Private First Class Bret "Skeeter" Burke, 19, of Pelican Rapids, Minnesota. "My nickname comes from our state bird," he said with a smile, knowing that Minnesota mosquitos inspired that joke. Burke was a go-along soldier in basic and at Riley, doing his work with little, if any, complaint. He had won an Army Achievement Medal and always struck me as a quietly patriotic citizen and prideful soldier who intended to make the Army his life. He still acted that way when we reconnected in September 1988 but had some constructive ideas, I thought, for Army leaders about training.

"They should have kept it more even," he said of the company training at Riley. "We came here and knew we were going to have to work hard for NTC. We did, here and in NTC. We did really good in NTC in December. We had a battalion commander's inspection in January. Then February to the end of March it was really slow." Drivers and track commanders worked on the M-113s, but the rest of the company did little. "Only thing to do was sleep. And you're not supposed to sleep while you're working.

So it was like working a full day and accomplishing absolutely nothing. You could get days off if you asked because there was nothing going on, but most of the guys just lay around.

"We could of done more on the tracks. I remember hearing in basic that it's better to have and not need than to need and not have. I felt we wasted so much time all through February and March, and then they killed us in the summer.

"I think they could plan better. It was work hard and then do nothing. Then work hard again. If they had only kept a steady pace, I think a lot of guys could have handled everything better."

As I listened to these and other lamentations by the young soldiers, I realized we really did have a different breed of soldier in this post-Vietnam Army. Every soldier just quoted went beyond his own personal problems and made the point that he wanted to learn more, that he wanted the Army to make better use of everybody's time, that he wanted to be a winner on a winning team. What a shame, I thought, that at least some Army leaders are failing to respond to these desires in this golden moment, which may never come again.

Having heard from scores of successful soldiers, ones who had weathered the storms of their first year of soldiering in a regular unit, I wanted to chronicle what had happened to the unsuccessful ones. Their stories too, I felt, would shed light on what went wrong within Charlie Company. These portraits emerged as I asked what happened to the eleven Charlie Company members who were already discharged or in the process of being ejected from the Army in the fall of 1988. I am not using their full names in order to avoid jeopardizing their new civilian careers.

## Joey, the Desperate Klinger

I knew Joey at Benning as a bright, if kooky, soldier whose mastery of the TOW antitank missile won him the "excellence in heavy antitank gunnery" award at Benning. The day I was going through the confidence course at Benning, Joey caught my eye, grabbed a live green lizard off a tree, put it in his mouth for my benefit, chomped down on the lizard's body while its green tail wriggled outside Joey's mouth. I laughed. Joey joined in. I considered him one of the company's characters, not a looney. He was staging a safe protest, as I saw it, against the uniform behavior the drill sergeants were trying to impose on everyone.

Joey came to Riley with the intention of doing his tour, putting away money for college and then going home to New York State. What first turned Joey off, according to Specialist Four John P. Brooks, one of his roommates and fellow TOW gunner, was Charlie Company's first deployment to the National Training Center. Brooks said that he and Joey felt their officers did not know how to use TOWs. The TOW crews were sent "up on top of a hill every day where we got killed every day," Brooks said. "Joey couldn't deal with that all our TOW section did was sleep. Joe told me, 'The Army's bullshit. Nobody cares about us. I'm getting out.' " Wasting time was intolerable to this young man with the unrealistically high expectations.

On top of that, the dispirited soldier hated to leave his girlfriend back home when it came time to break off Christmas leave and return to Riley, a desert in the middle of nowhere for most young soldiers, particularly because there were so few girls to date. Joey turned to drinking 151-proof Bacardi rum and Lord Calvert whiskey in his barracks room during the cold, slow days of January. Brooks said Joey realized he had gotten himself hooked on alcohol and made an appointment to get help. But his sergeant, according to Brooks, would not allow Joey to keep his alcohol-abuse appointment because the command had put top priority on servicing the M-113 vehicles at that time. Brooks said Joey lamented: "You try to get help and nobody cares. I'm going to get drunk." And he did, over and over again.

One night late in January, Brooks recalled, Joey got drunk on Lord Calvert, high on pot and inspired by Pink Floyd's rendition of "The Wall," which boomed out of the tape player in the room. He purposely broke a light bulb and ate the glass pieces, grinding them into granular bits with his teeth before swallowing them.

For reasons which neither Brooks nor Joey could explain afterward, Joey decided it would be neat to dive out the second-story window and into the arms of another soldier friend, Private Second Class Glenn P. Dowe, who would stand on the ground below to catch him. Brooks said when he saw Joey put a chair next to the window to serve as a springboard, he knew his roommate was serious. He said he tried to stop him. Joey donned a thick down parka, a hat and hiking boots and insisted he would make the dive. By this time Dowe had left his spot on the ground, Brooks told me, apparently deciding Joey would not jump after all. When Joey aimed himself toward the window, Brooks said he grabbed him. But Joey broke away and, as Brooks looked on with horror, dove right through a windowpane he had previously smashed with his fist. The window frame caught him at the waist, Brooks said, but Joey wriggled the rest of the way out. He landed on the cement ledge under the window and apparently bounced off it, smacking onto the snowy ground with enough force to knock himself out.

Because it was so cold outside, soldiers carried Joey inside the barracks to await the ambulance. Medics later scolded the troopers for moving Joey, saying the move could have killed him if his back had been broken. At the Fort Riley hospital, doctors determined that Joey had suffered only minor injuries, perhaps because the ledge had broken his fall and the thick down parka had cushioned the impact when he hit the snowy ground.

Back on duty a few days after his late January dive, Joey resumed drinking and made another suicidal gesture, apparently to provide additional proof that the Army should discharge him. He went into Junction City to visit Corporal Michael A. Austerman, a friend from Benning and leader of the company's TOW section, in Chief Austerman's trailer home. Austerman told me that Joey complained: "Nobody cares about me." Austerman said he tried to reassure Joey this was not true. He was driving the drunk soldier back to his barracks when Joey said, "I ought to jump out of this car." Then he did just that. Chief said he was going about 35 miles an hour at the time, heard a thump, slammed on the brakes and found Joey lying bruised but otherwise unhurt on the pavement.

These acts—along with hanging a Communist flag in his room, walking around the company area with his hat on backwards, his shoes unshined and his hands in his pockets—apparently convinced the command that everybody would be better off if Joey, unlike Corporal Klinger of *M*A*S*H* fame, were let out of the Army. If any further convincing was necessary, Joey provided it when Sergeant Major Wright asked him what he would do if he had to drive his track into combat: "Blow it up and walk the other way," Joey replied, according to a participant in the meeting.

The lesson I drew from Joey's experience is that the Army should make it easier for soldiers to get out of their enlistments so

221

that obvious misfits would not have to build a case against themselves through such desperate acts as diving through a barracks window or jumping out of a moving car.

If West Point cadets, who cost far more to train than privates and contribute almost nothing to the nation's fighting power while they are taking courses at the U.S. Military Academy, can resign from the service without penalty at anytime up to the start of their junior year—which was the policy as of 1988—why should not privates have the same kind of escape hatches available?

## Guy, 22, the Would-Be Carpenter

He grew up in a depressed Ohio town, kept getting laid off construction jobs, joined the Army in the belief he could make a career out of being a carpenter in uniform. He told me that his Army recruiter, in persuading him to sign up for the infantry, assured him he could switch to carpentry after completing basic and advanced infantry training at Benning. Guy swallowed his disappointment in being forced into a COHORT infantry training unit for three years but still worked hard at soldiering in the beginning. He continued that way for a while after joining The Big Red One at Riley, winning an Army Achievement Medal for his outstanding soldiering at the National Training Center. One hot day in the Mojave Desert, I asked Guy how he could keep digging foxholes hour after hour without letup: "I like to work," he replied. A few months later his sergeants were calling him "a lazy fat fuck."

Guy told me in a lengthy interview in his trailer home at Junction City in September 1988 when he was freshly out of the Army that he had developed conflicts with his sergeants. He said they singled him out for punishment by putting him on a weight-reduction program even though many of the sergeants were fatter than he was and dropped out of the company runs. Although Guy did not say so in our interview, Army rules require leaders to make overweight privates slim down.

Guy also stole $200 from a fellow soldier by using the bank pass card in the car he had borrowed. "I shouldn't of done that," Guy told me. "I had brought my wife up here and had all these bills to pay," he said. The victimized soldier was sitting next to Guy smiling when we talked about the theft. "I wouldn't have turned

222

him in to command," said the victim. "But the bank got into it and I lost control."

Guy was pouring cement for a construction firm for $8 an hour at the time of our reunion and hoped to move into carpentry. He sounded more disillusioned than shattered by his Army experience. "The best part was the people I met and the travel," he told me. "The worst was being lied to." He contended the Army had not fulfilled the bargain it made when he enlisted.

One of Guy's friends told me: "A couple months earlier they gave him a medal and told him how good he was and what a motivation he was to the other soldiers. Then they chapter him out because they say he's bringing the other soldiers down. They made a scapegoat of him because of his weight. Once they notice you're a bad boy, that's it. They'll stick it to you. Keep pushing you. Guy just gave up after that weight thing. He wanted out."

My own view was that Guy's failure was another indictment of COHORT's no-transfer policy. If he had been transferred from Riley once he began to slide to a job where he could have used his carpentry skills, I think he would still be a productive soldier.

## Dee, 18, the Street Fighter

This soldier considered himself a product of the street even though the part of New Jersey he came from was more suburbia than ghetto. He tried to intimidate fellow soldiers from Day One at Benning and usually succeeded. But he had a soft, friendly side and could soldier with the best of them when he wanted to. He was the father of a baby girl who was the center of his life. He told me at Benning that he had joined the Army "to make her proud of me." Dee, who was very physical himself, said he was inspired at Benning by Drill Sergeant Randy Stover who seemed able to do everything in the field and still listen like a big brother in garrison. Dee complained to me that there were no Stovers among the sergeants at Riley.

Dee decided early on at Riley that his platoon sergeants were picking on him. He became confrontational with them and with the black executive officer of Charlie Company. Dee told me in one session with the executive officer, who was no longer with Charlie Company when I returned there in September 1988, that he accused the officer of being "a fake nigger because you don't treat black people as if they're like you. You think you're better. Sir, you treat us blacks and people who are white and down-to-earth like they're nothing. That's not right. You kiss ass to everything that outranks you that comes by."

This militant black private, whom many commanders thought had great potential for leading troops, could not accept the premise that the officer-to-soldier relationship should be master-to-servant. He told me over dinner in Junction City after his year at Riley that "this Army isn't fair. Why can't you speak what you feel if you get in a room man-to-man? It always comes down to, 'I'm going to write you up because I'm an E-6 and you're a private.' That's not right."

Although this soldier had contempt for several of the junior sergeants over him, he had nothing but praise for First Sergeant Russell Snyder who was the top enlisted man in Charlie Company from the time the troops arrived at Riley from Benning in October 1987 until June 1988, when Snyder was replaced. Dee received ten days in the Riley jail for refusing to obey a lawful order. "Snyder told me, 'Do your ten days and then come out and make a fresh start as the good soldier you can be.' I respect that man to this day."

Dee said he tried to make a fresh start after serving his time, but "I was being burned for everything" by the sergeants he had told off before his confinement. "I needed a transfer so I could get away from those sergeants," he said. "But in COHORT you can't get out of your situation. I asked for a four-day pass to see my little girl who was sick. My sergeant wouldn't give it to me. He said I wasn't a super soldier. So me and Jamie took off in August. August was me. August was free. August was saying we're not taking the bullshit anymore. We started fighting back."

I asked Dee why he could bow to the iron authority of drill sergeants at Benning but rebelled at Riley, disobeying orders, going AWOL and slipping back into drugs as evidenced by urinalysis. He replied: "If only I had had somebody I could talk to like Stover. You know, ten to fifteen guys here still carry pictures of Stover around with them. He was the greatest. Without somebody like him, I couldn't find peace of mind."

Was this soldier salvageable? I asked one of Charlie Company's super soldiers who knew Dee well and was himself sensitive, mature and fair. "It was six of one and a half a dozen of the other," the super soldier said. "Both sides would have had to put a lot more time into it, but I think he could have been saved. Dee would have been a good leader. He's physical. He's big. He's always testing. But he can be reasonable. He'd walk down the hall on my side. I'd just say, 'Give me a break' and smile. He would move over."

My own view is that the combined grief the command and Dee suffered further indicted COHORT. If this soldier had been transferred to another unit for a fresh start, I believe there was a better than even chance he would have been rehabilitated. I also believe from talking to Dee when he was being chaptered out that there was a better than even chance he would have served an additional year honorably as a soldier if he knew he could get out of the Army at the two-year point in his four-year enlistment.

## Jamie, 19, Immature Rebel Without a Cause

He was bright, articulate, intolerant, impatient, immature, athletic. Son of a Navy captain, Jamie told me the only reason he had joined the infantry was because he believed it would be like the Rambo movies. He was crushed when the Army pushed him into a mechanized infantry unit rather than allow him to become an airborne Ranger. But he proved to be a highly skillful, if whiney, infantryman at Benning and continued to be that way at Riley for a while. But he could not accept criticism leveled by sergeants he considered inferior in intellect to him, as illustrated by this written exchange between Sergeant Willie L. Glover and Jamie:

Sergeant: "Private _____ was verbally counseled about his military appearance . . . _____'s uniform was extremely dirty, boots unshined. These types of actions will not be stood for in the United States Army . . ."

Private: "Other members of the squad sustain the same level of appearance and performance and yet receive no malicious documents such as given me. I feel that I maintain the 'average' appearance and represent the average soldier. If Sgt. Glover wants to give bullshit remarks and give counseling statements to everyone of my caliber, then he will need a hell of a lot of paper to counsel the rest of the company. I feel my appearance and attitude is standard as relative to the rest of the company and refuse to comply with someone else's perfectionist ego. I request to be put in a different squad."

Jamie continued to rebel, once in the spring of 1988 telling a sergeant who he felt was harassing him: "Sergeant, suck my dick!" This insubordination and lesser offenses drew him the unusually stiff sentence of thirty days in the Riley jail.

The once highly motivated "Rambo" told me he was locked up with prisoners who had committed far more serious offenses before receiving thirty-day sentences. He said he emerged from jail embittered and resolved to force the Army to discharge him. He told me he purposely missed a formation after serving his sentence to help the Army build a case for chaptering him out. He said his new First Sergeant told him: "You'll have to do something more drastic than that." Jamie then went AWOL in August with Dee and broke other rules. His actions provoked the chaptering out that was in process when we talked in September 1988.

Although this soldier got crossways with some of his sergeants, he and many other soldiers had nothing but praise for Sergeant First Class Roger Bernard, a former drill sergeant, who was one of the company's new NCOs who projected caring for his men. "He's great," said Jamie. "He was willing to help me to get out."

Battalion Command Sergeant Major Wright told me thirty days might have been overkill for the offense I described, noting that a sergeant could drive a private into doing almost anything to build a case. Wright was speaking theoretically, not second-guessing the sentence. The sergeant whom Jamie insulted told me, "I didn't want him to go to jail. I would have blown it off. But he did it in front of other NCOs and soldiers, so I had to write him up."

Of the eleven members of Charlie Company being kicked out of the Army, I discovered that fellow soldiers considered Jamie the easiest to salvage. One told me: "Jamie could have been saved if more time had been spent with him. But some NCOs just say, 'You've got a duty. Go do it.' All Jamie needs is for someone to put his arm around him and lead him along the right path. But instead of that, sergeants like Sergeant _____ think the old system will work. You've been naughty. You go to jail for thirty days. Then you're supposed to come out a brand-new person. But they just added fuel to the fire.

"I think if some of these NCOs had just treated these guys being chaptered out more like human beings than yelling at them and telling them they were dumb fucking privates, it would have straightened some of them out."

226

My own view is that this over-demanding but potentially skillful paratrooper would have succeeded in the Army if any one of these things had happened: (1) he had been allowed to pursue his paratrooper dream rather than be stuck in a dull mechanized unit in the middle of nowhere; (2) had been transferred out of Charlie Company once his troubles with his sergeants mounted; (3) had the two-year exit option available to him. But because the no-transfer policy of COHORT denied the command flexibility and Jamie refused to change, I believe chaptering the rebellious private out was the only viable option.

## Vinnie, 21, the Boy-Man Who Didn't Fit

I knew from talking to him at length in the Mojave Desert that he had spent most of his life trying to fit in somewhere. He told me he had hitchhiked up and down the West Coast looking for his niche. Once he became so depressed he seriously contemplated suicide. He found escape in drugs and in a woman named Mary who had three children and who he thought was his salvation. He told me he joined the Army because "I need a secure way to support my future wife and kids."

I found rough nobleness in Vinnie. He would work uncomplainingly day and night during those exhausting days at the National Training Center. As we jounced around the Mojave Desert in an M-113, Vinnie talked and sang of Mary and the wonder she was going to bring to his life when they got married over Christmas leave.

Vinnie was a hopeless romantic full of antics that few in the company understood or appreciated. But I thought of this boy-man with the big, trusting eyes as a puppy mystified by all the kicks he got. Vinnie brought his beloved Mary and their four children (she had three before they met and they had one together before they married) to Junction City to try to live on a private's pay. Of course they soon ran out of money. Vinnie wrote bad checks, failed to pay his rent for the crowded trailer, neglected to fill out all the forms to qualify for military assistance for his family. He had to wire home for the money to fly his wife and their children back to Oregon. This soldier who I thought would have been great in battle could not handle the twin demands in garrison of heading a family and soldiering. He missed formations and broke many other rules before the Army decided to chapter him out.

I talked to Vinnie in September 1988. He was still the lost puppy. He was getting kicked out of the first home where he thought he fit, the United States Army. I did not blame the Army. Rules are rules. But remembering how he sang through the miseries of the National Training Center in December, knowing he would have been a hell of a soldier at another time in another place, I felt like putting my arm around Vinnie and taking him home rather than say that wrenching goodbye to him at Fort Riley, the place he thought would be Camelot once Mary arrived, rather than another crossroads where he would crash and burn one more time.

## Mac, 19, the Grieving Private

He was a quiet, dedicated, respectful, diligent, low-visibility soldier from Pennsylvania who suddenly became an uncaring, heavy drinker at Riley with a streak of bad luck, including having the military police arrest him for drunken driving while he was asleep in his car in front of the barracks. He had told me at Benning that he joined the Army "because I thought it would be good for me." He told me at Riley in September 1988 that his experience at the NTC in April, when he went on only four missions in thirty days, convinced him that he was in a dead-end trade. "I realized this isn't going to get me anywhere." He told me he lost even more heart when his mother died in May; he was arrested for drunken driving in June, received counseling in July, came up positive in the drug urinalysis test in August. "I'm half glad I'm getting out," he told me. "They waste so much time and yet you have no time to yourself. I don't blame the Army" for what happened.

I did not blame the Army, either, for ejecting Mac, given his depressed mental state toward the end of his first year. I did wonder, however, if Army psychiatrists could have salvaged this once super soldier if they had gotten to him soon enough at Riley.

## Boo, 21, and Duke, 19—Deserters

These two seemingly motivated soldiers went home for Christmas leave and never returned to duty at Riley, ending up being dropped from Army rolls after deserting. Boo told me at Benning that he was grateful to the Army for rescuing him from his car-washing job and planned to make the military a career. Duke at Benning said of soldiering: "I love it." He wanted to become a paratrooper and had written on the questionnaire I had asked all the recruits to fill out: "Try to find me a way out of this COHORT deal. I don't want it!" At Riley, Duke was considered an eager-beaver soldier; a favorite of his platoon leader. I heard colorful stories of what happened to these two but could not verify the causes for their sudden behavioral change. The Army had no choice here.

## Vee, 19, the Wild Man

I had serious doubts at Benning about this young man's ability to adapt to military life. His compass just kept spinning once he got out from under the iron hand of the drill instructors at Benning and tasted the comparative freedom of Riley. He went AWOL, married a topless dancer, was jailed by civilian authorities, stopped being a soldier when he reached Riley. He seemed unbalanced. I thought the Army had no choice but to chapter him out.

## Wilkie, 18, Moonstruck Farmer

A dairyhand from upstate New York and son of a truck driver, Wilkie told me he joined the Army because he thought soldiering would be more fun than farming. But he apparently fell hopelessly in love with a young girl in Kansas and could not bring himself to return to duty. Repeated AWOLs and other offenses gave the Army no choice but to discharge him.

## Steve, 30, Who Drank a Little

This elder soldier who won an Army Achievement Medal at Riley either could not or would not stop drinking, making his discharge inevitable.

## Gee, 18, Motorcycle Cowboy

This Massachusetts soldier had found love in Kansas and was not going to Germany with the company no matter what, he told me in the fall of 1988. He said he intended to live with his girlfriend, a hairdresser in Manhattan, and do carpentry in between riding around on his prized possession, a motorcycle. He went AWOL shortly after our reunion. It seemed only a matter of time before the Army gave up on him and chaptered Gee out, which would bring the total ejections to twelve rather than the eleven listed above already accomplished or in process.

"It's nothing like I thought it was going to be," he told me in talking about his year of soldiering at Riley. "I pictured it being more Rambo style. I wish I had never joined. Right now I feel the NCOs and officers are out to burn me." He had four Article 15s when we talked and went AWOL again shortly afterward, generating a recommendation from his superiors to discharge him from the Army. "Best thing that happened to me was basic training. The sergeants there knew their stuff and taught it to us. Not here. Right now I don't care how I get out just as long as I get out. They're talking about sending me to MIC [Motivational Instruction Course]. Wouldn't bother me a bit because they say if you flunk out of MIC, they'll chapter you out. I tried to go with the flow; got my E-3 [private first class]. I do my job really good [as Dragon antitank gunner]; get the best scores in my squad. We're just in the field too much, which puts me in these phases where I don't give a shit. I blame myself basically."

I always found Gee a pleasant, bright, hard-working soldier who obviously went through mood changes during his drinking binges when he would pick fights and get beat up. He was match-thin. An exit option or transfer, I believe, would have salvaged much of the Army's investment in this soldier.

Setting my own feelings aside, most of the Charlie Company soldiers I interviewed at Riley contended at least three and perhaps as many as five of those ejected soldiers could have been saved through better leadership, more enlightened training, transfers and exit options.

I asked Specialist Four Brooks, whose abilities the Army recognized by awarding him the only ROTC scholarship won within the First Division while Brooks was with Charlie Company, to ponder the root cause of his company's unusually high losses and low morale. He was in the company from July 1987 until August 1988, when he went to the University of Tampa on an ROTC scholarship. This was the answer he gave me after pondering the question for several days:

"The reason was mainly the leadership from the NCOs at Riley. They had a lot of double standards. They would tell us to be the best soldiers we could be; then they would do just the opposite themselves, like coming on duty drunk and cheating on the PT tests.

"The command also kept promising us things and then taking it back, like a free day we would never get. We were promised in February that we would get six days off after doing service on the tracks. But the command then said we could have only two days off. The word was that it was afraid everybody would go AWOL if we got six days.

"The NCOs at Benning knew what they wanted from us and could make us want to do it. With only a few exceptions, the NCOs at Riley couldn't do that. Maybe because they didn't have the training the drill sergeants got. It wasn't their lack of military skills that was the real problem. It was the way they interacted with us. We got the feeling they didn't really care about us, so we spent most of our time trying to get the NCOs. We lost our incentive to work hard and stay in the Army."

While the NCOs were who they lived with day in and day out, soldiers also were shrewd judges of the commissioned officers who commanded them from the top of the company. Soldiers gave most of their officers nicknames, which were always incisive, sometimes devastating.

"Ranger Mac" was Captain Michael McMahon, who commanded the company from its formation at Riley in October 1987 until March 1988. He was a Ranger and was what the troops called "hard core" because of keeping the troops in the field so much, including in fiercely cold weather. The troops admired his professionalism in the field but found him stand-offish.

(McMahon's six-month tour as commander of Charlie Company departed from the COHORT concept of keeping a unit whole for an extended period.)

"Captain Chaos" was Captain C. Brandon Cholek, who took over Charlie Company from McMahon. The name stemmed from the chaotic training schedule that caused the troops such despair but, in fairness, may have been beyond his control. A private once checked through Cholek's pack before a long company hike and discovered it was lighter than the troops' because it did not contain several of the required items. This short weighting opened up a credibility gap and was the source of complaint at a company "bitch session."

"Custer's Last Stand" was Lieutenant John Kiser, commander of 2d Platoon, who led his troops into a trap at the National Training Center in December and had a proclivity for getting lost, especially at night.

"Book Smarts" was Lieutenant Eric Hungerford when he commanded 3d Platoon because of his obsession with going by the book. As one soldier put it with a smile, "If the enemy were attacking us, the L. T. [Lieutenant] would say: 'Attack. That's on page 37. Page 37. Return fire.'"

While looking through the privates' end of the telescope during my days of assessing Charlie Company at the one-year mark, I talked to several of their wives. Here I found another big gap between Army rhetoric at the top and practice at the bottom. Not one wife said she felt like she had been included in the company. They said neither officers nor senior sergeants showed much inclination to hold company-wide social affairs that included the wives. One wife astonished me when I asked what her biggest single regret was on the social front: "I would have liked to have met Captain McMahon. I heard a lot about him, but I never saw him." Several other privates' wives told me they had never met McMahon, either, nor been shown what Riley activities they might engage in instead of spending so much time inside depressing Junction City trailers waiting for their husbands to come in from the field.

Time can hang heavy for soldiers' wives locked up inside a Junction City trailer. One told me that she could not get a job in Junction City, partly because employers knew Charlie Company would only be in town one year before flying off to Germany.

232

Another reason, she said, is the long line of other military wives trying to get jobs in the military town. Unemployed and childless, the wife told me her typical day started at 9:30 A.M. because her soldier husband arose too early—at 5 A.M.—if he was home at all, walking out to the mailbox at mid-morning to see if anything was inside, watching television until it was time to get supper. If her husband had to spend the night in the field, the wife told me, she slept in another woman's trailer because she was afraid to stay alone in her own trailer.

Life for soldier wives with children can be difficult in military towns like Junction City, which are crowded with sex-starved soldiers. One mother told me she was often propositioned by soldiers even in places as public as supermarkets when she stood in line with her children.

"I don't have any feeling of being connected to the company and its wives," said the wife of a trooper the command considered a super soldier. "The only affair I went to was run by the First Sergeant's wife where she asked, 'What's your husband's rank? Then you sit over there.' They categorized the wives by rank. I didn't like it. The only other company functions I went to were briefings for wives on Germany"—before Charlie Company flew there from Charleston, South Carolina, in mid-October without the wives. The wives would join their soldier husbands later.

Sergeant Ronald Reichle, whom I had known from my first weeks with Charlie Company and who was one of the few NCOs still with the outfit a year later, told me as I moved up the chain of command trying to find out what had gone wrong that "for Captain McMahon, training was first for everything." Reichle was not being critical. He was just describing one commander's leadership style as he had lived it.

"That was his goal—to train constantly," Reichle said. "The stuff that normally goes on in a regular unit—like the sporting events to bring in togetherness after a major field problem—just wasn't done. They were way down on the list. He had this obsession about getting ready to go to war tomorrow morning.

"Now the Army teaches that the NCOs run the unit. That it's their people. That the officers just manage. But it was the philosophy of the chain of the command when Captain McMahon ran the company that the officers will get into the nitty-gritty, down in the NCO level and conduct and watch training.

"This led to a conflict, with NCOs saying: 'Well, if he's going to get into my job, why doesn't he just do it all. I'll go down and take a break.'

"Every new sergeant major who comes in here says, 'I see we have an NCO-officer problem here where the officers are getting into NCO business.'

"In normal units, as an NCO you don't see your platoon leader or your company commander unless you're in trouble or in the field. The platoon leader has too much else to do in garrison. But when we're in the field, it's his ball. But in garrison, it's the NCO's. They've thrown me for a loop here.

"I don't know where it all originated from. The previous battalion commander [Lieutenant Colonel Joseph G. Terry Jr.] had been in Vietnam. He knew the NCOs could do the job. You got the sense it was all the way up. It wasn't just one company commander. It was every company commander. It was every lieutenant that was told, 'This is what you will do.'

"McAfee [Lieutenant Colonel Lawrence McAfee Jr., commander of the Second Battalion of the Sixteenth Infantry Regiment to which Charlie Company was attached] is working his way out of it. He's trying to get out of the Fort Riley mode. It might have come from the old general. The NCOs, especially the young ones, are trying to relearn the NCO responsibilities to bring things back to the way they used to be."

Reichle said the troops were justified in complaining to me that duty at Riley was often dull for young tigers expecting to practice being Rambos. "With mechanized," he said, "it's vehicle, vehicle, vehicle. You do the same old routine. In light infantry, you don't have that vehicle you have to worry about being up 100 percent all the time."

The personable sergeant added that the infantry is the orphan at a base like Fort Riley where tanks and other armor dominate everything and everybody. "Infantry is always the orphan unless you're only infantry. Then everybody supports you. But on a post like this, when it comes to boring jobs like guard duty, who has to pull it? Infantry."

Reichle added that there was some truth in Trooper Linville's complaint that every new company commander puts a new load on the troops. "That's the problem of new commanders. He talks Vietnam. He's gung-ho. He says we're going to do this. We're going to do that. I want to make sure my men are highly trained. We're going to push until we get what I want. By the time he gets what he wants, it's, 'Adios. Bye-bye. I look good in front of the battalion commander. It has helped me. I've accomplished the things I wanted to accomplish, and now it's time to move on.'

"Boom! A new commander. Then it's Day One again.

"But after eighteen months [the time a captain usually spends in command of an Army company], a company commander is just beginning to learn his job. He should stay company commander until his next promotion—three or four years—so he would hand over a fully trained company to the next captain who comes in barefooted. A junior NCO has to stay four or five years in a unit to really learn his job. Who's to say a commander doesn't need that much time as well. It would give the officer time to mellow out. Time to get over his push-push."

Russell Snyder, Charlie Company's first sergeant from the time it arrived at Riley from Benning in October until he was replaced in June, agreed that the company had suffered from micro-management by its officers. But he made what I thought was a valid point after observing the company in the field: McMahon had inexperienced platoon leaders as well as inexperienced soldiers to train before the company went to the National Training Center in November and December 1987. I remembered hearing McMahon's constant counseling over the radios of the tracks I rode in at Riley and the National Training Center. "He's the best I've ever seen at training young officers," Snyder said of McMahon. An unwanted by-product of McMahon's effort was troops inside the tracks often feeling as if they were little more than training aids for those officers.

The always savvy soldiers could tell their platoon leaders did not know much more about the intricacies of mechanized infantry tactics than they did. The troops would tell me this over and over. I always thought it would have built unity, not shaken confidence any further, if the company officers had just come right out and told their soldiers, "Hey! We're all learning this together. Nobody's an expert out here." Several soldiers complained that their former executive officer took the opposite approach, telling them: "Anybody can do your job. But none of you can do my job."

Lieutenant John Kiser, commander of 2d Platoon and the only officer to stay put during Charlie Company's year at Riley, was a frenetic, short-fused leader whose master plan called for becoming a military chaplain after completing his infantry command and staff jobs. An ROTC cadet at the University of Kansas, he told

235

me that after graduating and receiving his Army second lieutenant bars in 1986, he chose the infantry because it was "human
intensive rather than equipment intensive."

He conceded his human relationships with many of his troops
were tense. One reason, he told me, was that "a big thing with
these guys is the double standard—'why can he do that and I
can't?' What I've been taught is that when you're a lieutenant you
don't have to explain your actions to soldiers. They have do stuff
without question; execute now and we'll explain it later because
in combat you don't have time to explain. I know when Captain
Cholek and Captain McMahon tell me to do it, I know I've got to
do it. Discipline has always been the problem" with the troops in
the company, he said over lunch at the Riley Officers' Club. He
said the Benning graduates reported to Riley underdisciplined.

As would be expected, the troops themselves disagreed with
Kiser's view on discipline. South Bronx Petersen's view was the
prevailing one: "Discipline in basic was all right. Then we got
here and at first they were too nice to us. They let us get away with
a little bit, and it spoiled some of the guys. Now all of a sudden
just before we go to Germany, they crack down real hard. You
can't do that. It's like raising a kid. If you spoil a kid rotten and
then crack down on him, you end up with a civil war in the family.
All of a sudden they're giving guys summarized Article 15s for
showing up a few minutes late for formation."

Captain Cholek, an ROTC graduate of William and Mary, in a
discussion in one of the old barracks at Camp Forsythe, said that
he did not blame the raw material for the company's problems. "A
soldier is a soldier," he said. "He'll do what needs to be done if
he's well led."

His impression of the ones inherited from McMahon, however,
was that they "were not pushed" in basic training and, he said,
"had developed some attitudes." He cited Soldier Dee, declaring
his misbehavior had prompted him to tell the soldier: "You say
you're off the block. Well, get off my block."

Like Sergeant Major Wright, Cholek said he believed the fundamental problem within Charlie Company was a middle-
management gap stemming from a shortage of noncommissioned
officers skilled at leading young troops. Unlike Wright, he felt
certain this gap would be closed when the super soldiers of
Charlie Company advanced into those leadership positions.

"They are starting to come through," he said of these soldiers on the way up. "They are my new leaders." While McMahon commanded the company, Cholek said, "Nobody did anything unless Mike McMahon said so. I've tried to loosen the reins to give junior leaders more opportunity to develop."

Cholek's reaction to Charlie Company's abnormally high loss rate was that it was better to get rid of the bad apples in the barrel before the company deployed from Riley to Germany even if that meant being shorthanded. "Once we get to Germany, things will really be good," he predicted.

Soldiers who had seen the training schedule for Germany doubted this because it called for so much time in the field.

Battalion Commander McAfee was the highest person in the chain of command at Riley with a working knowledge of the problems within Charlie Company. But he was looking at the company from a distance. He did not live its life. The lanky, low-key, affable, one-time mud soldier acknowledged, "I'm a little under strength in strong NCOs. We're looking at how we can improve our internal training program. We ask a lot of the NCO corps. All the hours they put in, the preparation for training and training itself. If they got in for money, they're in the wrong business."

I asked him if he agreed that commanders like himself and the soldiers trying to get out of their enlistments would be better off if there were an exit option. Only if the command could exercise a veto on a soldier's request to get out of the Army, he said. "Most company commanders have the Jesus syndrome. They need the time to work on soldiers. Nineteen- and 20-year-olds don't know what they want yet in life."

McAfee had a point, of course, but I felt he, like so many other officers and sergeants, did not fully comprehend how much today's teenaged volunteers want to be able to keep telling themselves that their service in the Army is getting them somewhere, even if their progress must be measured in inches. As long as they saw themselves improving, I felt, they would continue to put up with the discomfort, aggravation and loneliness of the toughest soldiering—that done by infantrymen. Did Tweety, Little and Big Henson, Chris Cashman, "Spank" Barker, West Virginians Murray and Adkins, College Boy Brooks, bad boys Glen and Budweiser and the other young volunteers who had had such high hopes for themselves in the Army still feel that way?

# 13. Volunteers Revisited

I found Tweety Selvester, the teenager who had suffered so much in growing up on his stepfather's farm in Lincoln, California, and during Shock Treatment at Fort Benning, with a big smile on his face at his off-duty hangout, the square at Aggieville, the college town outside of Fort Riley in The Little Apple—Manhattan, Kansas. His close-shaven blond head illuminated by the lights on the square reminded me of a giant lightbulb that moths in the form of teenaged girls had found and could not get close enough to. One girl after another embraced Tweety, offered him cigarettes and laughed as he shared his happiness with everyone crowding around him, including this intruder.

"Hey, I want you to meet this guy," Tweety said to his teenaged courtiers in jeans. "He has been doing everything with us and is writing a book about it. This is Mr. Wilson."

"No kidding," responded a tall, thin high school junior with the say-what's-on-your-mind manner of the Midwest. "Well, I want to get out of here and be a model. How about putting my picture in your book?"

I took her picture with Tweety and six other moths flying around this lamp of a boy-man-soldier. Then everybody went back to the Saturday night pastime on Aggieville's square of calling out to the people inside the cars driving round and round the town. Tweety and some of his soldier friends had rented a motel room on the edge of Aggieville. He was inviting everyone around him to stop by for a brew. I did not have the heart to remind Tweety that the management of that same motel was still a little tender about his buck-naked streaking through the courtyard in the wee hours a few months earlier.

Leaving Tweety to his fans on the square during those golden hours of his free time, I sat down with him later in a quiet corner of his new Army world and asked him about how he had changed in his recent passages from troubled teenager to trained soldier; from boy to man; from "stupid idiot" stepson to praised son.

"I look at things a lot different than I used to," Tweety began as my tape recorder spun. "Now that I'm in the military I have learned to appreciate the really small things in life that before I never even thought about, like a flush toilet and time to myself. When I think of all the time I wasted before I came in—

"I've learned there's so much more to life than the way I used to live it. When you're in the field, you can't get out. When you're in the barracks, you almost feel you're in jail because you're on the job all the time. But when you're out of the field and the barracks and get a little time off, everything is beautiful.

"I feel like I've aged about ten years. I'm much more responsible, most definitely. If I mess up, I can get nailed.

"Things with my dad and me are fine now. We do great. Just great. I think I did a lot of growing up, and he has just changed. I guess that's the way it happens. Maybe I'll find out one of these days.

"I've learned what the human body can put up with. It's amazing. You can just throw a big rucksack on your back, carry a 60 [M-60 machine gun], walk fifteen or twenty miles, live off what little food they give us or MREs, which amount to nothing, and just drive on."

All in all, I asked, are you glad you joined the Army and would you do it again?

"There's a couple of reasons I wouldn't have signed up if I had it to do over, but there are ninety-eight other reasons that make me glad I did. I know I would do it again.

"Going to Germany is going to be hard for me. I'm going to miss my mom really bad, and Teresa," his girlfriend back in Auburn who kept him afloat during the time his stepfather was cursing him for failing to do anything right on the ranch or in school or anywhere else.

"I don't want to leave them behind, but that's the way it's going to have to be. It's really hard being away. I need that love. My mom and I have always been very close.

"I'm trying to look at Germany as a great experience. I'm going to see as much as I can and make the best of it.

"If I stay in the Army after my four years, I've got to get some kind of guarantee that I'd be stationed in California at Fort Ord or Fort Irwin. None of this 'we'll see' stuff. This time it's got to be in writing.

"I still want to stay in the infantry if I stay in. If I'm going to join the Army, I want to be a soldier. I don't just want to be another person in BDUs [battle dress uniform]."

We talked about his trauma in basic training where the drill sergeants had ganged up on him in Shock Treatment and afterward because he was a klutzy, visibly vulnerable, homesick fat boy.

"You don't have to go that far to get a kid like I was when I came in to respect authority. About fifteen people in our company are still messed up from it. Now they just don't know how to deal with situations.

"What got me through basic were guys like Proctor, Remington, Hollands [Kevin J. Hollands, 19, of Reading, Michigan] and you, Mr. Wilson. You don't know how nice it was to be able to talk to someone who was not in the Army. I was really stressed. Talking to you—well, I just can't thank you enough."

It was like hearing my own son suddenly say thanks for being there when he needed me. I looked away as my eyes filled. Tweety and I had shared so much as we bridged the generation gap. We both knew we soon would be going separate ways, never again to feel the closeness he had just spoken.

I asked the same questions of Aaron Henson, the black soldier who had felt the sting of racial prejudice in his hometown of Tyler, Texas, and joined the Army in the belief he was escaping the hurt. But he found basic training at Benning so intolerable that he drank a bottle of window cleaner in hopes of ending his misery. He struck me as being at peace with himself when we reunited at Riley after his traumatic first year in the Army. I could tell just by watching the way he interacted with his fellow soldiers that he had finally learned how to go with the flow. He was no longer the raging volcano I had seen at Benning. We talked on the side porch of the barracks at Camp Forsythe.

"I've growed up a lot," Henson said. "Matured a lot. I'm taking things more seriously. Before I came in it was, 'Hey, forget it,' when something went wrong with the job I had. Now if I had a job it would be, 'I need this job,' and all that.

"The worst thing has been being away from home and all the mess-ups here at Riley. Maybe the rest of the Army has the same mess-ups. I might come in again if I had it to do over. But not the infantry. They ought to make it more entertaining, more real like. The best part has been learning to be more responsible."

I remembered, as Henson and I sat in the sun talking, what Captain Jim Fleenor had told me at Benning when he rejected the psychologists' recommendation to kick Henson out of the Army after he had drunk the glass cleaner: "If ever there was a kid I could save, Little Henson was him."

Fleenor had also extricated Henson from a scrape with military policemen outside the Sand Hill post exchange, led the private to his own car, drove Henson back to the barracks. This company commander never said a word during the tense drive from the PX to the barracks. Fleenor's silent treatment shouted louder to Henson than all the shouts of the drill sergeants put together. He had let down the captain who had taken such a personal interest in this mixed-up teenager. Henson never let Fleenor down again. He finished basic with no more rebellious acts. At the time I had thought Fleenor was wrong in not following the psychologists' advice and keeping Henson in the Army. Fleenor proved right. He would have been proud to learn that Henson in his one year at Riley had won an Army Achievement Medal and had been promoted to private first class.

"Aaron?" answered Chris Cashman, his best friend in Charlie Company, when I asked him how he thought the once-troubled soldier was holding up. "He's even playing the game of soldier—pressing his uniform and everything. The other day I told him that with all this enthusiasm he must be planning to reenlist. He rolled on the ground laughing."

"And how about you?" I asked Cashman, the rugby player who discovered he had stayed in Australia too long and joined the Army to keep his young family afloat.

"Oh, I'm putting up with it," said this super soldier with two Army Achievement medals and the stripes of Specialist Four on his collar. He told me that he would never go in the infantry again.

He said his year at Riley had demonstrated how little time infantrymen get with their family even in peacetime.

I asked his wife, Kerry, as we chatted together in the family trailer in Junction City how she thought the Army had changed Chris in one year.

"The Army's made him more assertive. It used to drive me crazy the way his friends walked all over him."

"The Army didn't change me as much as they wanted to," interjected Chris. "I'm older and more set in my ways. I'm more forceful than I used to be. But you sort of have to be more assertive when you get rank. I don't mean to brag, but I was well mannered when I came in. It took a lot of getting used to the way people shoved other people around and never said, 'Excuse me.' I kind of had to put my manners away.

"I keep thinking I'll be 31 years old when we get out after my four years and four months in the Army. And still with no trade. We could be right back where we were before unless I stayed in the Army, got out of the infantry and got a trade."

I had to agree with a laugh as we sat together discussing the past year that not many civilian employers were panting to hire an expert infantryman no matter how good he was with the M-16 rifle.

For all their hardships, Kerry reminded Chris, "the Army enabled us to make it. We had too much family hanging over us in Australia. But when we got to California, we found we couldn't make it. We didn't want to go back to Australia defeated."

Chris and Kerry had the mattress from their double bed spread out on the living floor of the trailer so they could watch television at night without waking up their two children in the bedroom of the trailer. That way, either parent could just drop off to sleep in front of the TV without walking to the back of the thin, tight trailer off the highway. I was humbled by how little this decent, hard-working couple was asking from life. They would settle for just a little piece of the American dream. A job, a home, a place where the family could be together. Kerry told me it was tough being alone in the trailer during all the nights when Chris was in the field. She said she had been invited to only one company social function during her year at Riley. I left the Cashmans feeling warmed by their friendship but chilled by the Army's failure to make them feel part of its family.

Steve Henson, the tall black idealist who vowed to go back to his native Baltimore some day to be a policeman "to do good," told me his year of soldiering "made me a better person. Sergeant [Roger] Bernard told me one time. 'No one is going to look out for you unless you look out for yourself.' "

His asthma attacks in the field had impelled the command to transfer Steve to driving a 2½-ton truck, a "deuce and a half," much of the time rather than hump around the prairie. I asked him if Riley had burned him out the way it had burned out so many other soldiers.

"No. I don't mind working. A lot of guys did get burned out. I deal with it, that's all."

His mother, Betty, told me that she felt grateful to the Army for teaching her often impatient son "how to deal with it. I look at him now and say, 'Wow!' I'm so proud of him. He has improved. Before he just didn't care. Now he seems to worry about his buddies even more than himself. And he's proud of being in the military. He thinks before doing something and says to himself, 'I better not do that' because he doesn't want to smear the military. He's prepared to accept responsibility. That's good. He's also ambitious. He's been taking reading courses at Riley. He told me he's now up to the college level and will keep taking courses in Germany. He still wants to be a policeman. The Army has been good for Steve."


Ty Barker, who joined the infantry "to be something more than a little fat kid," told me he felt good about what he had been able to accomplish in his year in the Army but regretted the command at Riley had wasted so much of his time when he would rather be home with his wife, Rhonda.

"I wanted a career and to make a life for ourselves," he said of himself and Rhonda. "I had looked around for jobs. You had to be this; you had to be that." He said the best part of Riley as an M-113 driver was learning the tricks of battlefield survival at Riley's advanced infantry school, which took less than three weeks because the training was well planned and executed. The worst, Barker told me during several sessions in his trailer home in Cottonwood trailer park in Junction City, was being away from Rhonda so much for no good reason.

Rhonda told me most of her days at Riley amounted to "watch TV and wait for Ty. The worst part of being here is that I know there's nothing to do. I never know when he's coming home. Time goes by really slow. You can go to the Wal-Mart just so many times.

"I'm scared to death when he's away. I jump at every little noise in the trailer," which cost the couple $190 a month without utilities and up to $289 a month during the winter when heating bills were high.

"I learned a lot because I don't have Mom. I learned how to pay bills.

"I had heard so much about how the Army was a family. But it hasn't been that way at all. They should get more involved with the wives. They're always saying family first. I've never been invited to anything social. I've never seen Captain McMahon. I don't know what he looks like. I would have liked to have met him because I heard so much about him."

I asked this 21-year-old wife of a soldier whether Charlie Company or its parent battalion had any kind of wives' club she could have joined for something to do and moral support. "Not that I know of," she replied. "No one has ever said anything about it, and I don't know how to find out. Somebody should have let me know what there was."

"The thing about Riley," Barker told me as we parted, "is that there is nothing for a young soldier's family to do here. Topeka is the closest place where you can do something."

Drive a few hundred yards away from Barker's trailer, passing banged-up cars sitting on blocks in weedy rectangles off to the side of the trailer park's main roads, and you come to the trailer home of Specialist Four Murray and his wife, Ruth. She is a tiny slip of a woman. When we talked in the fall of 1988 about her first year away from home, her first year of being a mother, her first year of being an Army wife, she seemed too vulnerable to me to stay night after night by herself with her baby in a trailer bounded by the Junction City Highway, the parking lot for a raucous tavern, and other trailers. But she said she had hung in there. Like Rhonda Barker and Kerry Cashman, she said she never felt the embrace of the Army as she struggled with her loneliness.

"He's got a job," Mrs. Murray told me in giving the best part of her Army experience. "Him being away" was the worst, she added. Murray nodded in agreement as we sat together in their trailer living room. "When I came in," he said, "I had this image that you could focus your life around your family. Ruth doesn't like to take the baby in for shots. I can't get off to come home and do stuff like that even when we're in garrison."

Has the Army been good for this once happy-go-lucky wrestling champion from a tiny town in West Virginia? I asked Ruth. "He's gotten more serious. Instead of hanging around with his buddies, he comes home. He also worries more than he used to. He never used to worry about how we would pay for things. He worries about that now, but he doesn't tell me."

I could sense the deep love these two hometown sweethearts had for each other. She looked to him for guidance in everything she did and said. He smiled back at her encouragingly. They would make it. And they would stay loyal to the Army, I felt sure, giving back far more than they took from the Army he had served so well in this first year.

Norman Adkins, the other Smurf wrestler from West Virginia, who had signed up to be an Airborne Ranger only to be forced into a COHORT mechanized unit, told me at Riley that he was no longer sure he would make the Army a career, given his disappointment with his first year with The Big Red One. The all or nothing-at-all workload and tedium of Riley had deflated him, the once gung-ho infantryman who had won two excellence awards at Benning told me at the end of his first year at the fort. He said if he became rejuvenated during Charlie Company's two years in Germany and made sergeant in that time, he might still make the Army his career, hopefully as the Airborne Ranger he signed up to be in the first place.

"He's restless, gets mad easily—that's not Norman A.," his mother said despairingly when asked how her son had changed after his first year at Riley. "He told me that he got so tired of them telling him one thing and doing another and all the bull." She said Norman just felt like ending it all. "I told him, 'Norman, it's not worth it. Don't do that. If you don't like it, you can get out somehow.' He said, 'No. No.' He would finish. But it's not what he thought it would be. I guess they give them the runaround all the time. That's what they all seem to say. It's real aggravating for them. If he liked it, I could feel better about it all."

I heard good news and bad news when I checked up on the two "mended men" I had interviewed at length at Benning, Budweiser and Glen. Budweiser, with difficulty, had continued on the high road he had taken when he joined the Army. He was in Germany most of his first year maintaining and then driving the Bradley Fighting Vehicle. He had been promoted to private first class, proof he had performed well.

"The best thing that ever happened to him," enthused Budweiser's mother when I talked to her after his first year in uniform. "The Army is not for everybody, but it has been great for [him]. It's helped him to grow up. He writes us these great letters, saying he realizes that life is not just a game. He has told us that he did not believe the things we told him when he was growing up but now realizes they were true. He got in a hot argument with his sergeant and then he just took off, like he always did with us. But he said he remembered us telling him that when he wronged somebody, he should go back to that person and make it right. That's what he did with the sergeant. He told us that doing that saved his neck.

"We're so proud of [our son]. He's got everything. He could conquer the world if he wanted to. He's interested in college now. But he has been so homesick. And he got blinded with shrapnel for a while, and he so wanted to be home then. But he's all right now and can't wait to come home for his leave."

Glen told me he did well at Fort Hood, Texas, for a while but gave up on the infantry after spending so much time in the field. "We got back from a thirty-day field problem on a Thursday in late February," Glen told me. "We worked until 10 P.M. Friday cleaning up the vehicles. Then they told us to be back at 6 A.M. Saturday to go back out in the field. I didn't show up." He went AWOL for more than a month, was caught and chaptered out of the Army under less than honorable conditions.

"It was my fault, not the Army's," Glen told me. "I screwed up. I think I could have made it in the Army if I had gone into something besides the infantry. When I got to Fort Hood from Benning I found it was so laid back compared to basic. Guys would not show up for formation and never be reported. I missed days without anybody sending papers forward that I had been AWOL. In one formation there were only nine guys out of the twenty-three in our platoon who showed up. Nothing happened to anybody. If we had done stuff like that at basic the drill sergeants would have put us before a firing squad.

"Then everything suddenly changed and we were out in the field all the time. In the winter the mud would sometimes be up to your knees. I drove that Bradley all over the place; went back in to clean it up, and then back in the field again. I just decided in February I wasn't going to go out there again.

"I'm glad I joined. It helped me understand how much I screwed up before I went in and how much home means to me. I wasn't prepared enough for what was going to happen," said the young man who had joined the Army at age seventeen under threat of going to jail if he stood trial for an assault he had committed. Glen said his time in the Army had enabled him to kick his drug habit.

John Brooks, who joined the Army in the belief it offered the best opportunity for him to finish the college education he had started at the University of Maryland but did not have money to finish, told me that his success at Fort Benning "made me feel real good about myself. It gave me confidence and the discipline I was after."

After he got to Riley, however, he said disillusionment with the Army came in three stages. The first was his conviction at the National Training Center that his officers did not know how to employ the TOW antitank weapon he had been trained to use. The second wave of disillusionment came after Christmas at Riley, he said, when the work load was all or nothing at all and no superior seemed interested in arranging his hours so he could take college courses. The third wave was the conclusion that some officers and sergeants really did not care about his health and welfare or that of his fellow soldiers, subjecting them unnecessarily, in his view, to frostbite in the winter and breaking promise after promise about time off if they did this or that first. Brooks, like Sergeant Major Wright, did not fault the soldiers in Charlie Company, declaring they were a good bunch to be with. "The trouble was leadership; especially the sergeants," he said. Brooks won an ROTC scholarship and left Charlie Company in mid-August 1988. He told me that he felt happy about the Army enabling him to pursue his dream of a college degree but sad that so many of his fellow soldiers he was leaving behind were not realizing their dreams.

One sunny morning as I shuttled back and forth between trailer parks, Camp Forsythe and my motel in Junction City interviewing soldiers on their first year with a regular Army unit, I stopped off in Heritage Park in the heart of the cold-looking town. I found an inscription on the park's monument to Vietnam War dead that gave Junction City a bit of grace. I decided the words applied to all mud soldiers—the living as well as the dead. Mud soldiers are so often kept away from where they want to be and from whom they want to hold. The words were written by Major Michael Davis O'Donnell of Springfield, Illinois, shortly before he was killed at the age of 24 in Vietnam on March 24, 1970. I set down his words here as a final salute to mud soldiers past, present and future:

*If you are able,*
*Save for them a place inside of you.*
*And save one backward glance*
*When you are leaving for the places they can no*
*longer go.*
*Be not ashamed to say you loved them,*
*Though you may or may not always have.*
*Take what they have left*
*And what they have taught you with their dying.*
*And keep it with your own.*
*And in that time when men feel safe to call the war*
*insane,*
*Take one moment to embrace those gentle heroes*
*You left behind.*

# 14. Recommendations

Just as the world changed for the United States and its Army in 1966 because of the Vietnam War and the decision to switch from the draft to the All-Volunteer Force, so is the world changing in 1989 for the country and its post-Vietnam Army as a different set of pressures push against them.

One of these pressures is the reoriented Congress that convened in 1989. The lawmakers are more afraid of the federal deficit and other cracks in the national economy than they are of the Russians. Barring war, the days of steadily increasing defense budgets are over, putting the Army in a bind.

To pay for all the weapons it has already ordered and wants to buy in the future, the Army will have to stay small and probably get smaller. There is not enough money in sight to buy the weapons and still keep the present force of 772,000 men and women on the active duty payroll.

Another pressure is coming from Europe where many North Atlantic Treaty Organization partners are pressing for mutual U.S.-Soviet troop withdrawals. General E. C. Meyer, a former Army chief of staff, predicts two U.S. Army divisions will be withdrawn from Europe and demobilized within the next few years.

While a smaller Army would seem to make recruiting easier in the future because there would be fewer vacancies to fill, this will not necessarily be so. The pool of young men and women to recruit will shrink in the 1990s. This will generate more intensive competition within the American marketplace for the best and brightest people within this smaller pool.

This competition for quality people will be further intensified if national service legislation now being pushed through Congress becomes law. The legislation would require men and women aged 18 to 26 to serve in some community or state enterprise, like a hospital, or in the armed services before they could obtain government money to continue their education. Civilian service would be for one year and military duty for two years under the legislation sponsored by Senator Sam Nunn, a Georgia Democrat, and Representative Dave McCurdy, an Oklahoma Democrat. The civilian volunteer would receive a $10,000 government grant for college, vocational school or a business after serving one year. A two-year military volunteer would receive $24,000.

If some form of this national service legislation becomes law, as seems likely, the Army will be competing not only with its brother services and industry for high-quality young people, but with communities and states as well.

The Army must find ways to compete successfully in this broadened marketplace to keep up its fighting power while losing manpower. It must find ways not only to attract high-quality young people but to hold them. Neither the nation nor the Army can afford the attrition caused by the kind of leadership that inflicted so much pain and disillusionment on the soldiers in the Charlie Company I followed and many outfits like it.

The big challenge for Army leaders, as I see it, is to force an attitudinal change toward soldiers in that great middle body of leaders between private and general. The Army's junior and middle managers must lean farther toward their volunteer soldiers or lose them. Too many of these sergeants and officers in the middle do not seem to realize that marketplace competition, if nothing else, makes it in the Army's interest for them to treat volunteer soldiers like valued employees with alternatives rather than like serfs with no place to go.

In hopes of helping the new American Army we all depend on to be all it can be, I have set down a number of recommendations inspired by my year-long, inside look.

## Send Young Officers Through Basic with Troops.

Requiring officers shortly after being commissioned to go through seven weeks of basic training with today's volunteers would force them to learn what these new soldiers are all about. I was appalled during my year inside the Army at the depth of ignorance young officers had about this new breed of soldier. They did not know, or seem to care in many cases, the backgrounds, hopes and fears of these young men they may some day try to lead in the kind of battle Johnny Libs of the old Charlie Company fought.

Like it or not, times have changed. Army leaders are competing to attract and hold talent in the enlisted ranks. The soldiers want to see themselves appreciated, to be told how they are doing, to be put on the fast track to somewhere if they excel. If they are not treated as valued employees, they will quit spiritually first and physically next, as an unacceptably high percentage of soldiers in Charlie Company did.

The officers going through basic under my concept would wear no insignia, sleep in the barracks with the troops and eat with them, do everything they did—including accepting the punishment of Army drill sergeants the same way Navy officers in training to become aviators accept the punishment of Marine drill sergeants. The firebreak between officer and enlisted would be re-established after basic.

My year inside today's Army told me that many young officers and sergeants really do not like or respect apprentice soldiers. Some, I found, fear them. They are afraid to get too close to their soldiers, to learn anything about or from them. These officers and sergeants do not project caring; they project an "all for me" quality which soldiers resent. Basic training would help to identify these qualities, hopefully prompting superiors to direct those officers' careers away from troop leadership.

## Make Training More Fun

Most young people join the Army in hopes it will be more fun than the jobs they could get at home. The Army could go a lot further in fulfilling this desire while providing valuable training by taking such steps as these:

• Building ranges behind the barracks for contests in grenade throwing, low and high crawl races and laser shooting galleries.

• Providing computerized war games, such as an infantryman against a tank, and interesting training films in the form of cassettes of such exciting but instructive operations as the invasion of

251

Normandy in World War II, the Inchon landing during the Korean War and Vietnam search-and-destroy tactics. Modern barracks have television sets and often VCRs but virtually nothing related to the profession of arms to play on them. Even paperback books with a military orientation for the lounges in Army barracks would be an improvement over the deserts of nothingness I found in day rooms at Fort Benning and Fort Riley where the troops often longed for something meaningful to fill their time.

• Inserting in training schedules more fun activities, such as squads slipping through the woods under their own enlisted leaders' command to knock out "enemy" machine-gun nests. These exciting and instructive exercises virtually stopped once the troops I followed left Benning.

• Requiring company commanders to hold more sports competitions, family picnics and other unifying recreational events since they seem to have lost the zest for doing these things on their own. Take something else out of their schedules or bring back the polo ponies so the officers would have to practice riding for the weekend match, enabling the sergeants to run their units with less interference.

• Forbidding sergeants or officers to read lessons to troops out of training manuals, especially in the cold and wet. If they cannot teach any other way, find leaders who can. I spent hours listening to sergeants and officers read to me and the troops out of field manuals and doubt if any of us learned anything.

• Appointing a panel of civilian experts to assess Army training with an eye to determine whether it is suitable for today's brighter soldiers. How many hours, for example, are needed to teach these volunteers to shoot straight? How many to get in and out of an armored vehicle? Would we have better marksmen for the same investment by compressing the initial training and then conducting practice firings every week after that? I found much of the Army training, especially that at Fort Riley with M-113s, excruciatingly boring and the troops told me they felt the same way.

## Safeguard Soldiers

The six members of Delta Company who were hospitalized for heat exhaustion, the near fatal heat struck suffered by Stephen Granoth, and Steven Henson's brush with death after becoming chilled and wet suggested to me several simple precautions against extreme hot and cold weather, including:

- Equipping every platoon with a radio that could be used to call for help or medical advice.
- Suspending troop training when it is too hot or too cold. When did the peacetime Army gain this compulsion to operate like workaholics?
- Deploying roving medics to units in the field when the weather is unusually hot or cold. The medics should have a line of communication to the battalion commander to alert him to health-threatening situations.

## Liaison with Soldiers' Families

No mother of a soldier should suffer the frustration and stonewalling encountered by Irene Granoth when she tried to find out how and why her son, Stephen, was almost killed by a heat stroke. Such suffering could be minimized and some lawsuits avoided by designating a high-ranking officer in the Inspector General's office whom family members could query when they were concerned about relatives in the Army. Incoming recruits should be given a postcard to send home bearing the name, address and telephone number of this liaison officer. This would be in the spirit of General Carl E. Vuono, Army Chief of Staff, who tells his officers: "Parents send their sons and daughters to us to return them better than they left. We are entrusted with their sons and daughters, and we cannot let them down."

## Provide Exit Options for Volunteers

If West Point cadets, who cost far more to train than privates and contribute little to the nation's fighting power while they are taking courses at the U.S. Military Academy, can resign from the service without penalty at any time up to the start of their junior year—which has been the policy—why should not privates have the same kind of escape hatches available?

Soldiers who quit would lose their military benefits unless they joined reserve units. Historically, National Guard and Army reservists have been allowed to serve six months of active duty or less and then complete their military obligations by drilling at reserve units near their homes. This policy documents that military leaders consider only a few months of continuous active duty valuable.

After interviewing several trainees at Benning who found the Army so intolerable that they attempted suicide to end their torment, learning about Joey jumping out of his barracks at Riley, and talking to scores of privates about whether volunteers should be able to volunteer out of the Army as well as in, I concluded the Army would be better off by allowing soldiers to exercise exit options made as part of four-year enlistments, perhaps at the one-year and two-year points.

I believe such exit options would: (1) encourage more young people to take a chance on the Army and join it; (2) avoid the kind of misery Joey and his superiors endured before the present chaptering-out process ran its course; (3) encourage more soldiers who would otherwise go AWOL or misbehave to perform well knowing they could get out of the Army with honorable discharges if they stuck it out to the exit mark, the light at the end of their tunnel; (4) telegraph to Army leaders those units that had a higher than normal number of soldiers trying to get out, perhaps identifying a problem in time to solve it; (5) encourage leaders at all levels to make their training more fun, interesting and instructive to avoid a highly visible exodus of disillusioned volunteers; (6) instill greater pride in the soldiers who chose to remain in the Army under the "we don't want you if you don't want us" philosophy. The Marines have capitalized on this desire for being special by advertising they have room for only "a few good men."

Specialist Four Cashman reinforced my views by asking me during one of our many chats at Riley: "Why can't they just let guys who really want to get out, get out—instead of making them feel like such scum and lowlife?"

## Develop Career Patterns for Winning Battles

My two weeks of watching battles at the National Training Center convinced me that modern high-speed warfare requires officers and sergeants to spend years mastering it, not run a rifle company for eighteen months and then move on to check another block in the established career pattern. Given the smaller, more manageable Army the United States will field in the 1990s, I recommend:

• Putting officers and sergeants who demonstrate outstanding abilities in combat exercises on career paths that would enable them to run platoons, companies and battalions for three years or more at a time without losing out in promotions for failing to go to war colleges or fill staff jobs.

• Transferring more of the promotion powers from computerized personnel centers to individual battalions so they can manage their outfits like a winning coach manages his football team. Battalion, company and platoon leaders and senior sergeants must have more authority to determine who goes where to do what before this small Army of the 1990s can achieve maximum fighting power.

• Raising the retirement age of one percent of the officer corps from 55 to 60 to determine if this would result in getting more for the Army out of its best and brightest.

I set down these recommendations not with the idea of faulting the dedicated men and women who wear Army green or our institution but in the hope of making their lives more fulfilling and the Army of the future even better than it is today.

# 15. View from the Top

My immersion in the great national experiment called the All-Volunteer Force convinced me that the soldiers at the very bottom and the generals at the very top agree on what it takes to make the post-Vietnam American Army succeed: enlightened leadership. But it became obvious to me in my vertical study of one part of this new Army and a horizontal look at the rest of the force that there is a great middle body of Army leaders who either do not know or are unwilling to admit that they are competing in the commercial marketplace for quality young men and women.

Once recruiters succeed in signing up these sought-after people, thanks in large part to today's relatively generous military pay and benefits for untrained teenagers with no more than a high school diploma, Army leaders must lean toward this talent or lose it.

If soldiers perceive their leaders do not care about advancing them as promised by the recruiting slogan, "Be all you can be, join the Army," and do not treat them with consideration and respect or make their work fulfilling, the once enthusiastic volunteers will find a way to quit, as happened in Charlie Company and other outfits in 1987 and 1988.

Present and former soldiers can be the biggest help or biggest hindrance to Army recruiting as they go back to their home neighborhoods and relate their experiences in uniform. In 1987, Army recruiters signed up 104,000 male volunteers. In 1988, they recruited 91,000, or 13,000 fewer. This drop suggests that the

word is spreading that the Army does not live up to its advertising, although this is only part of the problem.

As President Bush takes over the White House, he is faced with a
government so deep in debt that Congress is unlikely to raise
military pay and bonuses to overcome the reluctance of young
people to join the Army. Although the Army is shrinking in
size—772,000 on active duty in 1988 compared to 1.57 million in
1968, the year of the Vietcong and North Vietnamese Tet offensive—and thus requires fewer volunteers, this small Army
must be high quality. It will fight the first battles in any next war.
And the first battles are apt to be the decisive ones.

This already small Army, which probably will become even
smaller in the 1990s because of the budget crunch, is likely to be
outnumbered if it goes into battles. Therefore, the soldiers within
this small Army must be motivated, ready, skilled and well led if
they are to win. Leadership that drives quality people out of the
Army or reduces the winning qualities in the soldiers who stay in
the service is not only bad leadership but perilous leadership for
the Army and the country.

The Charlie Company of 1987 and 1988 was neither the best nor
the worst unit in the new American Army. Nor was it the whole
American Army. But Charlie Company soldiers were the whole
Army in the sense they typified the backgrounds, hopes and fears
of the trigger-pullers on the point who would fight the first battles
of any next war. Therefore, Army leaders needlessly risk the
future of their institution and the country it is sworn to defend if
they do not address the grievances of these ordinary soldiers.

One four-star general who understood this in 1988 was General
Maxwell R. Thurman, commander of the United States Army
Training and Doctrine Command. A bachelor, he was married to
the Army and spent his thirty-four years in uniform trying to
make it better. Another four-star general who understood that
battles are won or lost by mud soldiers was the top soldier of them
all, General Carl E. Vuono, Army Chief of Staff in 1988 when I
completed my year of chronicling Charlie Company.

Thurman in talks at his headquarters at Fort Monroe, Virginia,
and at his home there stressed that the top leaders of the Army
were indeed fervently dedicated to making the American soldier
all that he can be. But, as in any organization where there are
thousands of people with competing personalities and goals and
styles and biases and agendas, the job of guiding the Army along

257

the same road, no matter how clearly marked, is impossible to do without missteps. Thurman, after listening to the lamentations of Charlie Company soldiers, promised to consider my ideas for addressing them, including sending officers through basic training with soldiers and incorporating exit options into four-year enlistment contracts. He was especially disturbed over the evidence that wives were not being made to feel like members of the Army family. He promised to do some exhorting to push Army leaders back on the road he and others have spent their lives mapping and marking.

On such specifics as the leadership gap described by Battalion Sergeant Major Wright, Thurman said that although this is true for the near term, "the guy is unduly pessimistic" about the long-term prospects for closing this gap.

"The gap exists in older E-5s [buck sergeant] and E-6s [staff sergeants]. In 1979," when Army leaders were struggling to fill empty spaces in the ranks of the all-volunteer Army, "upper and lower mental categories were not in our lexicons."

"We've only been in the halcyon days of recruiting since 1983," Thurman continued. He said this means the best and brightest of the post-Vietnam Army are just beginning to rise into the rank of E-6, staff sergeant, where they help lead platoons. "There is every indication that the NCO corps is getting brighter. We're keeping a good percentage of the high-quality kids. They will become the NCOs of the future." To hasten the closing of the leadership gap that hurt Charlie Company and other units, Thurman launched new programs to improve the training of NCOs, particularly their capability for leading troops in combat. "Getting the leadership dimension is very difficult," he told me.

General Carl Vuono, like Thurman, loves his soldiers and winced when I told him of their disappointments at the National Training Center and at Fort Riley. He agreed, too, that it might be a good idea to send freshly commissioned officers through the unique crucible of basic training so these future leaders would understand their soldiers, body and soul. And this four-star champion of the invisible mud soldier out on the point grasped instantly what I was talking about when I warned that many commanders were unwittingly abusing and dispiriting their soldiers because these new volunteers would let themselves be overworked before they went AWOL or did something else disruptive to force the command to recognize their anger and frustration.

"The leaders have got to understand that they have kids who are so motivated that they will do anything they want," Vuono told me. "This puts a responsibility on the leader's shoulders. There are rewards for this" kind of dedication by the troops. "If next weekend is a long weekend, you have to pay off with a long weekend. You cannot give them an expectation and not carry it out."

This sensitive, thoughtful general said it is more difficult in some ways to lead bright troops than dull ones because it is often difficult to tell when you have stretched them too little or too much. He said the enlightened leader of this new breed of soldier must ponder, "How far can you stretch them? How much can they do and how much do they want to do? These kids want to be challenged. They want to know what the standard is and whether they met it. And if they did not meet it, they want to know why.

"You know," reflected the leader of all American soldiers in 1988, "when you get quality soldiers, the leader's job is tougher. How can we insure that the officers really know what makes these kids tick? That's an interesting idea," sending young officers through basic training with the soldiers they will ask to follow them.

I went to Fort Leavenworth in Kansas, the Harvard Business School of Army leadership training for officers, to hear Vuono lecture newly chosen commanders of battalions and brigades. As I listened to him tell these officers how he wanted them to lead privates, I realized I had come full circle. For this four-star general was saying the same things as the privates of Charlie Company when it came to discussing how troops should be led. These were the main points in Vuono's Sermon on the Mount, delivered with fervor as he paced back and forth in front of the commanders seated before him in a Fort Leavenworth classroom:

## Training the Soldier

"A leader is responsible for planning the training. He's responsible for the execution of the training, and he's responsible for the assessment of the training. That's a leader's job.

"The troops expect it to happen. When it doesn't happen, and we don't explain why, they're going to say to themselves, 'What kind of organization am I in?' You've got to do pre-execution checks. If you don't do them, something will not happen."

The four-star general launched into an example that the troops of Charlie Company had lived over and over again in slightly varied forms during the long winter of 1987 and 1988 in Kansas.

"It's January" in Germany. "It's cold. You can't get the medic track out of the motor pool. So what happens? The training doesn't happen at 8 o'clock. It starts at noon.

"Then you drive out in your Hum-Vee and say, 'How are things going?'

"Sergeant Vuono says, 'Everything is going great, sir. We got a little late start. We'll finish everything.' You hop back in your Hum-Vee and say everything is great and go back.

"What you don't know is that the training was supposed to end at 1500 [3 P.M.] because in January in Germany it gets dark early. The troops were all going to get back, get their weapons cleaned, and be dismissed by 1700 [5 P.M.] or 1730.

"But because we started late, because we didn't do our pre-execution checks, instead of finishing at 1500 we didn't finish until 1700. But the time we got back, it was 1800 [6 P.M.]. By that time everybody is upset, including the troops.

"And the only person who can't complain is the trooper. But down inside he's seething. If he's married and living away from the caserne, instead of getting home at 1800, it's about 2000 [8 P.M.] when he walks in the house.

"Now you tell me what he thinks. Now you tell me that's not your fault. That's the kind of thing that happens in our Army if you're not careful. And that's the kind of thing you can prevent by your pre-execution checks where you get together and lay out what it is tactically you want to accomplish and then administratively have everything lined up. That is not too mundane for a battalion commander to be involved in. . . .

"I'm not a believer in training inspection. I would not allow a training inspection in any organization I commanded. I would not allow the S-3 to get out his clipboard or the G-3 trainer to get out with his clipboard and check off. That's an inspection, and that's something we don't need in training."

I recalled as I listened to Vuono that troops had complained about being dogged for not having their chin straps buttoned out in the field.

"The kind of soldiers we have today want to train hard. They want to train tough. They want to know what the standard is, and they want to know whether they met it. They want the training planned and executed the way we said we would. They know the difference between good training and ho-hum training. And it relates right back to you. If you think I'm a zealot for training, I am."

## Even Out the Work Load

"Your program has to be sustained," Vuono warned. "It cannot be a jerky program. It has to be a constant program."

## Let Soldiers Try Commanding

"On the kind of battlefields we're going to fight on, you're going to be decentralized. So you've got to practice decentralization."

I recalled here the story Private Second Class Glenn P. Dowe had told me when his lieutenant was "killed" in the National Training Center "war" against the Russians. The lieutenant's MILES sensor gear was ringing, signifying he had been shot. "I went over to him and said, 'Sir, give me the radio.' He said, 'I'm not dead. There's just something wrong with the MILES.' Our leaders never give us a chance to try leading. Who would take charge in a real war?"

## Caring for the Family

"Your wife is your best friend and your strongest critic. Your spouse had a choice, but your children had the luck of the draw. Nothing they could do about it. You have a responsibility. They know you're embarking on one of the most important parts of your career. You must be considerate of them. Sometime they're going to need you. And you better be there listening. Talk to them. Listen to them. Take leaves while you're in the Army. Nobody is indispensable. You're better for me and your Army" by taking time off.

How the lonely soldiers' wives in the Junction City trailers would have agreed with the general here.

After I left Vuono, I reflected on how closely the agreement between privates and generals like Thurman and Vuono resembled the situation I had encountered in 1971 while talking to black Navy boiler tenders in Navy destroyers and admirals at the Pentagon. Both acknowledged racial relations were strained and wanted to ease them. But the polarization blew up in the form of sit-down strikes and sabotage before Admiral Elmo R. Zumwalt Jr. navigated the Navy through this most difficult passage with sensitivity and brilliance.

Seventeen years later, after looking deep into the bottom of the Army, I believe the Army must guide its way through an equally difficult passage. It must train this small Army of willing soldiers without overworking them to the point they give up on themselves, their leaders and the Army. By the time such troop abuse becomes highly visible, it may be too late to stop it. I sounded this warning about invisible troop abuse to a conference of generals held at Fort Monroe in October 1988.

But the generals dare not let it go at that. They have the command responsibility for this all-volunteer Army. Their job is to fix what is wrong, and our job as citizens is to insist that they do it. For the American Army is not a case of "They vs. We." It is our Army—all of ours. The American Army already is the government's best social-betterment program. But we all need to do more for the heart of this Army—the soldier who has volunteered to carry our burden.

# Acknowledgments

Although I am indebted to far more people that I can list here, I would at least like to express my gratitude for the cooperation extended to me by such active-duty Army leaders as General Carl E. Vuono, Army Chief of Staff; General Maxwell R. Thurman, commander of the U.S. Army Training and Doctrine Command; Brigadier General Richard S. Siegfried, who commanded the United States Army Infantry Training Center while I was at Fort Benning, Georgia, in 1987; Col. Jose R. Feliciano and Lieutenant Colonel Gordon R. Lam, respectively commanders of the First Infantry Training Brigade and the Second Battalion of the Fifty-fourth Infantry Regiment while I was at Benning; Captain James R. Fleenor II, commander of Delta Company when I followed it through basic and advanced individual training at Benning; Second Lieutenant Keith Raines, Delta Company executive officer; First Sergeant Edward D. Williams of Delta Company.

Army information officers at the Pentagon whom I would like to single out for special thanks include Major General Charles D. Bussey, Brigadier General Clyde Hennies, Colonel F. William Smullen III, Lieutenant Colonel James Fetig, Major Gregory A. Rixon. Army information officers in the field whom I would like to salute include Lieutenant Colonel Robert E. Pilnacek, civilians Richard J. McDowell and Bill Walton at Fort Benning, and Mark Meseke at Fort Riley, Kansas; Major Mark Dutton at the National Training Center at Fort Irwin, California; Colonel Anthony F. Caggiano at the U.S. Army Training and Doctrine Command at Fort Monroe, Virginia; Lieutenant Colonel John C. Garlinger at the Army Command and Staff College at Fort Leavenworth, Kansas.

Many Army officers in the retired community lent their support, encouragement and expertise to this endeavor. At the top of any short list must go Colonel John B. Keeley, whose love of the mud soldier and the Army never blurred his keen analytical capabilities, which made this book closer to the bull's-eye than it could otherwise have been.

263

Charles S. Gardner III, fellow journalist, made extremely helpful suggestions for the text.

In reconstructing Charlie Company's battle of April 11, 1966, I received unstinting help from retired General William E. DePuy, Colonel William D. Hathaway, Colonel Bibb A. Underwood, Lieutenants John W. Libs and Martin L. Kroah Jr., Sergeant First Class Charles Urconis and Specialist Four Phillip Hall.

At Scribner's, I am indebted for the support and verve of my editor, Edward T. Chase.

And on the home front go my deepest thanks of all. For there my wife, Joan, with her usual grace put up with the long absences and general turmoil associated with writing a book.

George C. Wilson
4875 Potomac Avenue N. W.
Washington, DC 20007
(Letters answered)

# The Graduates

The author followed these men through their infantry training at Fort Benning, Georgia. They graduated from the United States Army Infantry Training Center on October 9, 1987, as members of Delta Company, Second Battalion, Fifty-fourth Infantry Regiment, First Infantry Training Brigade, and then joined their regular Army units. About half of the graduates went to Fort Riley to form Charlie Company, Second Battalion, Sixteenth Infantry Regiment, First Infantry Division (Mechanized). The ages shown are as of graduation day.

Alton M. Adams, 18, Selma, NC
Norman L. Adkins Jr., 18, Seth, WV
Guy D. Aldrich, 21, Norwalk, CT
John Alvarez, 18, Kermit, TX
Michael A. Austerman, 23, Elizabethtown, IN
Joseph E. Ayers, 19, Ballston Spa, NY
Donald J. Bailey, 18, Milwaukee, WI
Michael L. Ballard, 18, Lone Grove, OK
Marty L. Banks, 18, Bowling Green, KY
Ty J. Barker, 21, Fremont, CA
Daniel J. Becker, 18, Cedar Lake, IN
William C. Best, 20, El Paso, TX
Jeffery L. Birge, 20, Oak Park, IL
Patrick E. Blair, 18, Springfield, OH
David F. Blas, 18, Guam
David A. Bohmann, 18, San Antonio, TX
Joseph E. Booth Jr., 25, Houston, TX

Walter J. Boothe, 18, Monterey Park, CA
Jeffery M. Boutwell, 19, Osceola, IA
Edgar S. Bowdish Jr., 18, Falls Creek, PA
Derrick S. Brevard, 17, Bloomfield, NJ
Kevin D. Brewton, 18, Beatrice, AL
Dennis P. Brice, 18, Goodwell, OK
John P. Brooks, 19, Berlin, MD
Nathaniel R. Brown, 18, Medford, OR
Bret A. Burke, 18, Pelican Rapids, MN
Christopher R. Burks, 18, Tiffin, OH
Robert J. Burns Jr., 18, Bloomfield, NJ
Gregory L. Burt, 18, Everett, WA
Danny L. Cartwright, 18, Uniontown, OH
Lance R. Carver, 18, Glennville, CA
Christopher S. Cashman, 26, Santa Rosa, CA
Rafael C. Castro, 19, Nogales, AR
Michael S. Chicvorka, 19, Endicott, NY
William H. Clark Jr., 18, Laurel Hill, NC
Daniel J. Clifford, 18, Las Vegas, NV
Fred D. Cole, 18, West Plains, MO
Javier Cornejo, 22, Los Angeles, CA
Tandyn D. Cutler, 20, Ellensburg, WA
Ken G. Darnall, 19, Brunswick, OH
Terry J. Daubenspeck, 19, Carson, WA
Keith R. Devey, 18, Sacramento, CA
Patrick N. Dickerson, 21, Hungerford, TX
Anthony L. Dilk, 18, Dayton, NV
Rodney D. Donaldson, 20, Lakewood, NJ
Glenn P. Dowe, 18, South China, ME
Raymond T. Durgan, 19, Port Gibson, NY
Brian A. Edmisten, 18, Ripley, OH
Gregory A. Elliott, 23, Galena, KS
Travis Fishel, 18, Houston, MN
Richard S. Florczyk, 18, Horseheads, NY
Russell K. Florian Jr., 18, Dolgeville, NY
Marcus D. Foreman, 18, Southlake, TX
Earl G. Fulcher, 18, Heathsville, VA
Jeffrey A. Fullerton, 18, Huntsville, OH
Scott B. Fulmer, 23, San Antonio, TX
Christian A. Gambotz, 18, Palos Park, IL
Edward W. Giroux, 17, Weymouth, MA
James W. Gordon Jr., 18, Orange Park, FL
Mark A. Grant, 20, Madras, OR
Edward S. Green, 18, Williamston, NC
Keith A. Groves, 18, Oakdale, CA
Jeffery N. Hall, 20, Frederic, WI
Eric S. Harbour, 18, Troy, OH

Michael T. Hart, 18, Solvay, NY
James D. Henderson, 18, Burke, VA
Aaron K. Henson, 20, Tyler, TX
Steven Henson, 19, Baltimore, MD
Dean E. Herod, 20, Greensboro, PA
Wayne T. Hewlett, 18, Durham, NC
Michael A. Hill, 18, Blaine, MN
Kevin J. Hollands, 18, Reading, MI
Kevin W. Hoop, 18, Fort Dodge, IA
Harold D. Hudson, 18, Omaha, NE
Andrew G. Hymers, 18, Norfolk, VA
Todd J. Jaramillo, 18, DeSoto, TX*
Timothy D. Jefferies, 18, El Paso, TX*
Thomas W. Jenner Jr., 18, Seattle, WA
Derek Johnson, 19, Theodore, AL
Ronald M. Johnson, 21, Chicago, IL
Jason A. Kachuck, 18, Fremont, CA
Christian C. Keck, 18, Portland, OR
Floyd D. Kennedy, 19, Lindale, TX
Scott J. Kiltoff, 18, Seattle, WA
Frank R. Knight, 18, Pueblo, CO
Vailes D. Knox Jr., 18, Baltimore, MD
Kevin M. Kolasinski, 18, Duluth, MN
John P. Korkue, 22, Jamesville, NY
Raymond R. LaGrange, 18, Amsterdam, NY
Robert S. Larson, 18, Blaine, MN
Michael W. Leach, 18, Carlsbad, NM
Jeffrey S. Lillibridge, 25, Jesup, IA
Travis S. Linville, 18, Grand Junction, CO
Frank H. Logan III, 18, Medford, MA
John A. Madsen, 18, La Vista, NE
Brian K. Majchszak, 18, Chicago, IL
Daniel S. Manfull, 20, Burney, CA
Steven C. Martin, 18, Woodland Hills, CA
Michael D. Mathews, 18, Riverton, IL
Michael D. Matthews, 19, Omaha, NE
Robert R. McBride, 18, Roscoe, TX
Robert G. McCain, 19, Longview, WA
Raymond N. McDaniel Jr., 21, Esmont, VA
John R. McGinnes, 20, Monmouth, IL
Leonard R. McLaughlin, 18, Coraopolis, PA
James L. Mericle, 22, Buffalo, NY
John R. Miller, 18, Edgewater, FL
William J. Miller, 18, Pittsburgh, PA
Phillip A. Moore Jr., 18, Modesto, CA
David S. Murray, 20, New Cumberland, WV

* Held over at Benning a few weeks to complete requirements.

Robert E. Myers, 18, Columbia, MD
Steven M. Natole, 18, Virginia Beach, VA
Paul A. Neher, 19, Wolcottville, IN*
David W. Nicholas, 20, Beaumont, TX
G. R. Norton, 17, Sinton, TX
Lawrence W. Noyes Jr., 18, Levant, ME
Cuauhtemoc T. Olivo, 19, Phoenix, AZ
Carlos A. Ollison, 22, Gladewater, TX
Johnny R. Parks II, 17, Balch Springs, TX
Mark E. Peet, 18, Windsor, NY
Philip J. Perkins, 18, Havana, IL
Sean G. Petersen, 19, Tintah, MN
Daniel A. Pinkowsky, 19, Black Creek, WI
Scott W. Prescott, 19, Bolingbrook, IL
James E. Proctor II, 20, Indianapolis, IN
John P. Quinn, 26, Medway, MA
Gary A. Ramsey, 19, Lakeville, OH
Edward M. Reiner Jr., 27, Valhalla, NY
Lester J. Remington, 18, Burton, MI
Agustin R. Rios, 18, Colton, CA
David D. Rittenhouse, 18, Dalton, GA
Orlando Rivera, 19, Waterbury, CT
Brian M. Roads, 18, Omaha, NE
Daniel J. T. Ross, 19, Silver City, NV
Jimmy L. Russell Jr., 18, Gray, GA
John D. Ryan Jr., 18, Angola, IN
Michael P. Sampson, 19, Bradford, OH
Stephen M. Sears, 18, Marietta, GA
Kristian C. Selvester, 18, Lincoln, CA*
Eric J. Serrano, 20, Syracuse, NY
Jason W. Shiflet, 18, Monroe, MI
Mike C. Shipley, 18, Englewood, CA
Michael F. Simmons, 18, Warren, ME
Gregory T. Sisson, 20, Soldotna, AK
Michael J. Smith, 18, Bakersfield, CA
Darrell G. Snell, 18, Broaddus, TX
Clyde S. P. Sowers, 20, Temple, TX
Kevin E. Squires, 18, Holmes Beach, FL
Eddie E. Statemann, 17, Bullhead City, AR
James J. Stephenson, 27, Harrison, ID
Sean K. Stewart, 19, Greenfield, MA
John M. Stone, 26, Florence, SC
Anthony L. Suddoth, 20, Zion, IL
Timothy N. Tasse, 18, Worcester, MA
Andrew E. Thomas, 19, Austin, TX
Neal B. Thomas, 20, Troutville, VA
Brian S. Trotter, 17, Roanoke, VA
Robert D. Underhill, 18, Pinckney, MI

267

ACKNOWLEDGMENTS

John F. Utley, 18, Diamond, OH
Darren L. Vinaas, 19, Anaheim, CA
Robert C. Vogel, 18, Norwalk, OH
Frederick E. Waddell Jr., 19, Temple Hills, MD
Jeff A. Warren, 19, Pierceton, IN
Anthony W. White, 18, Linton, IN
Brian C. Wilcox, 18, Drakesville, IA
Scott A. Wilcox, 18, Caneadea, NY
Barry Williams, 21, Shreveport, LA
Jeffrey L. Williams, 18, Claypool, IN
Michael S. Willyard, 20, Amarillo, TX
Stephen Wing, 29, Brandon, FL
John F. Wolfe, 23, Smithfield, PA
Thomas D. Woodruff, 18, West Lake Village, CA
William L. Wright, 18, Cedartown, GA
Gaylon S. Yocham, 24, Midland, TX
Robert E. Young, 18, Fair Oaks, CA
Timothy E. Zikas, 18, Papillion, NE

# Index